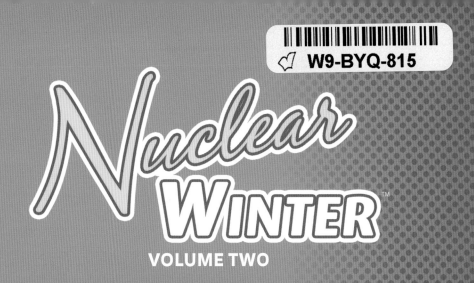

Nuclear WINTER™

VOLUME TWO

BOOM! BOX™

BOOm! Box™

NUCLEAR WINTER Volume Two, January 2019. Published by BOOM! Box, a division of Boom Entertainment, Inc. Nuclear Winter is ™ & © 2019 Caroline Breault. All rights reserved. BOOM! Box™ and the BOOM! Box logo are trademarks of Boom Entertainment, Inc., registered in various countries and categories. All characters, events, and institutions depicted herein are fictional. Any similarity between any of the names, characters, persons, events, and/or institutions in this publication to actual names, characters, and persons, whether living or dead, events, and/or institutions is unintended and purely coincidental. BOOM! Box does not read or accept unsolicited submissions of ideas, stories, or artwork.

BOOM! Studios, 5670 Wilshire Boulevard, Suite 400, Los Angeles, CA 90036-5679. Printed in China. First Printing.

ISBN: 978-1-68415-303-9, eISBN: 978-1-64144-156-8

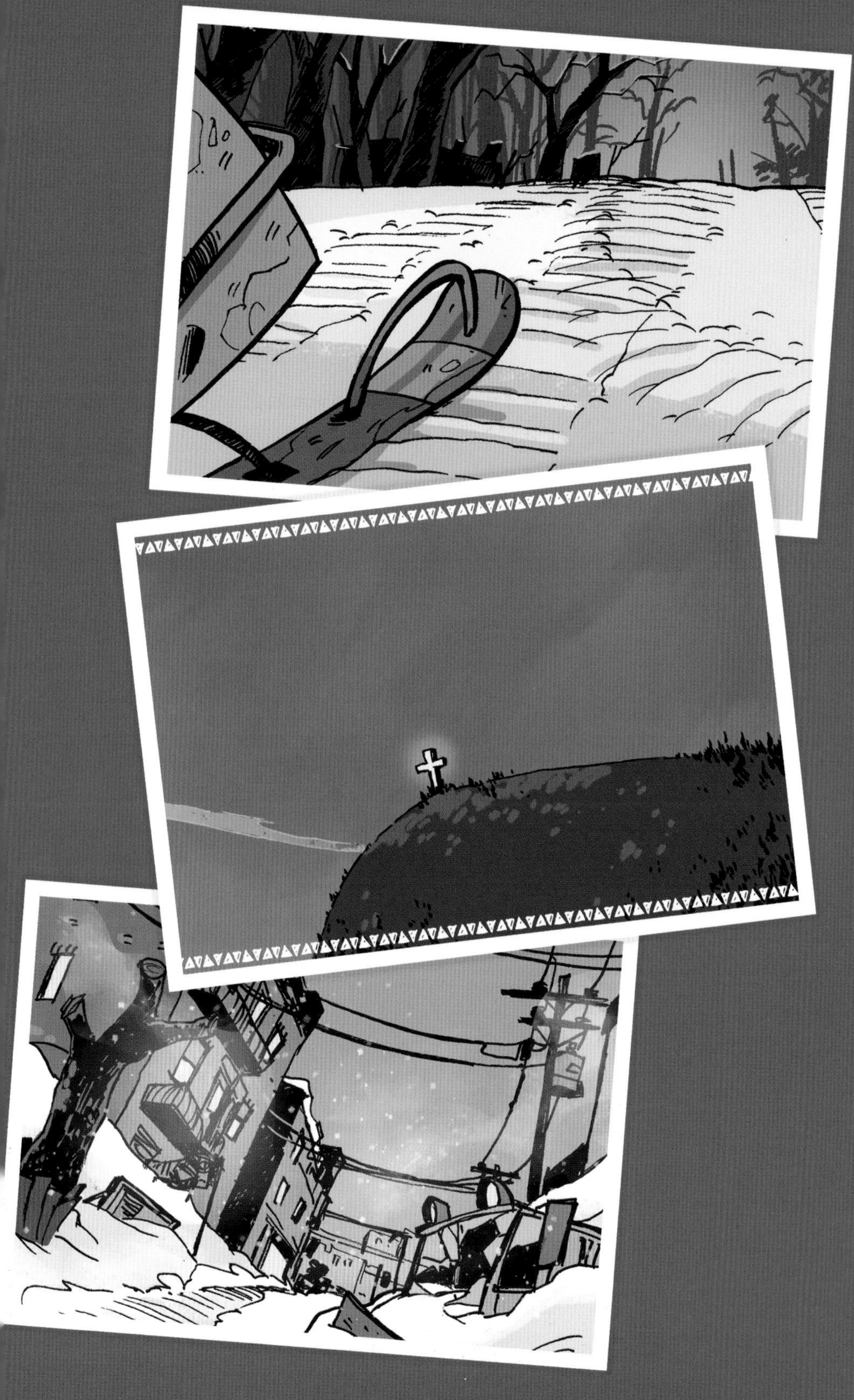

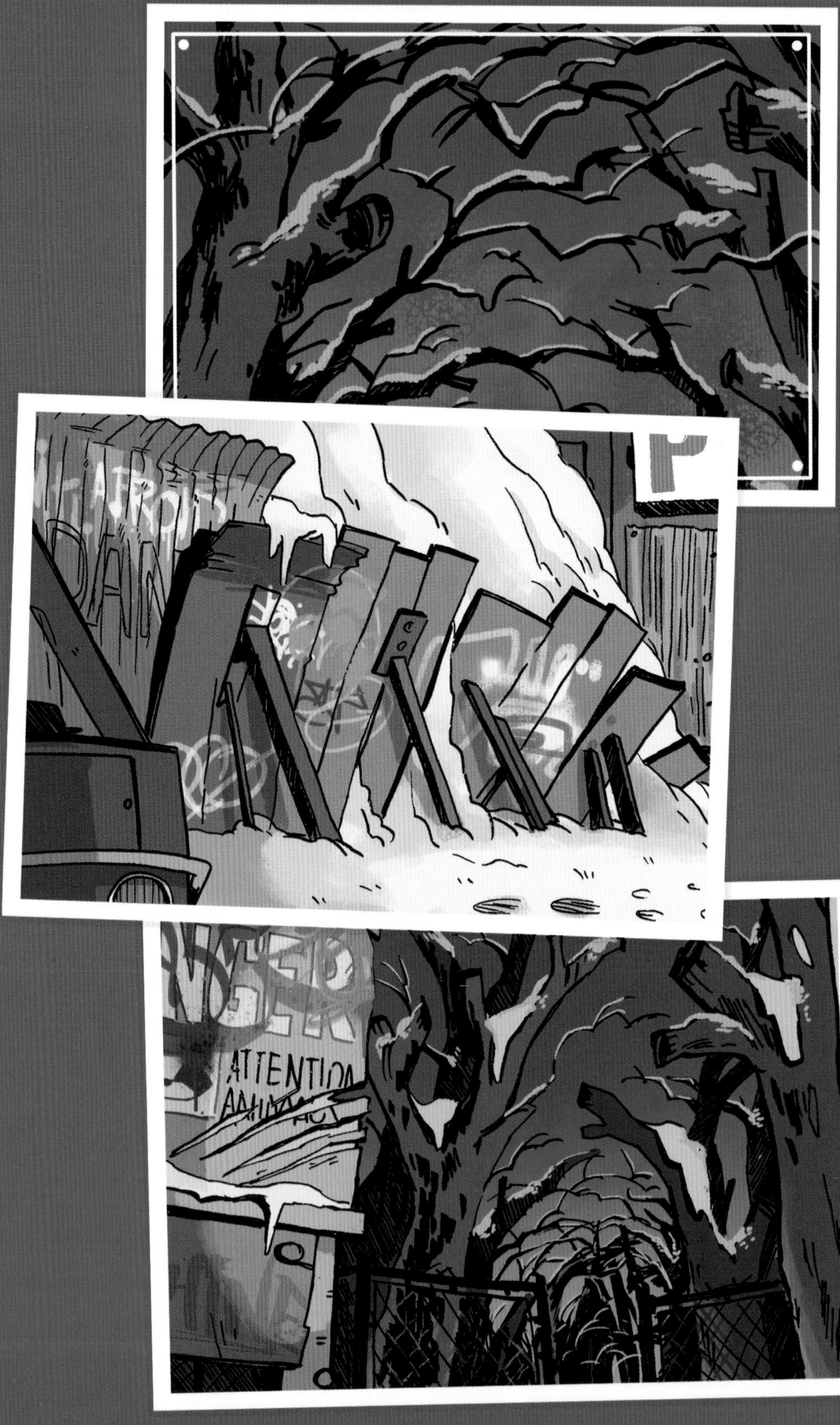
ATTENTIO

Written & Illustrated by
Cab

English Translation by
Edward Gauvin

Letters by
Deron Bennett

Designer
Kara Leopard

Assistant Editor
Michael Moccio

Editor
Shannon Watters

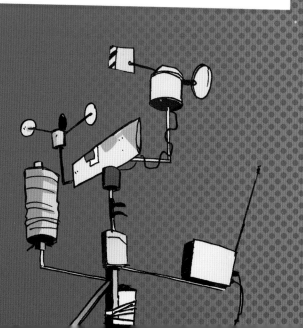

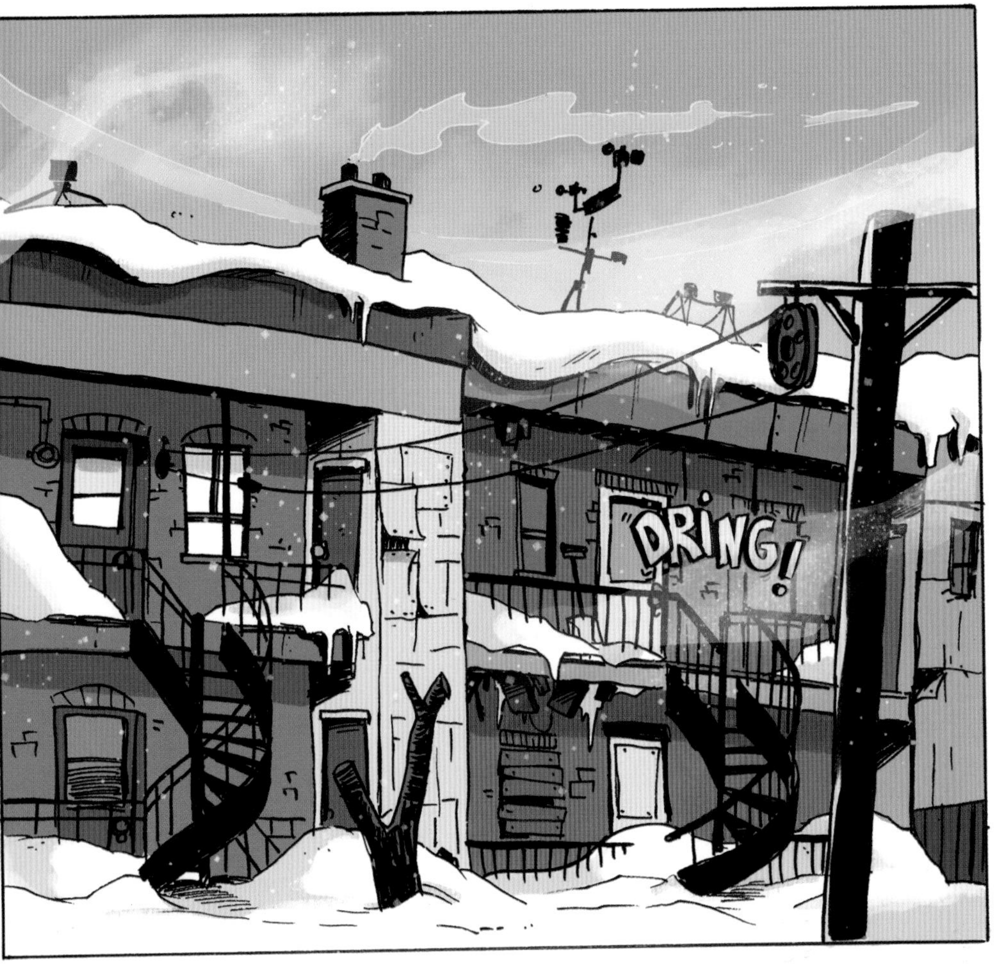
DRING!

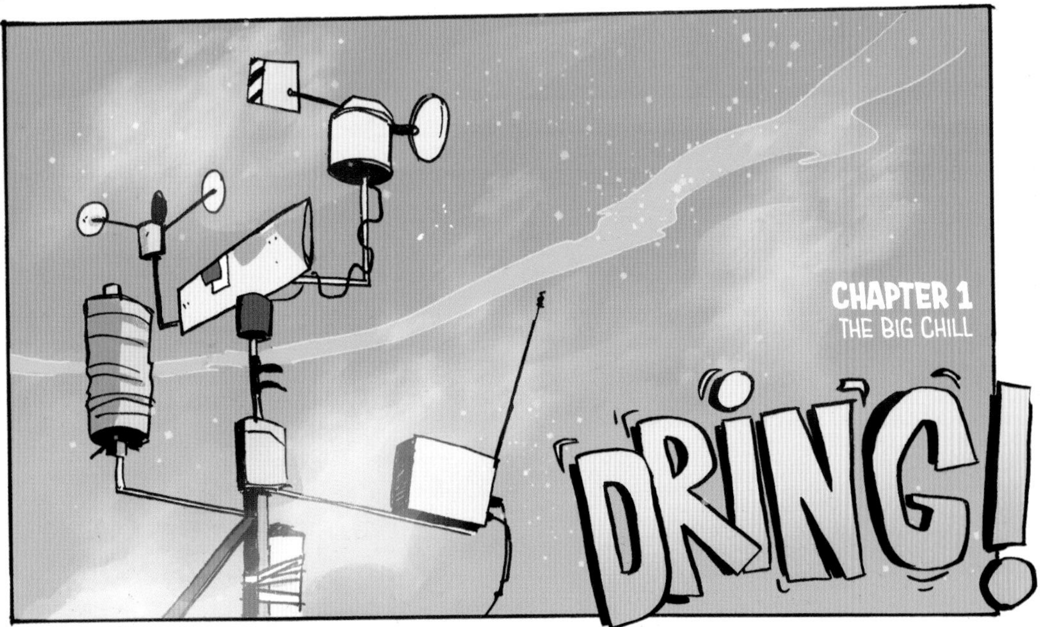
DRING!

CHAPTER 1
THE BIG CHILL

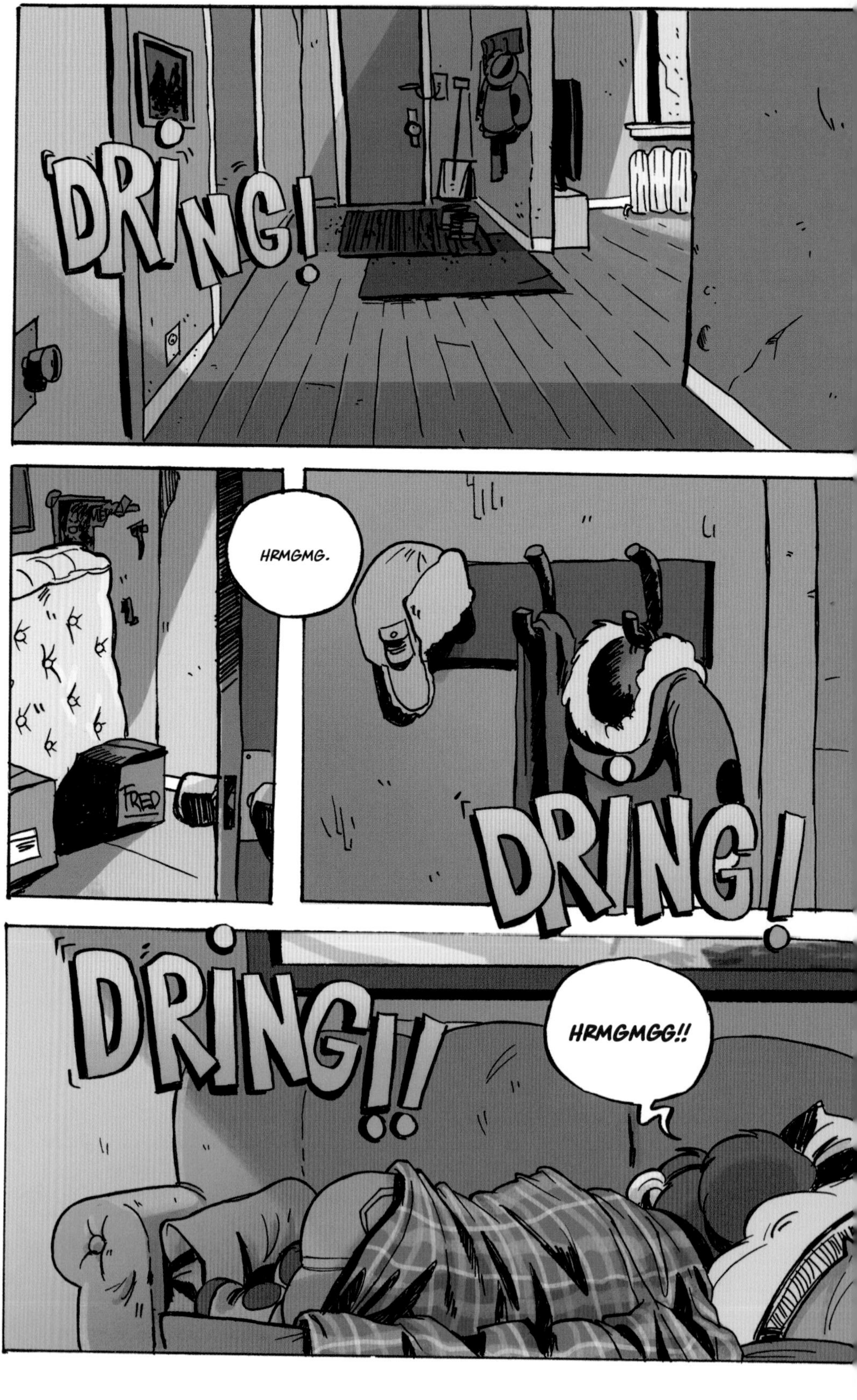
DRING!
FRED
HRMGMG.
DRING!
DRING!!
HRMGMGG!!

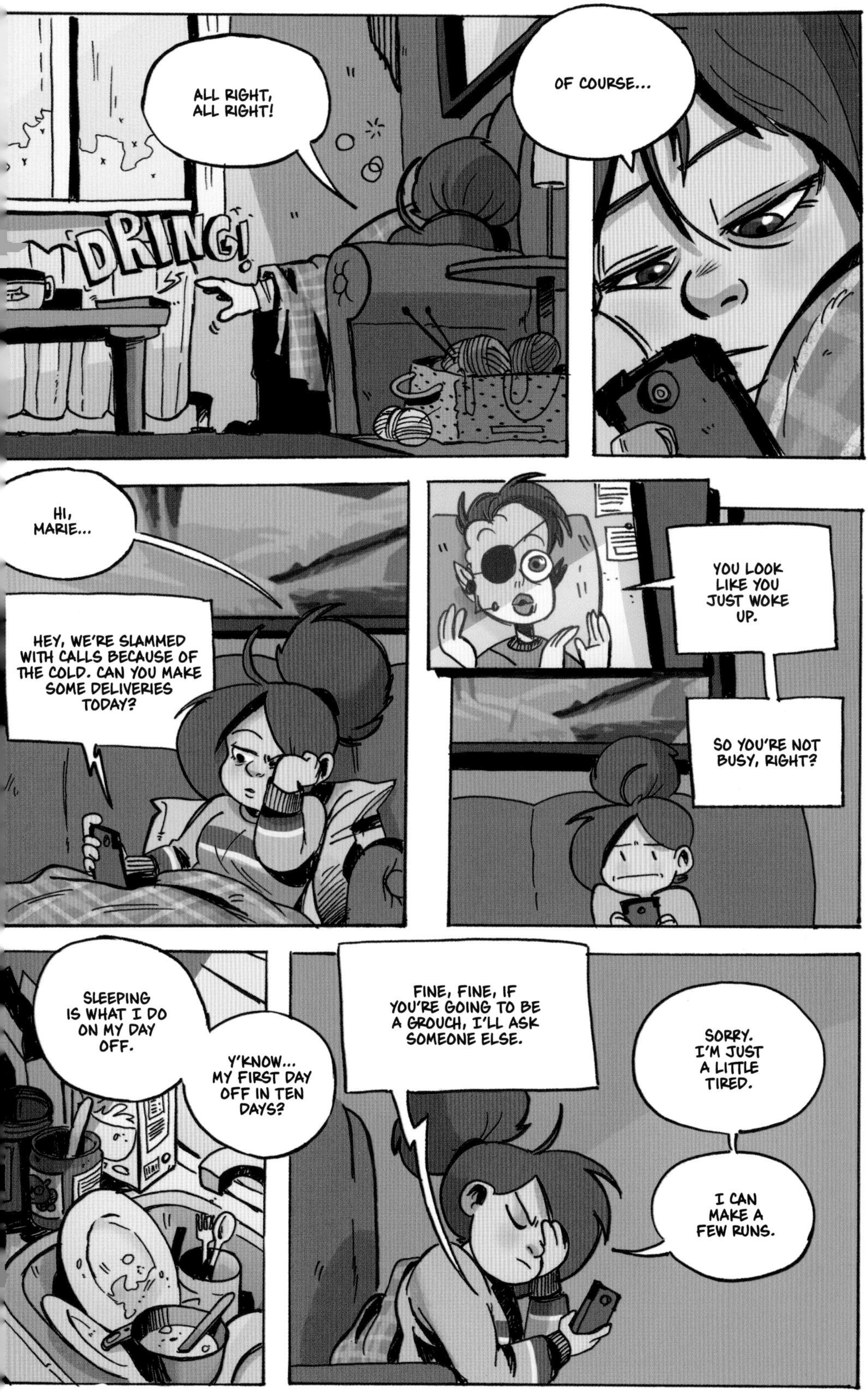
DRING!
ALL RIGHT, ALL RIGHT!
OF COURSE...
HI, MARIE...
HEY, WE'RE SLAMMED WITH CALLS BECAUSE OF THE COLD. CAN YOU MAKE SOME DELIVERIES TODAY?
YOU LOOK LIKE YOU JUST WOKE UP.
SO YOU'RE NOT BUSY, RIGHT?
SLEEPING IS WHAT I DO ON MY DAY OFF.
Y'KNOW... MY FIRST DAY OFF IN TEN DAYS?
FINE, FINE, IF YOU'RE GOING TO BE A GROUCH, I'LL ASK SOMEONE ELSE.
SORRY. I'M JUST A LITTLE TIRED.
I CAN MAKE A FEW RUNS.

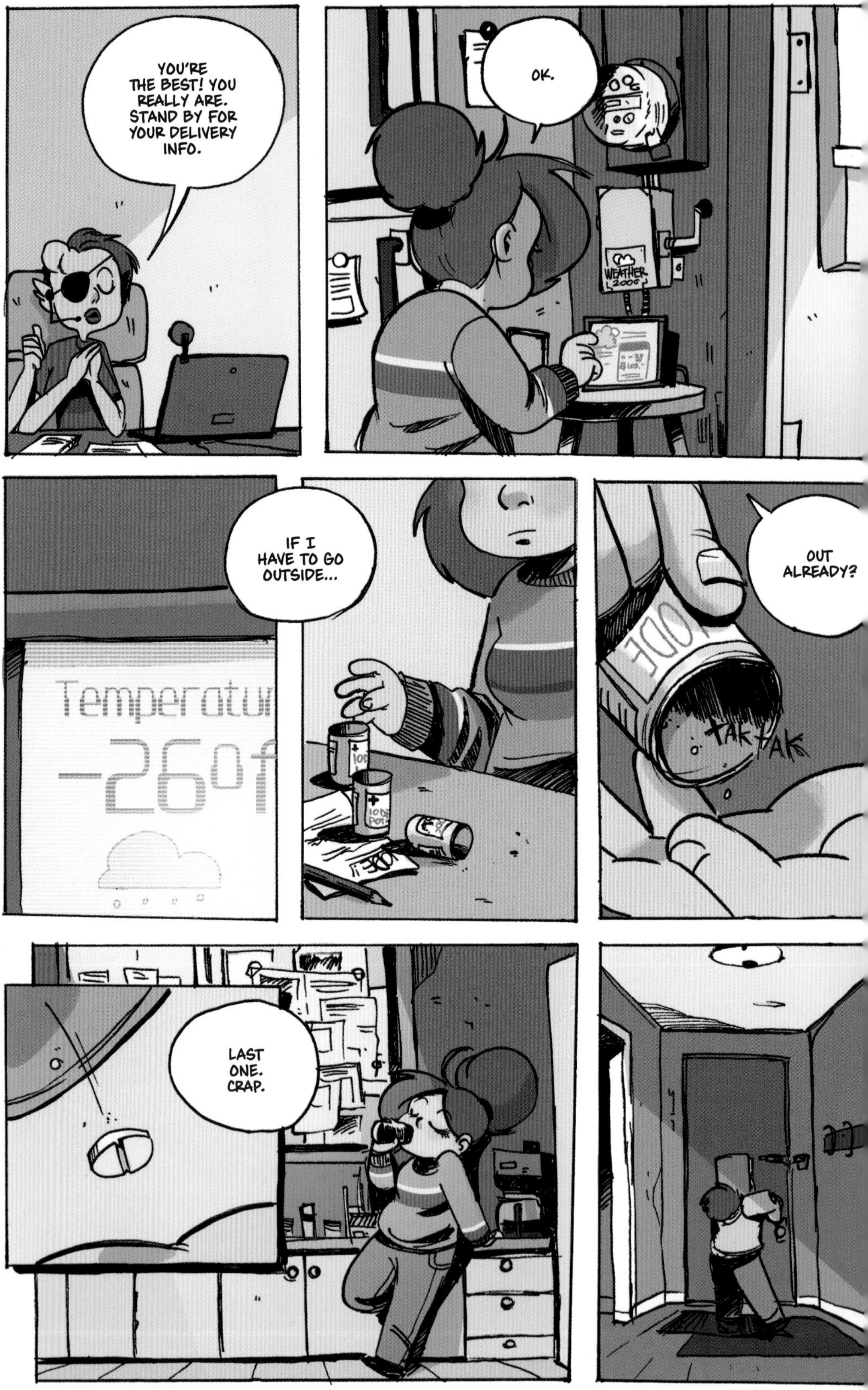
YOU'RE THE BEST! YOU REALLY ARE. STAND BY FOR YOUR DELIVERY INFO.
OK.
WEATHER 2006
Temperatur
-26°f
IF I HAVE TO GO OUTSIDE...
OUT ALREADY?
TAK TAK
LAST ONE. CRAP.

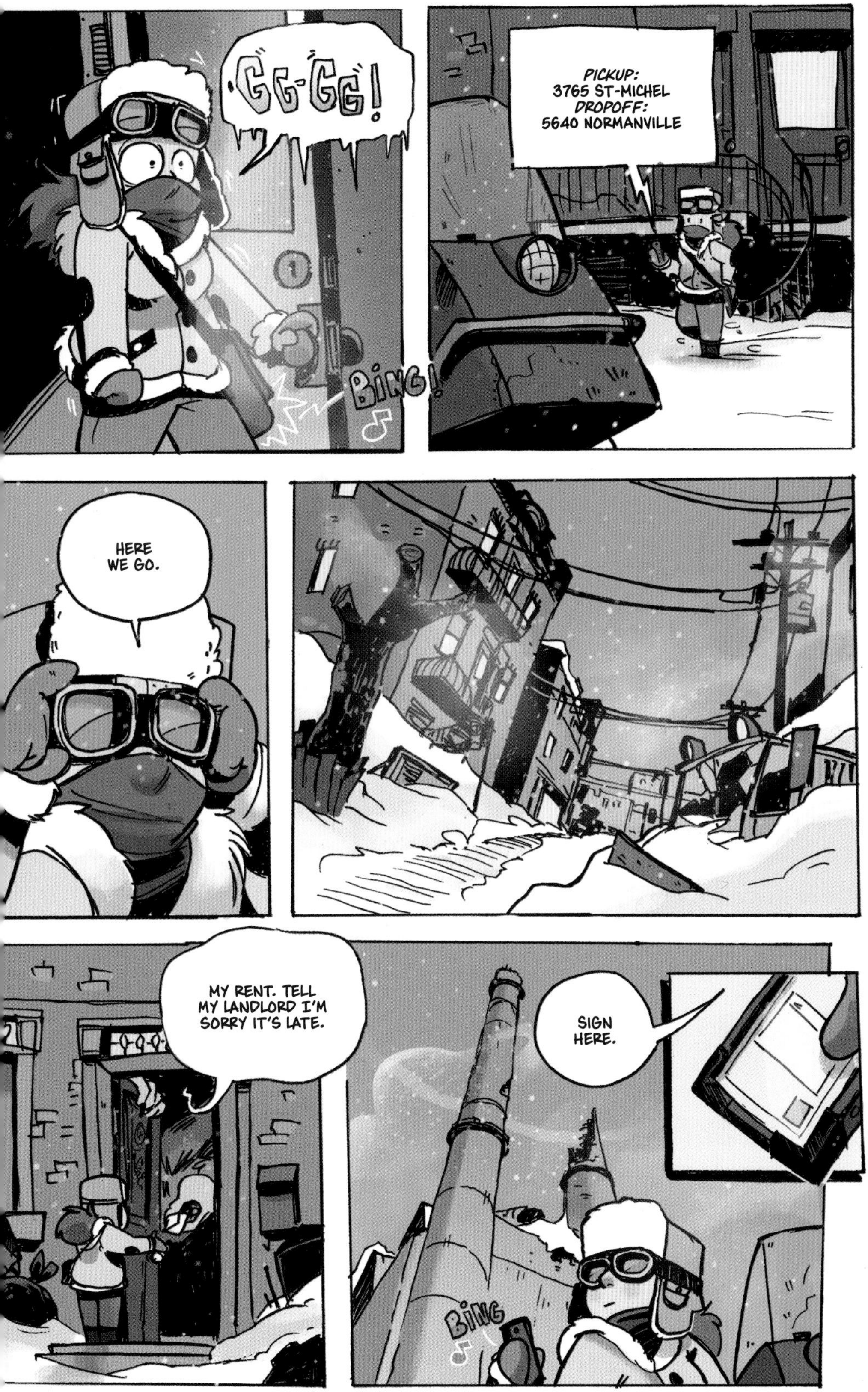
GG-GG!
BING!
PICKUP:
3765 ST-MICHEL
DROPOFF:
5640 NORMANVILLE
HERE WE GO.
MY RENT. TELL MY LANDLORD I'M SORRY IT'S LATE.
SIGN HERE.
BING

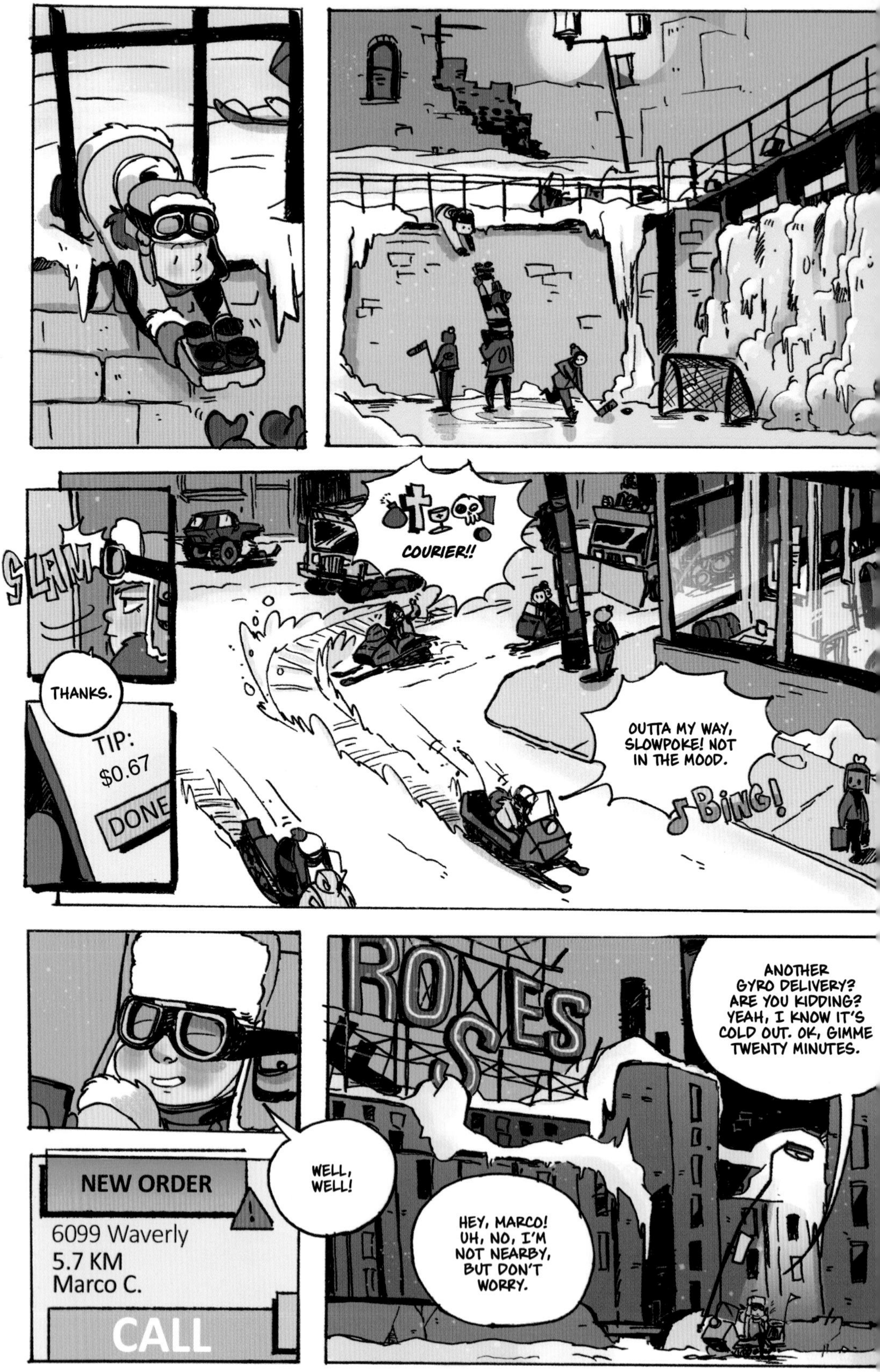

SLAM
THANKS.
TIP:
$0.67
DONE
COURIER!!
OUTTA MY WAY, SLOWPOKE! NOT IN THE MOOD.
BING!
NEW ORDER
6099 Waverly
5.7 KM
Marco C.
CALL
WELL, WELL!
HEY, MARCO! UH, NO, I'M NOT NEARBY, BUT DON'T WORRY.
ANOTHER GYRO DELIVERY? ARE YOU KIDDING? YEAH, I KNOW IT'S COLD OUT. OK, GIMME TWENTY MINUTES.

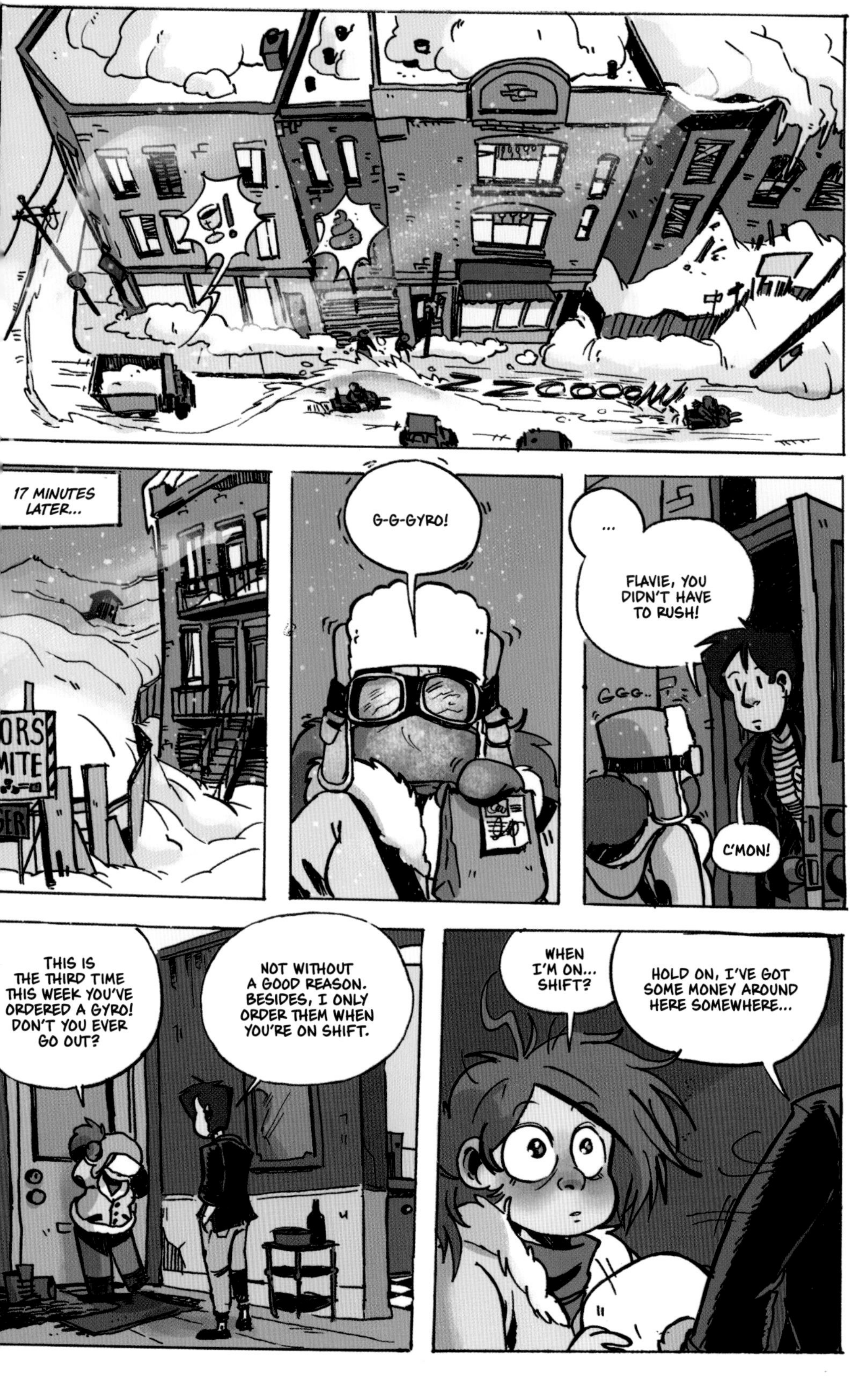
ZZZOOOOM!!
17 MINUTES LATER...
G-G-GYRO!
...
FLAVIE, YOU DIDN'T HAVE TO RUSH!
GGG..
C'MON!
THIS IS THE THIRD TIME THIS WEEK YOU'VE ORDERED A GYRO! DON'T YOU EVER GO OUT?
NOT WITHOUT A GOOD REASON. BESIDES, I ONLY ORDER THEM WHEN YOU'RE ON SHIFT.
WHEN I'M ON... SHIFT?
HOLD ON, I'VE GOT SOME MONEY AROUND HERE SOMEWHERE...

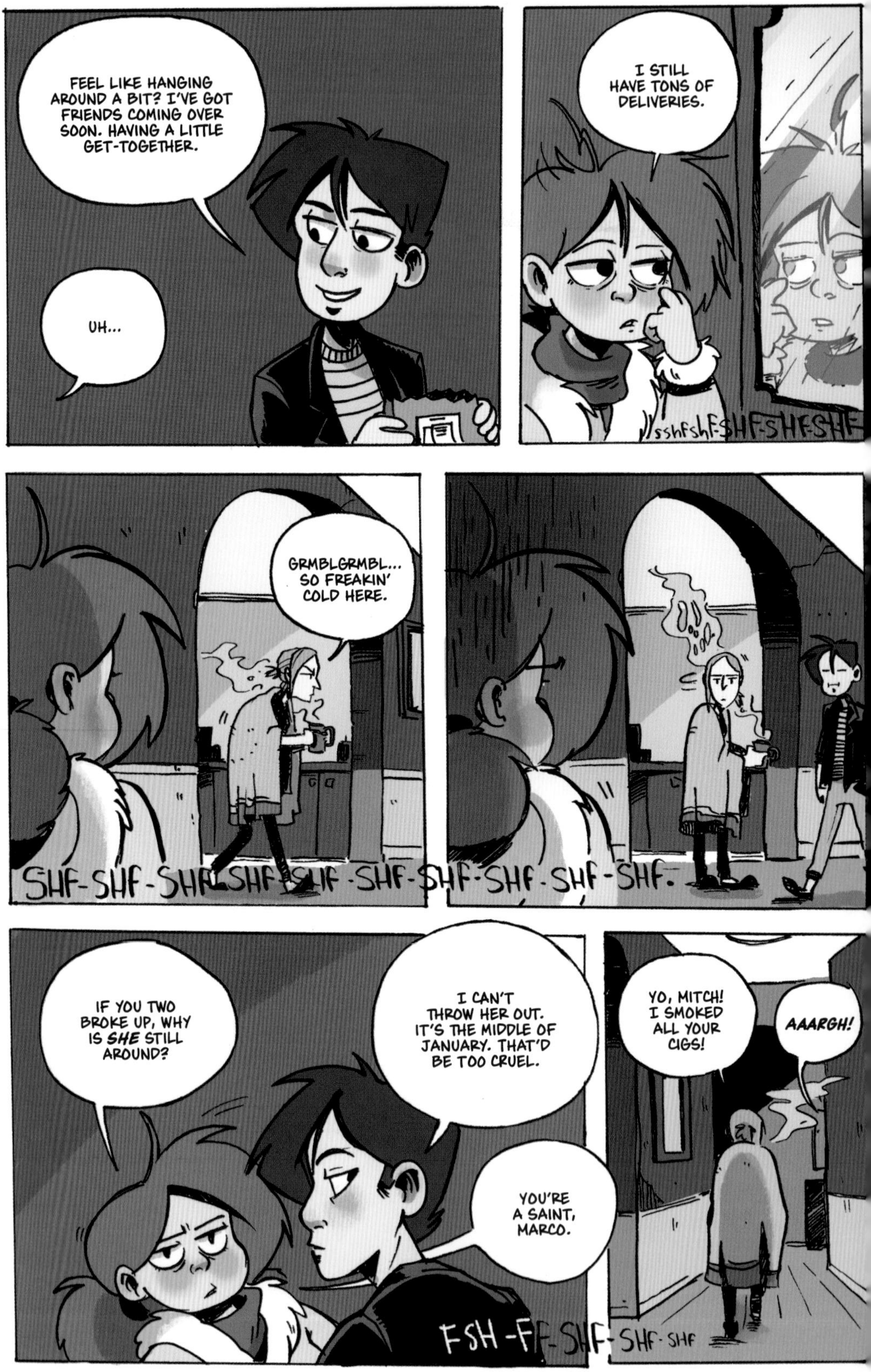
FEEL LIKE HANGING AROUND A BIT? I'VE GOT FRIENDS COMING OVER SOON. HAVING A LITTLE GET-TOGETHER.
UH...
I STILL HAVE TONS OF DELIVERIES.
sshfshf-SHF-SHF-SHF
GRMBLGRMBL... SO FREAKIN' COLD HERE.
SHF-SHF-SHF-SHF-SHF-SHF-SHF-SHF-SHF-SHF.
IF YOU TWO BROKE UP, WHY IS SHE STILL AROUND?
I CAN'T THROW HER OUT. IT'S THE MIDDLE OF JANUARY. THAT'D BE TOO CRUEL.
YOU'RE A SAINT, MARCO.
FSH-FF-SHF-SHF-SHF
YO, MITCH! I SMOKED ALL YOUR CIGS!
AAARGH!

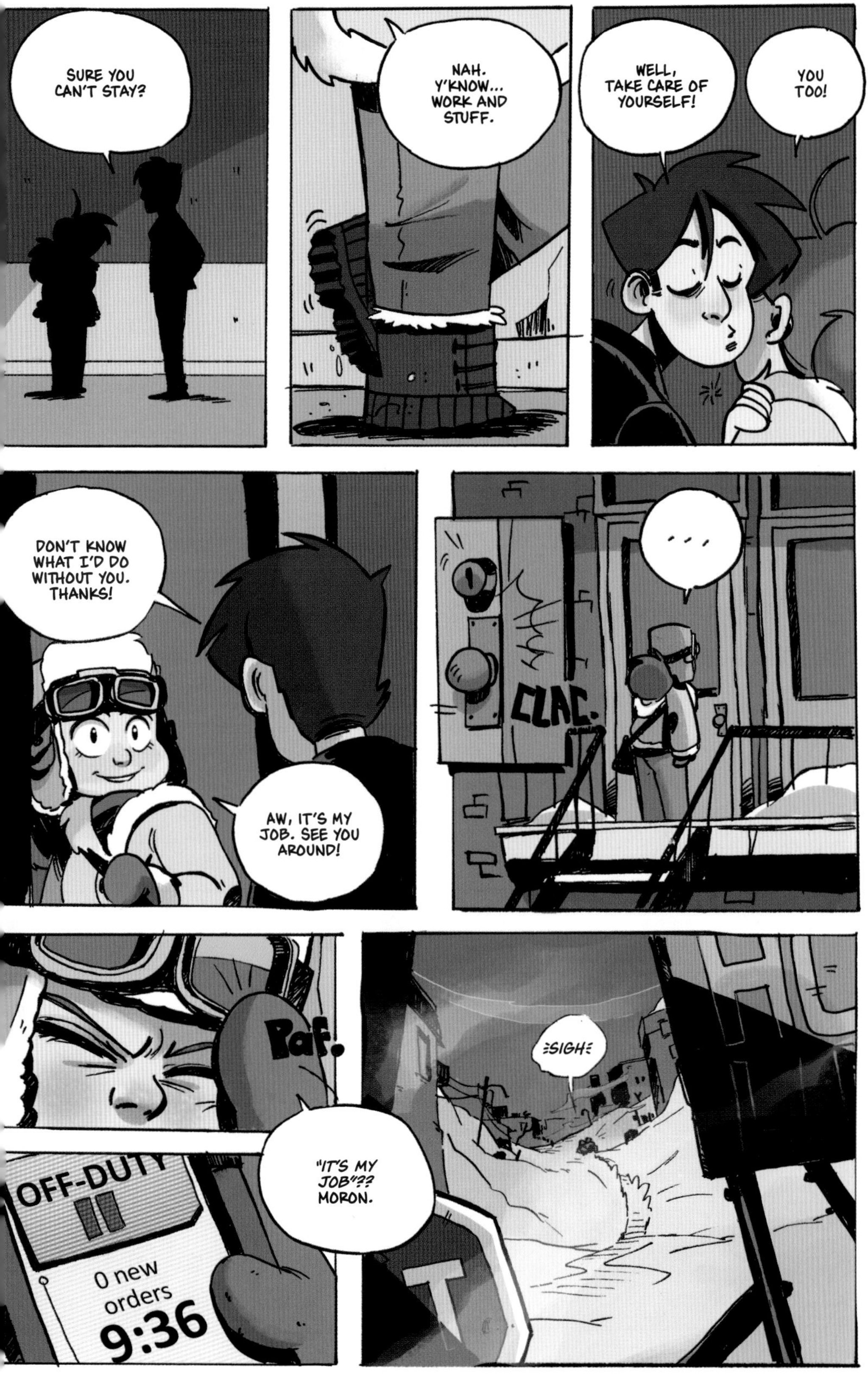
SURE YOU CAN'T STAY?
NAH. Y'KNOW... WORK AND STUFF.
WELL, TAKE CARE OF YOURSELF!
YOU TOO!
DON'T KNOW WHAT I'D DO WITHOUT YOU. THANKS!
AW, IT'S MY JOB. SEE YOU AROUND!
...
CLAC.
Paf.
OFF-DUTY
0 new orders
9:36
"IT'S MY JOB"?? MORON.
SIGH

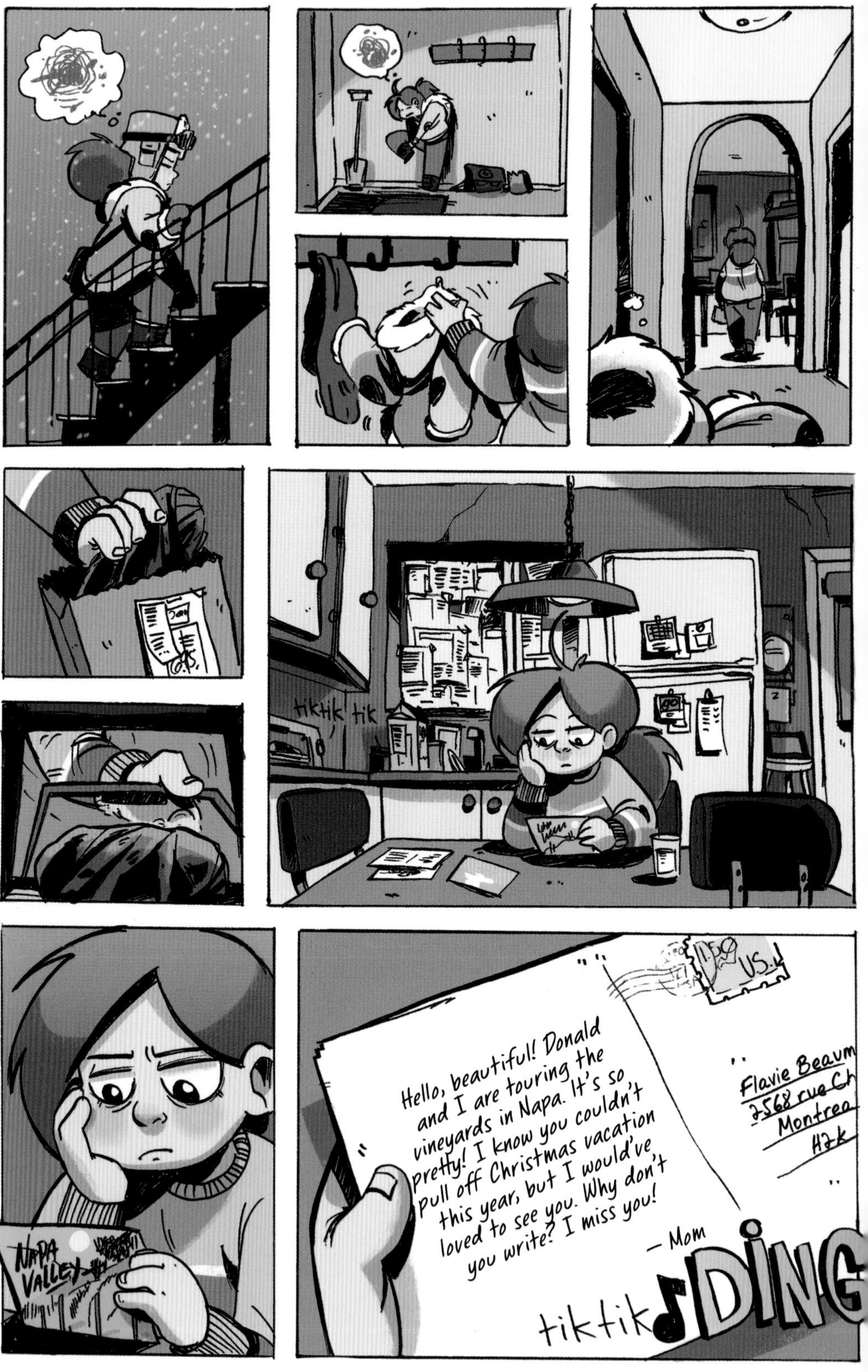
tiktik tik
NAPA VALLEY
Hello, beautiful! Donald and I are touring the vineyards in Napa. It's so pretty! I know you couldn't pull off Christmas vacation this year, but I would've loved to see you. Why don't you write? I miss you!
— Mom
US.
Flavie Beaum
2568 rue Ch
Montrea
H2K
tiktik DING

HOT, HOT, HOT!!

SO HUNGRY

TOC TOC!!

BANG

BA

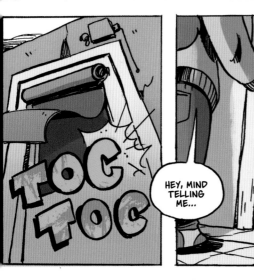

TOC TOC

HEY, MIND TELLING ME...

WHAT'S THE BIG IDEA?!

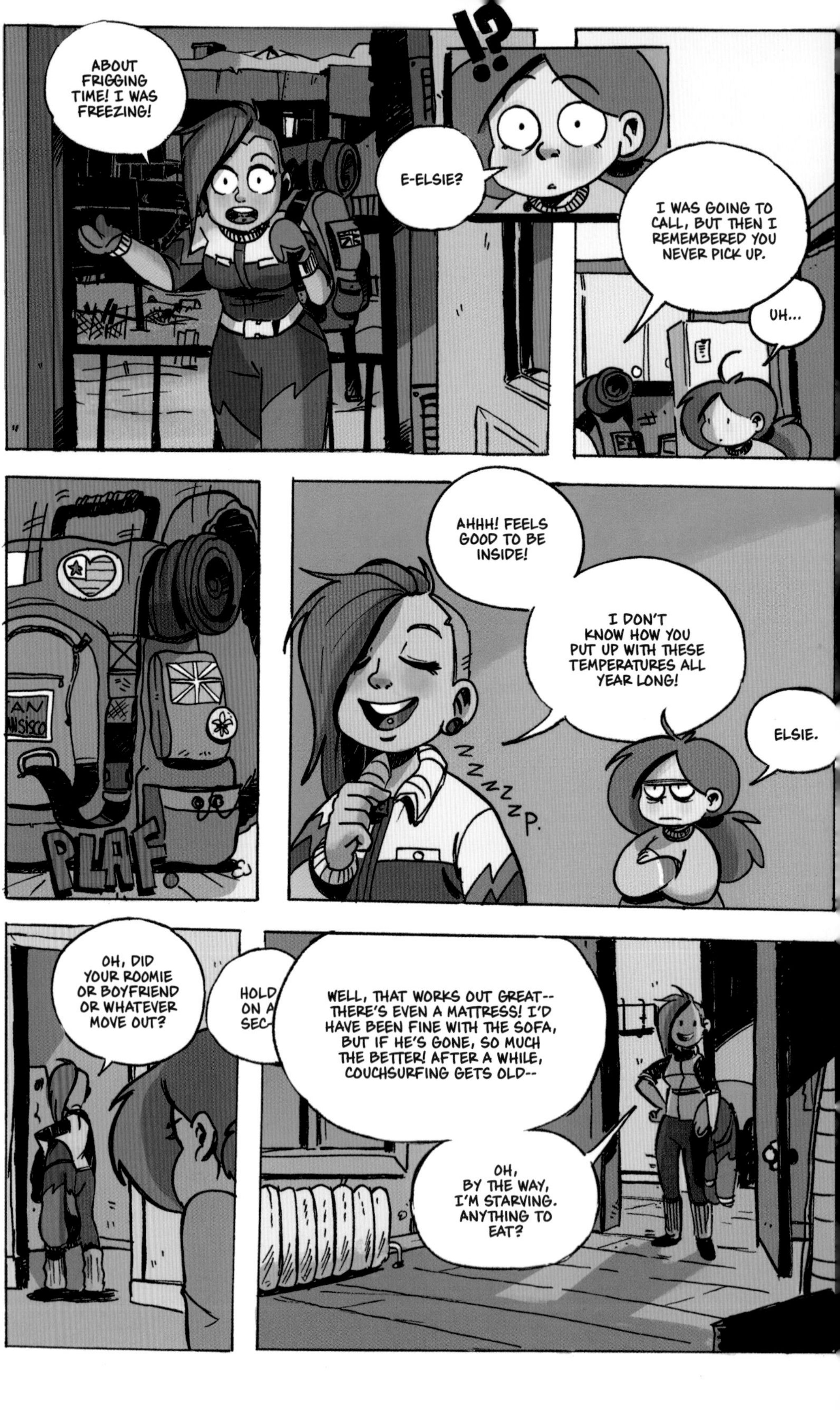
ABOUT FRIGGING TIME! I WAS FREEZING!
!?
E-ELSIE?
I WAS GOING TO CALL, BUT THEN I REMEMBERED YOU NEVER PICK UP.
UH...
PLAF
AHHH! FEELS GOOD TO BE INSIDE!
I DON'T KNOW HOW YOU PUT UP WITH THESE TEMPERATURES ALL YEAR LONG!
ZZZZZP.
ELSIE.
OH, DID YOUR ROOMIE OR BOYFRIEND OR WHATEVER MOVE OUT?
HOLD ON A SEC--
WELL, THAT WORKS OUT GREAT-- THERE'S EVEN A MATTRESS! I'D HAVE BEEN FINE WITH THE SOFA, BUT IF HE'S GONE, SO MUCH THE BETTER! AFTER A WHILE, COUCHSURFING GETS OLD--
OH, BY THE WAY, I'M STARVING. ANYTHING TO EAT?

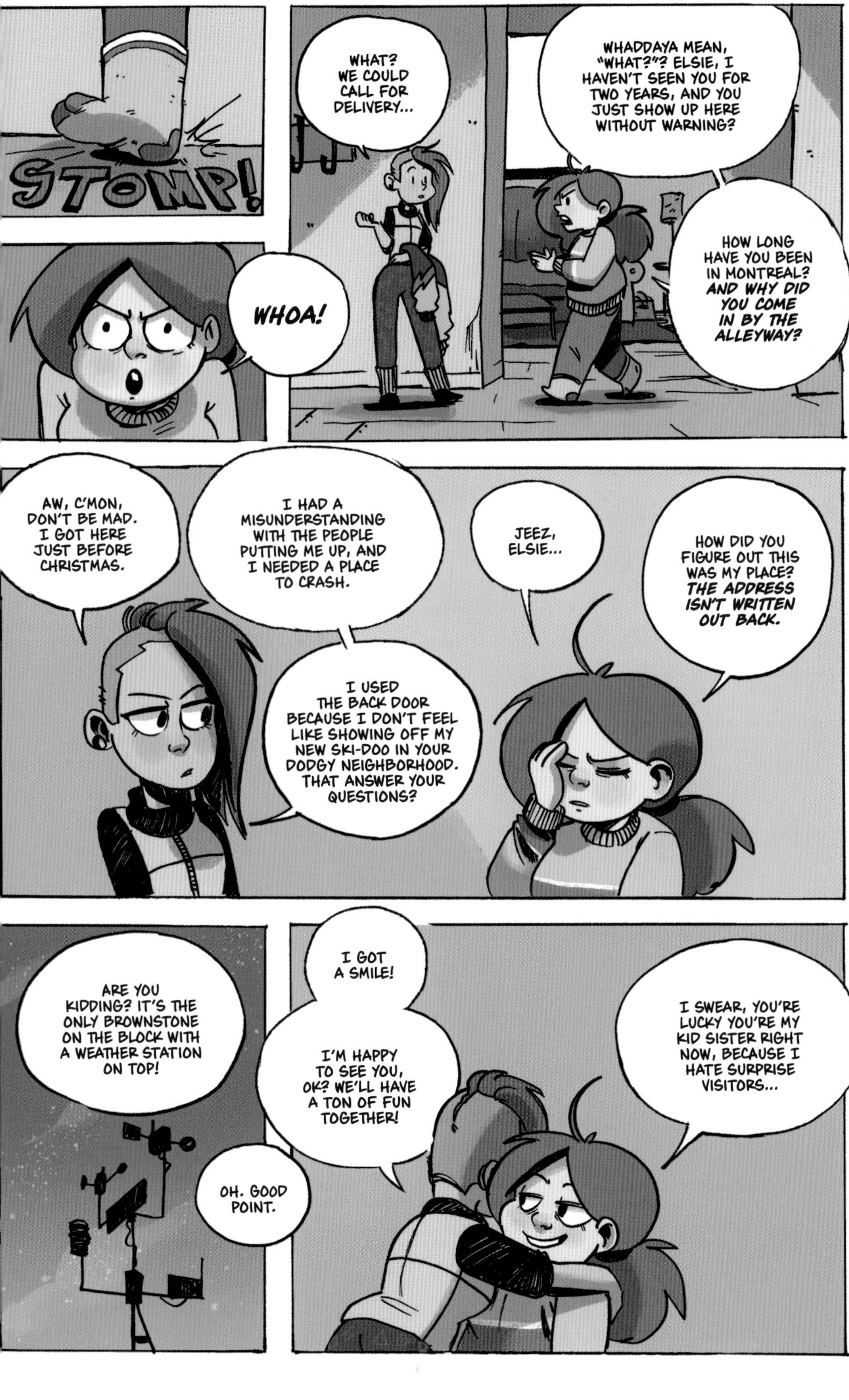
STOMP!
WHOA!
WHAT? WE COULD CALL FOR DELIVERY...
WHADDAYA MEAN, "WHAT?"? ELSIE, I HAVEN'T SEEN YOU FOR TWO YEARS, AND YOU JUST SHOW UP HERE WITHOUT WARNING?
HOW LONG HAVE YOU BEEN IN MONTREAL? AND WHY DID YOU COME IN BY THE ALLEYWAY?
AW, C'MON, DON'T BE MAD. I GOT HERE JUST BEFORE CHRISTMAS.
I HAD A MISUNDERSTANDING WITH THE PEOPLE PUTTING ME UP, AND I NEEDED A PLACE TO CRASH.
I USED THE BACK DOOR BECAUSE I DON'T FEEL LIKE SHOWING OFF MY NEW SKI-DOO IN YOUR DODGY NEIGHBORHOOD. THAT ANSWER YOUR QUESTIONS?
JEEZ, ELSIE...
HOW DID YOU FIGURE OUT THIS WAS MY PLACE? THE ADDRESS ISN'T WRITTEN OUT BACK.
ARE YOU KIDDING? IT'S THE ONLY BROWNSTONE ON THE BLOCK WITH A WEATHER STATION ON TOP!
OH. GOOD POINT.
I GOT A SMILE!
I'M HAPPY TO SEE YOU, OK? WE'LL HAVE A TON OF FUN TOGETHER!
I SWEAR, YOU'RE LUCKY YOU'RE MY KID SISTER RIGHT NOW, BECAUSE I HATE SURPRISE VISITORS...

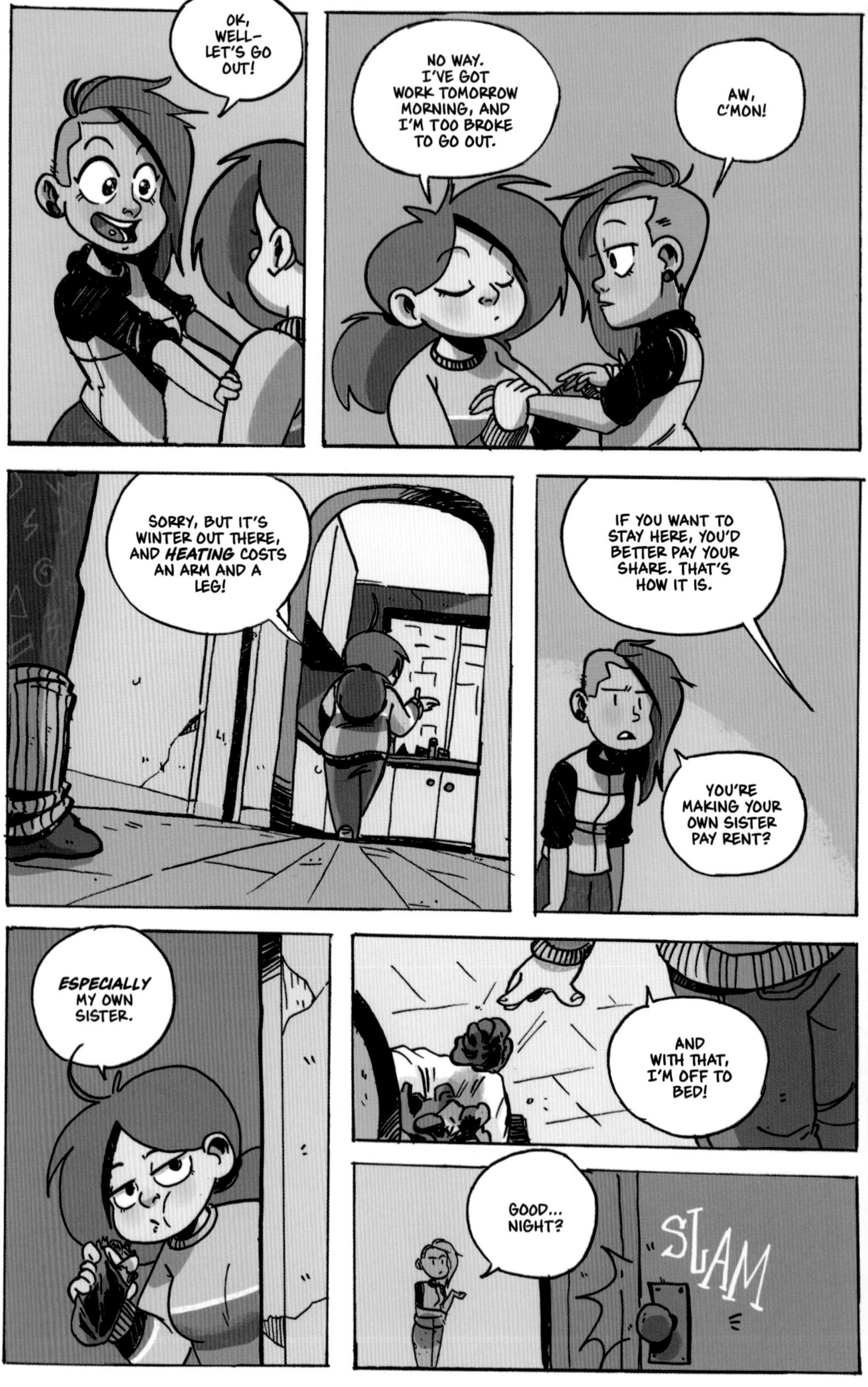
OK, WELL- LET'S GO OUT!
NO WAY. I'VE GOT WORK TOMORROW MORNING, AND I'M TOO BROKE TO GO OUT.
AW, C'MON!
SORRY, BUT IT'S WINTER OUT THERE, AND *HEATING* COSTS AN ARM AND A LEG!
IF YOU WANT TO STAY HERE, YOU'D BETTER PAY YOUR SHARE. THAT'S HOW IT IS.
YOU'RE MAKING YOUR OWN SISTER PAY RENT?
ESPECIALLY MY OWN SISTER.
AND WITH THAT, I'M OFF TO BED!
GOOD... NIGHT?
SLAM

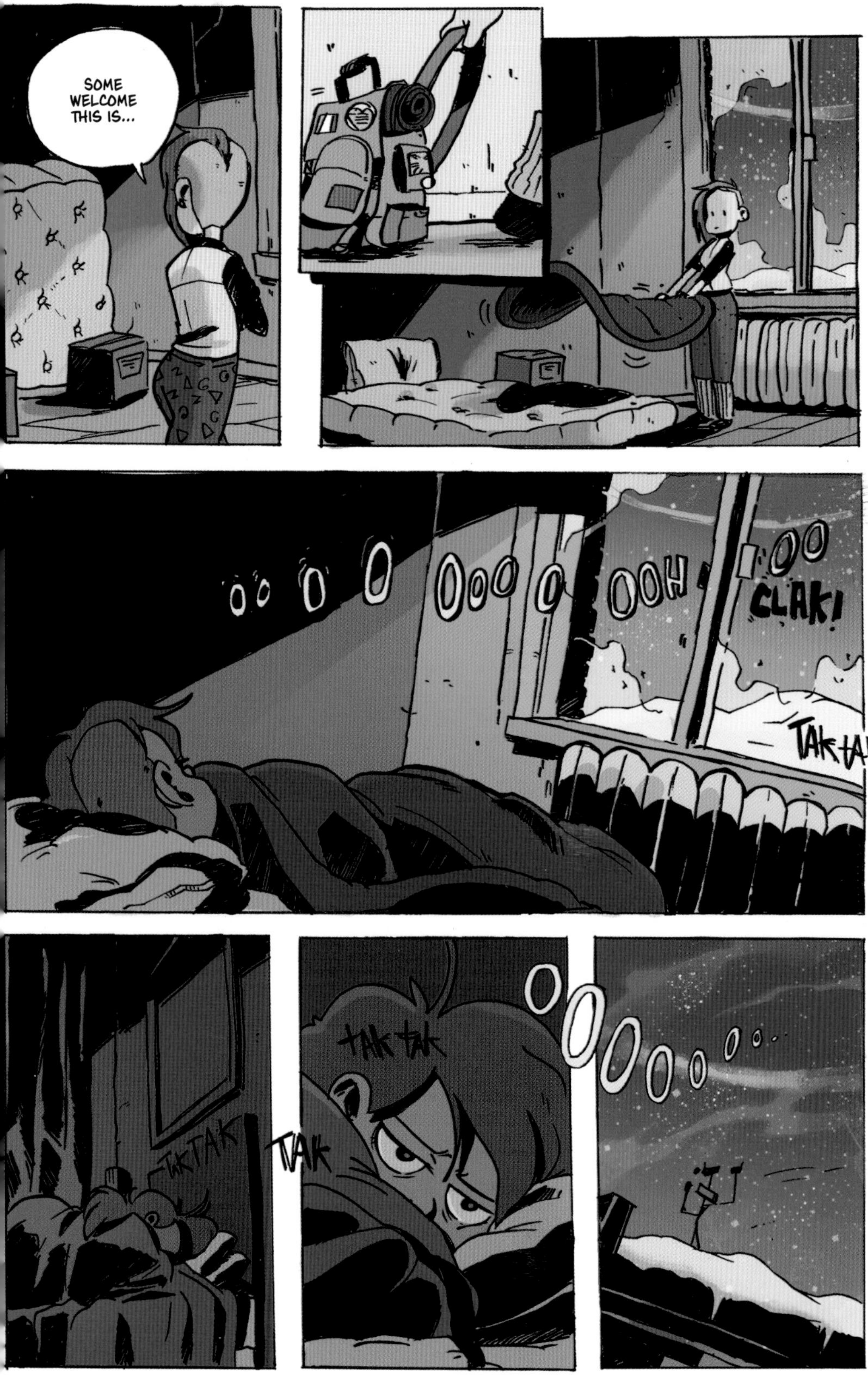
SOME WELCOME THIS IS...
OOOOOOOOOOOOH
CLAK!
TAKTAK
TAKTAK
TAKTAK
TAK
OOOOOOOOO..

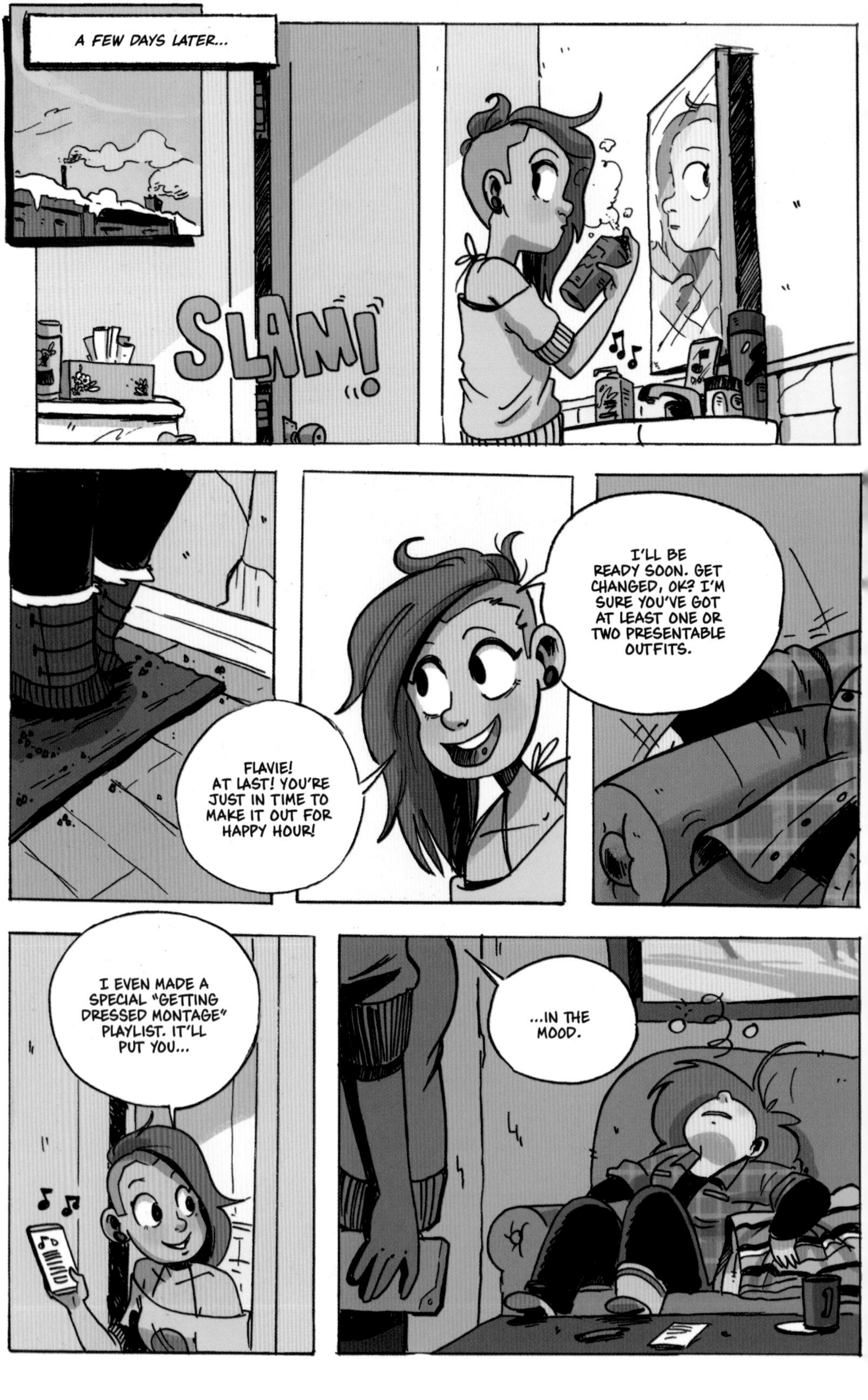
A FEW DAYS LATER...
SLAM!
FLAVIE! AT LAST! YOU'RE JUST IN TIME TO MAKE IT OUT FOR HAPPY HOUR!
I'LL BE READY SOON. GET CHANGED, OK? I'M SURE YOU'VE GOT AT LEAST ONE OR TWO PRESENTABLE OUTFITS.
I EVEN MADE A SPECIAL "GETTING DRESSED MONTAGE" PLAYLIST. IT'LL PUT YOU...
...IN THE MOOD.

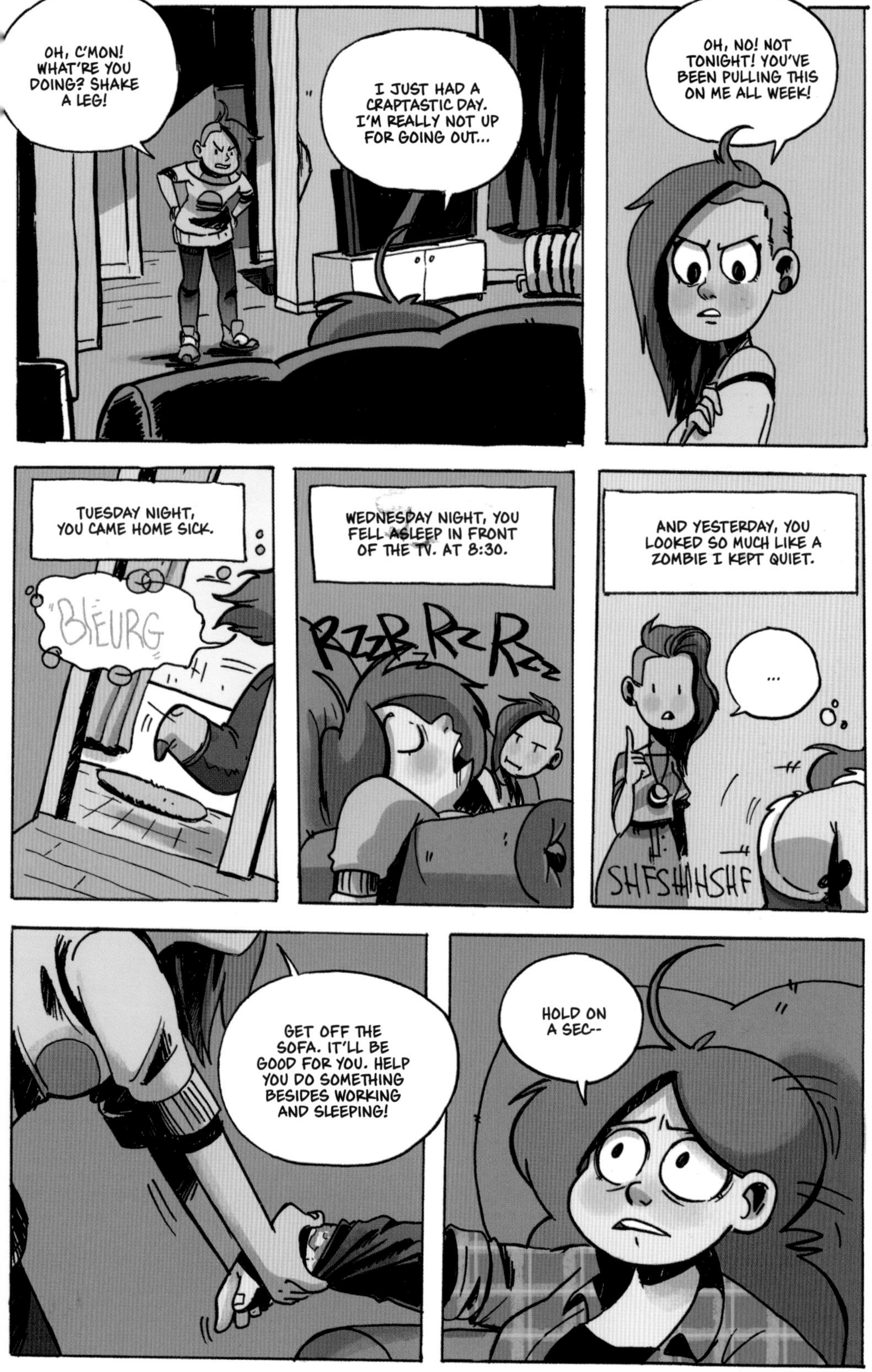

OH, C'MON! WHAT'RE YOU DOING? SHAKE A LEG!
I JUST HAD A CRAPTASTIC DAY. I'M REALLY NOT UP FOR GOING OUT...
OH, NO! NOT TONIGHT! YOU'VE BEEN PULLING THIS ON ME ALL WEEK!
TUESDAY NIGHT, YOU CAME HOME SICK.
BLEURG
WEDNESDAY NIGHT, YOU FELL ASLEEP IN FRONT OF THE TV. AT 8:30.
RZZBRZZRZZZ
AND YESTERDAY, YOU LOOKED SO MUCH LIKE A ZOMBIE I KEPT QUIET.
...
SHFSHHHSHF
GET OFF THE SOFA. IT'LL BE GOOD FOR YOU. HELP YOU DO SOMETHING BESIDES WORKING AND SLEEPING!
HOLD ON A SEC--

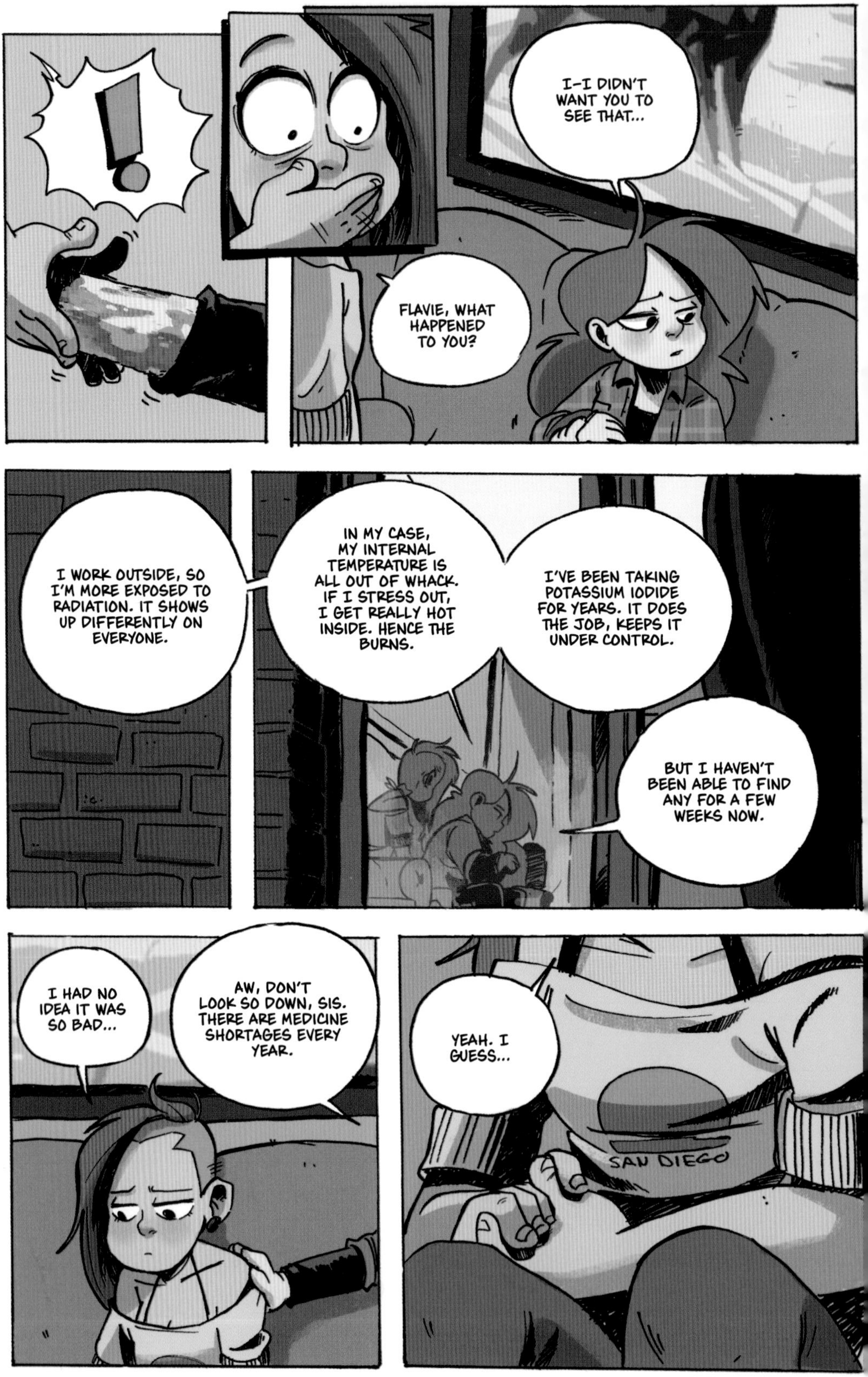
!
FLAVIE, WHAT HAPPENED TO YOU?
I-I DIDN'T WANT YOU TO SEE THAT...
I WORK OUTSIDE, SO I'M MORE EXPOSED TO RADIATION. IT SHOWS UP DIFFERENTLY ON EVERYONE.
IN MY CASE, MY INTERNAL TEMPERATURE IS ALL OUT OF WHACK. IF I STRESS OUT, I GET REALLY HOT INSIDE. HENCE THE BURNS.
I'VE BEEN TAKING POTASSIUM IODIDE FOR YEARS. IT DOES THE JOB, KEEPS IT UNDER CONTROL.
BUT I HAVEN'T BEEN ABLE TO FIND ANY FOR A FEW WEEKS NOW.
I HAD NO IDEA IT WAS SO BAD...
AW, DON'T LOOK SO DOWN, SIS. THERE ARE MEDICINE SHORTAGES EVERY YEAR.
YEAH. I GUESS...
SAN DIEGO

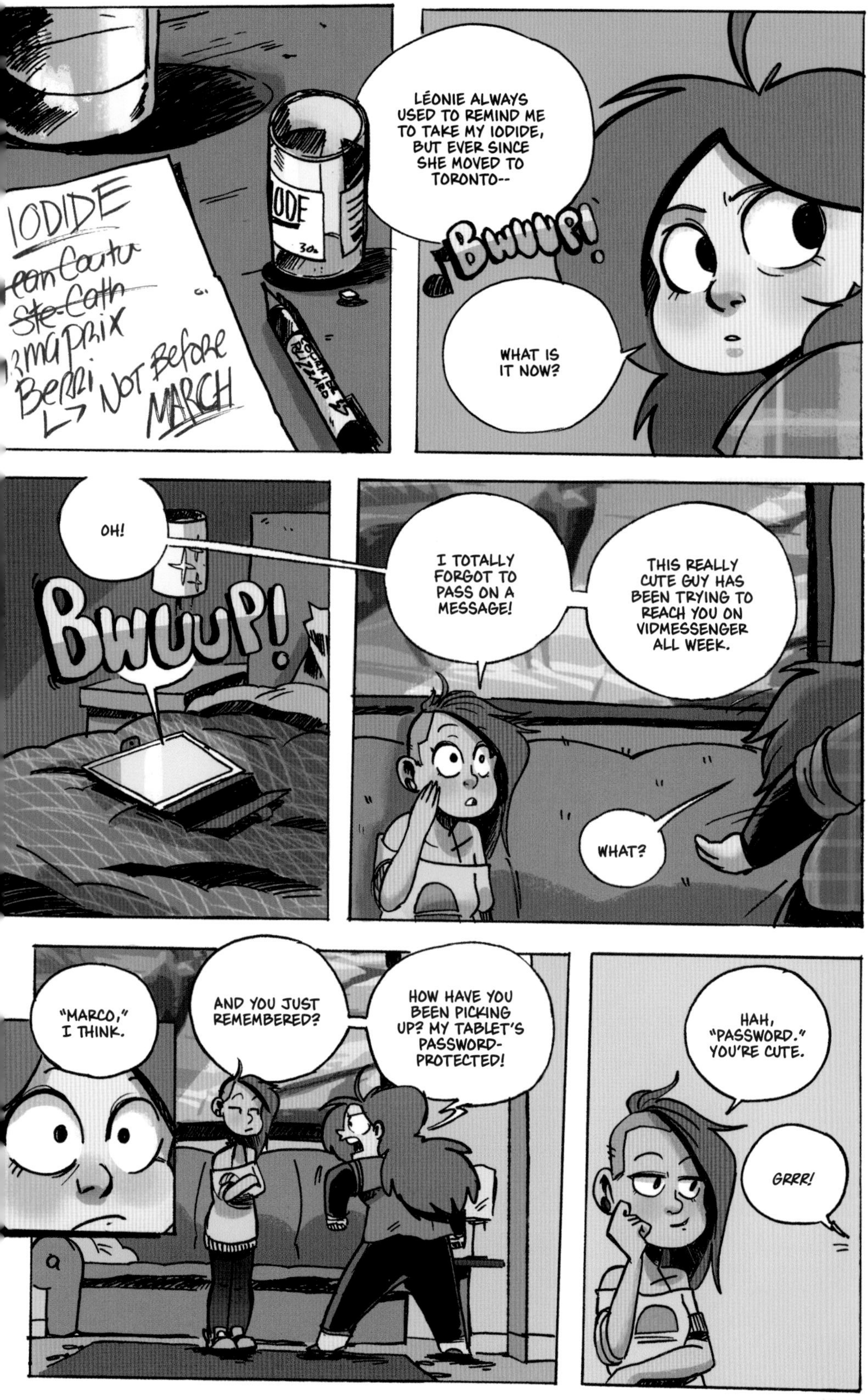
IODIDE
ean Coutu
Ste-Cath
13 maprix
Berri
└> NOT BEFORE MARCH
ODE
LÉONIE ALWAYS USED TO REMIND ME TO TAKE MY IODIDE, BUT EVER SINCE SHE MOVED TO TORONTO--
BWUUP!
WHAT IS IT NOW?
OH!
BWUUP!
I TOTALLY FORGOT TO PASS ON A MESSAGE!
THIS REALLY CUTE GUY HAS BEEN TRYING TO REACH YOU ON VIDMESSENGER ALL WEEK.
WHAT?
"MARCO," I THINK.
AND YOU JUST REMEMBERED?
HOW HAVE YOU BEEN PICKING UP? MY TABLET'S PASSWORD-PROTECTED!
HAH, "PASSWORD." YOU'RE CUTE.
GRRR!

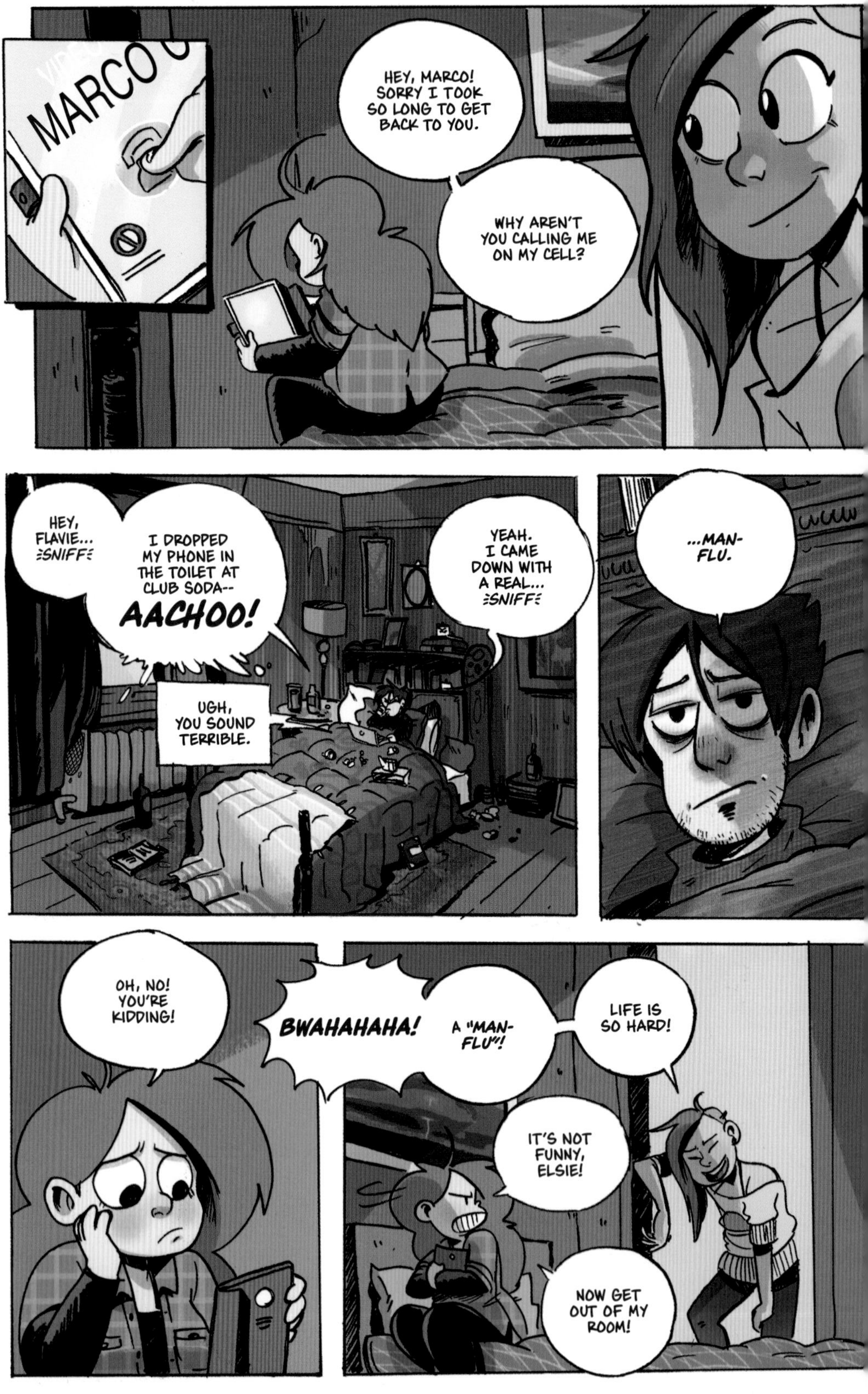
MARCO
HEY, MARCO! SORRY I TOOK SO LONG TO GET BACK TO YOU.
WHY AREN'T YOU CALLING ME ON MY CELL?
HEY, FLAVIE... SNIFF
I DROPPED MY PHONE IN THE TOILET AT CLUB SODA--
AACHOO!
UGH, YOU SOUND TERRIBLE.
YEAH. I CAME DOWN WITH A REAL... SNIFF
...MAN-FLU.
OH, NO! YOU'RE KIDDING!
BWAHAHAHA!
A "MAN-FLU"!
LIFE IS SO HARD!
IT'S NOT FUNNY, ELSIE!
NOW GET OUT OF MY ROOM!

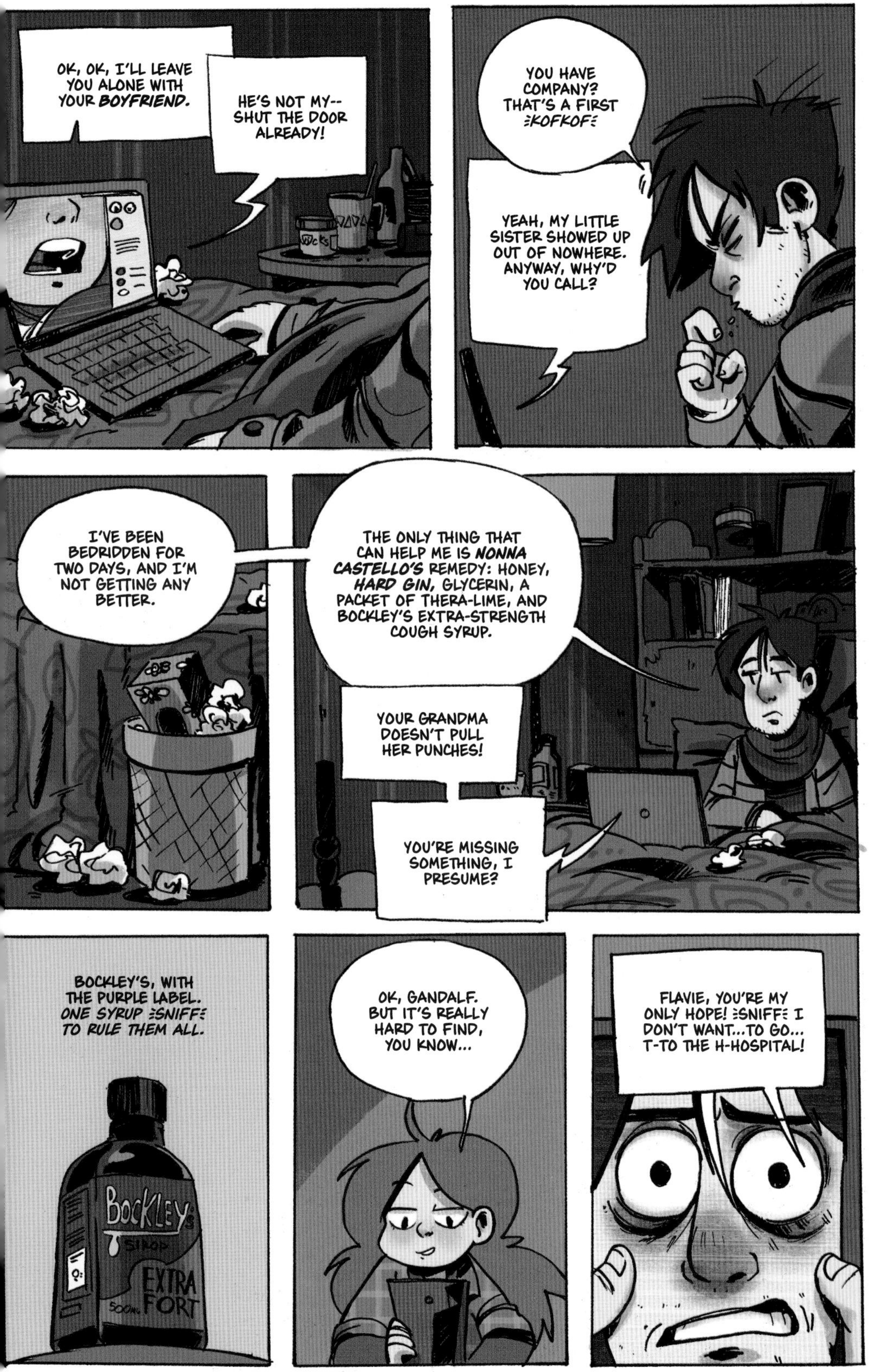
OK, OK, I'LL LEAVE YOU ALONE WITH YOUR *BOYFRIEND.*
HE'S NOT MY-- SHUT THE DOOR ALREADY!
YOU HAVE COMPANY? THAT'S A FIRST ⩶KOFKOF⩶
YEAH, MY LITTLE SISTER SHOWED UP OUT OF NOWHERE. ANYWAY, WHY'D YOU CALL?
I'VE BEEN BEDRIDDEN FOR TWO DAYS, AND I'M NOT GETTING ANY BETTER.
THE ONLY THING THAT CAN HELP ME IS ***NONNA CASTELLO'S*** REMEDY: HONEY, ***HARD GIN,*** GLYCERIN, A PACKET OF THERA-LIME, AND BOCKLEY'S EXTRA-STRENGTH COUGH SYRUP.
YOUR GRANDMA DOESN'T PULL HER PUNCHES!
YOU'RE MISSING SOMETHING, I PRESUME?
BOCKLEY'S, WITH THE PURPLE LABEL. *ONE SYRUP* ⩶SNIFF⩶ *TO RULE THEM ALL.*
BOCKLEY'S
SIROP
EXTRA FORT
500ML
OK, GANDALF. BUT IT'S REALLY HARD TO FIND, YOU KNOW...
FLAVIE, YOU'RE MY ONLY HOPE! ⩶SNIFF⩶ I DON'T WANT...TO GO... T-TO THE H-HOSPITAL!

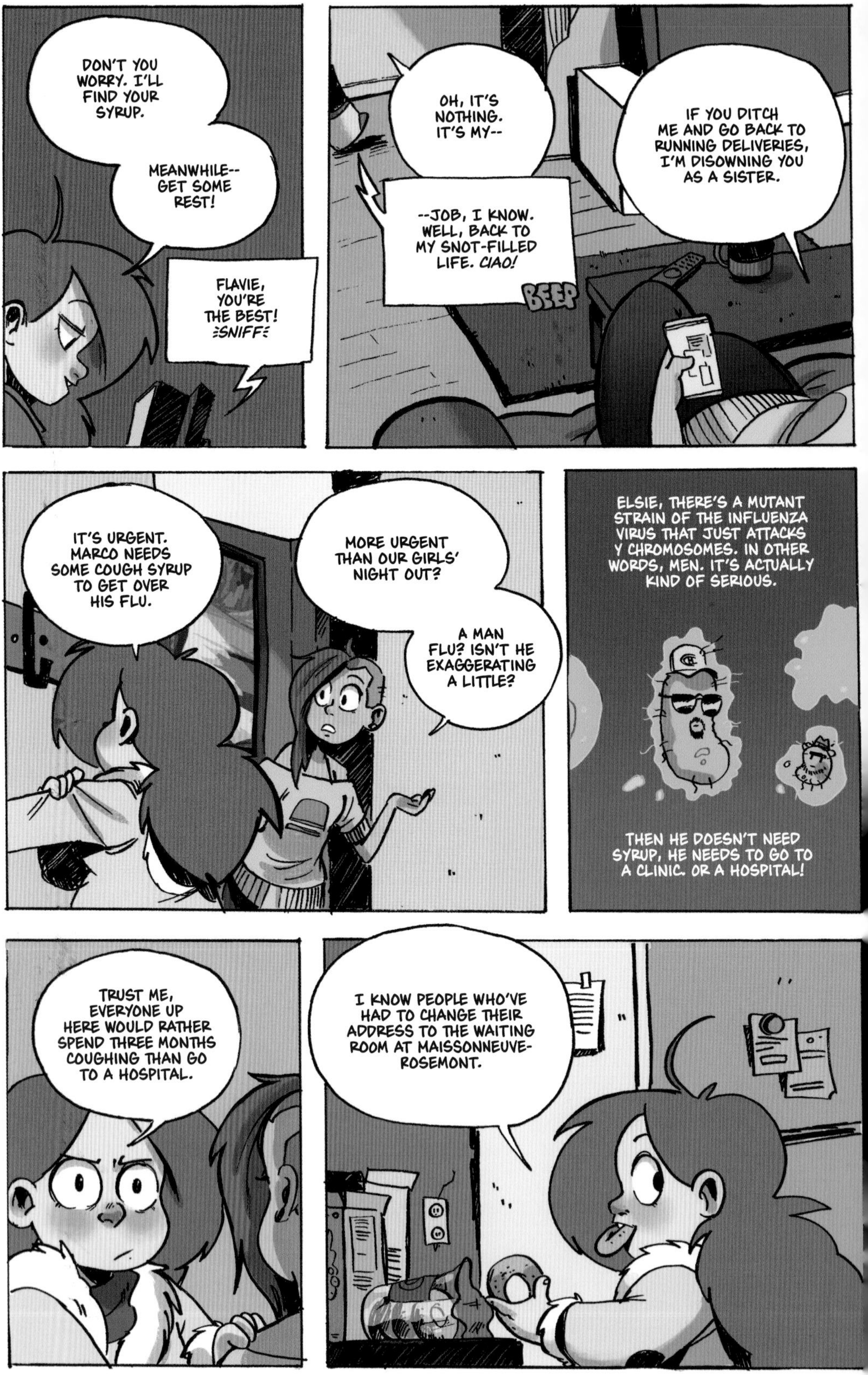
DON'T YOU WORRY. I'LL FIND YOUR SYRUP.
MEANWHILE-- GET SOME REST!
FLAVIE, YOU'RE THE BEST! SNIFF
OH, IT'S NOTHING. IT'S MY--
--JOB, I KNOW. WELL, BACK TO MY SNOT-FILLED LIFE. CIAO!
BEEP
IF YOU DITCH ME AND GO BACK TO RUNNING DELIVERIES, I'M DISOWNING YOU AS A SISTER.
IT'S URGENT. MARCO NEEDS SOME COUGH SYRUP TO GET OVER HIS FLU.
MORE URGENT THAN OUR GIRLS' NIGHT OUT?
A MAN FLU? ISN'T HE EXAGGERATING A LITTLE?
ELSIE, THERE'S A MUTANT STRAIN OF THE INFLUENZA VIRUS THAT JUST ATTACKS Y CHROMOSOMES. IN OTHER WORDS, MEN. IT'S ACTUALLY KIND OF SERIOUS.
THEN HE DOESN'T NEED SYRUP, HE NEEDS TO GO TO A CLINIC. OR A HOSPITAL!
TRUST ME, EVERYONE UP HERE WOULD RATHER SPEND THREE MONTHS COUGHING THAN GO TO A HOSPITAL.
I KNOW PEOPLE WHO'VE HAD TO CHANGE THEIR ADDRESS TO THE WAITING ROOM AT MAISSONNEUVE-ROSEMONT.

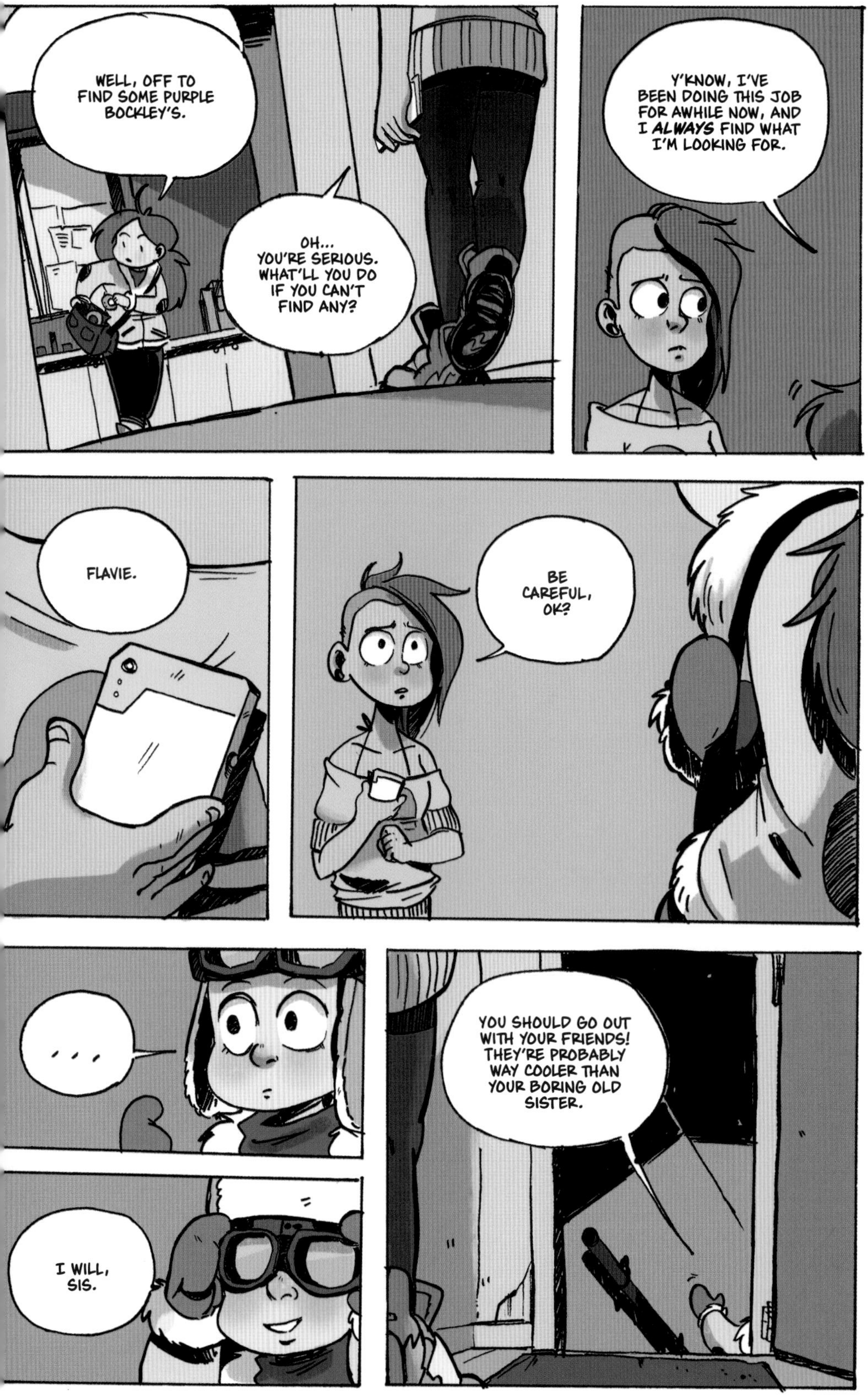

WELL, OFF TO FIND SOME PURPLE BOCKLEY'S.
OH... YOU'RE SERIOUS. WHAT'LL YOU DO IF YOU CAN'T FIND ANY?
Y'KNOW, I'VE BEEN DOING THIS JOB FOR AWHILE NOW, AND I *ALWAYS* FIND WHAT I'M LOOKING FOR.
FLAVIE.
BE CAREFUL, OK?
. . .
YOU SHOULD GO OUT WITH YOUR FRIENDS! THEY'RE PROBABLY WAY COOLER THAN YOUR BORING OLD SISTER.
I WILL, SIS.

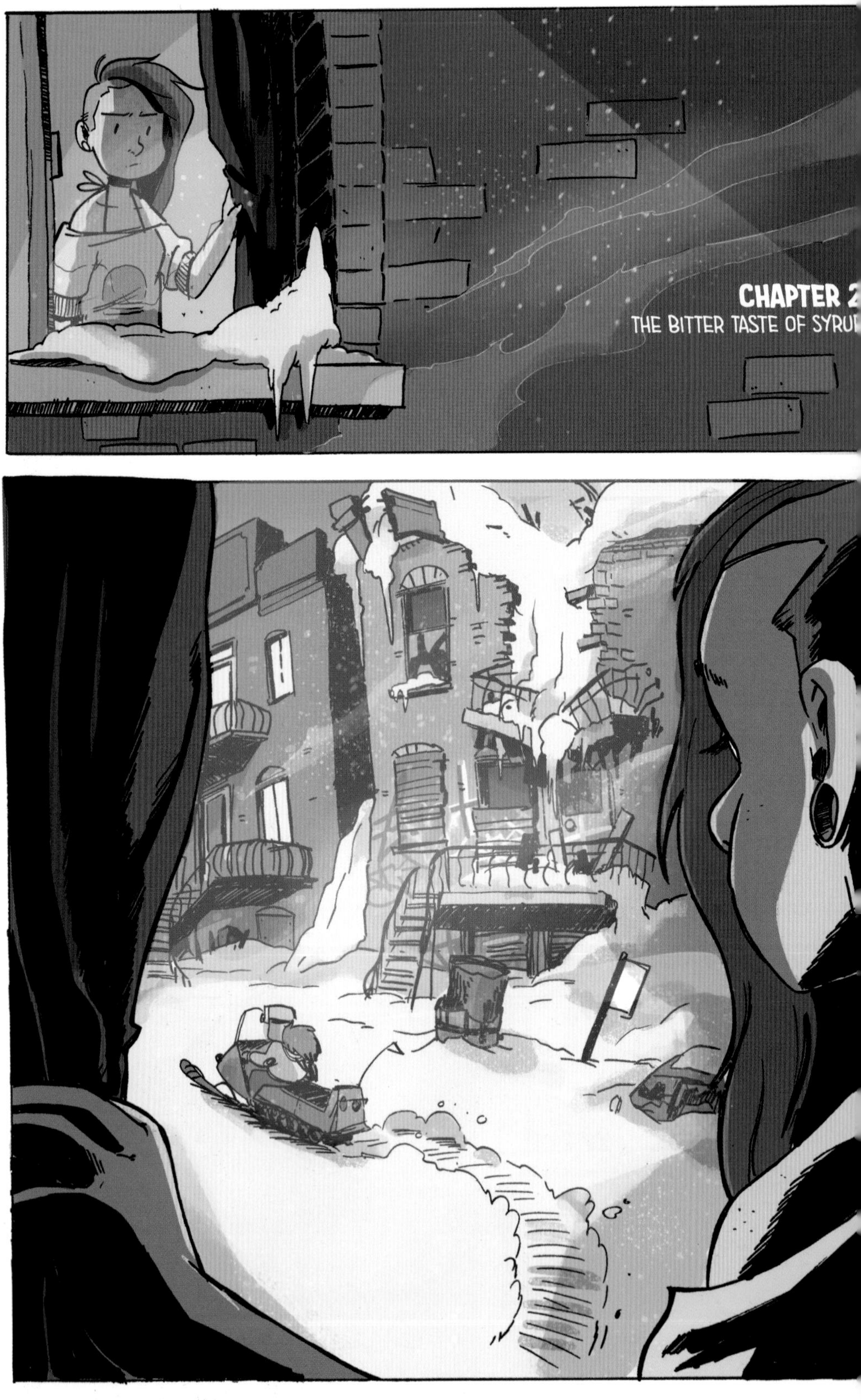
CHAPTER 2
THE BITTER TASTE OF SYRUP

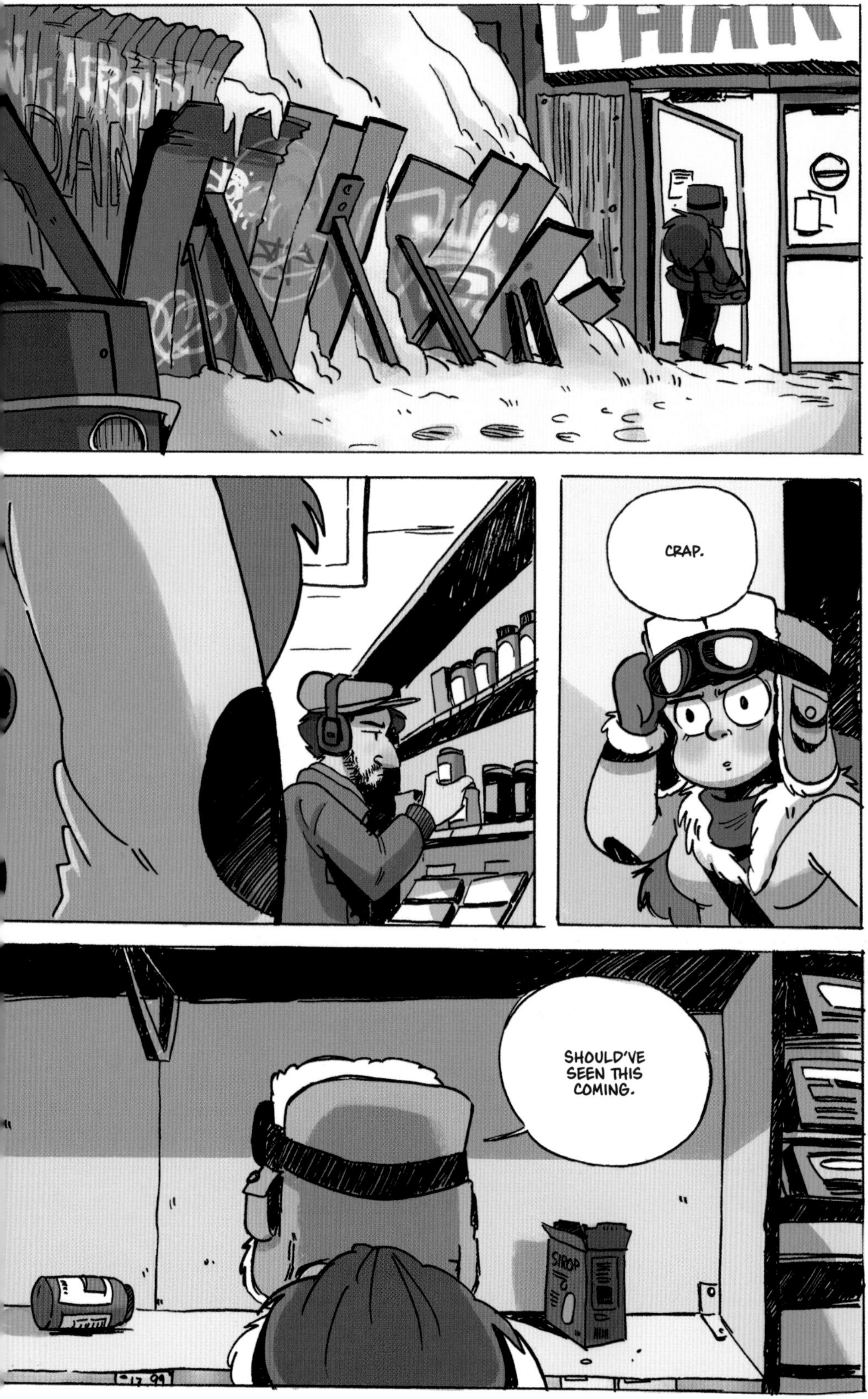
PHAR
CRAP.
SHOULD'VE SEEN THIS COMING.
SIROP

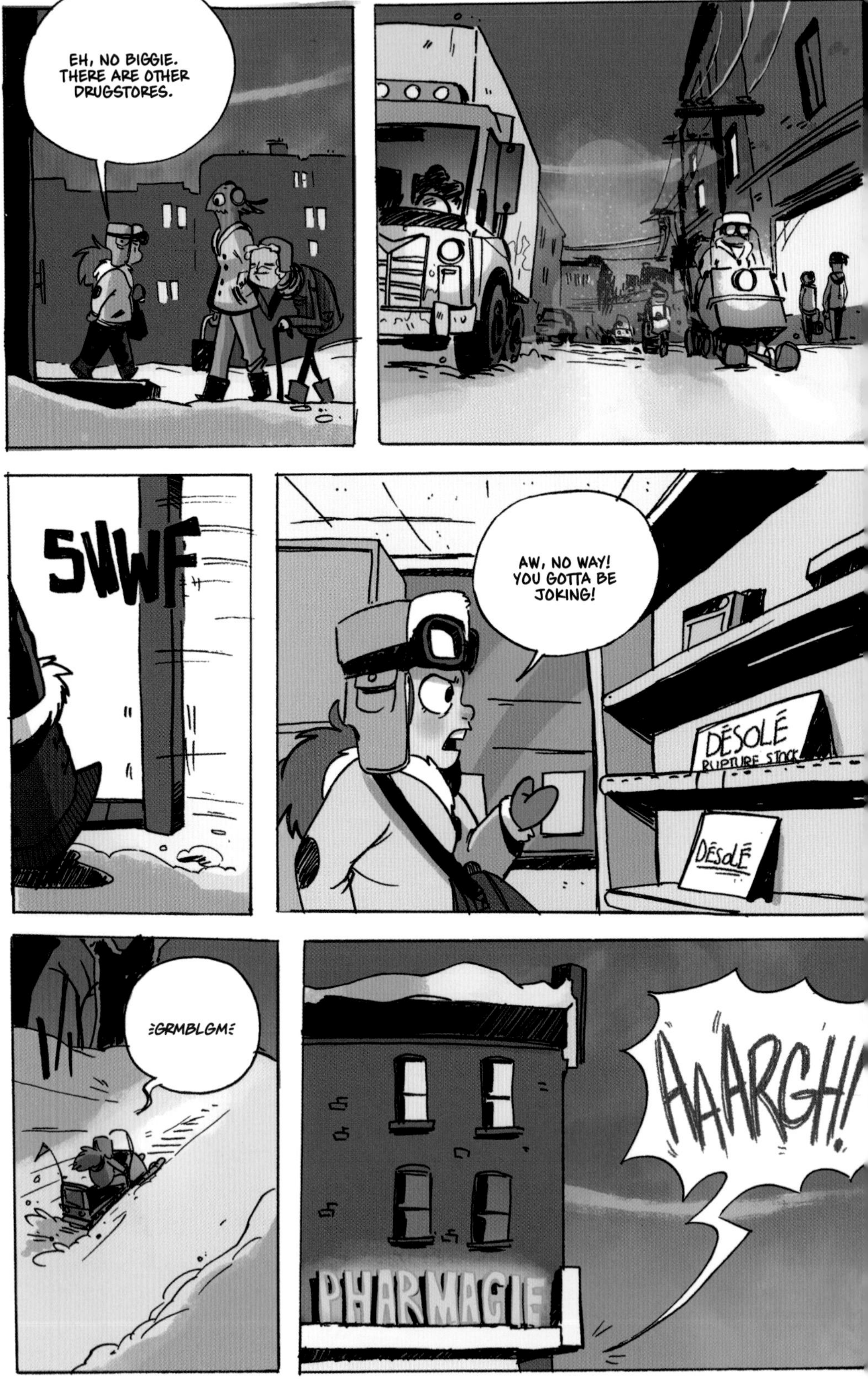
EH, NO BIGGIE. THERE ARE OTHER DRUGSTORES.
SWF
AW, NO WAY! YOU GOTTA BE JOKING!
DÉSOLÉ
RUPTURE STOCK
DÉSOLÉ
GRMBLGM
PHARMACIE
AARGH!

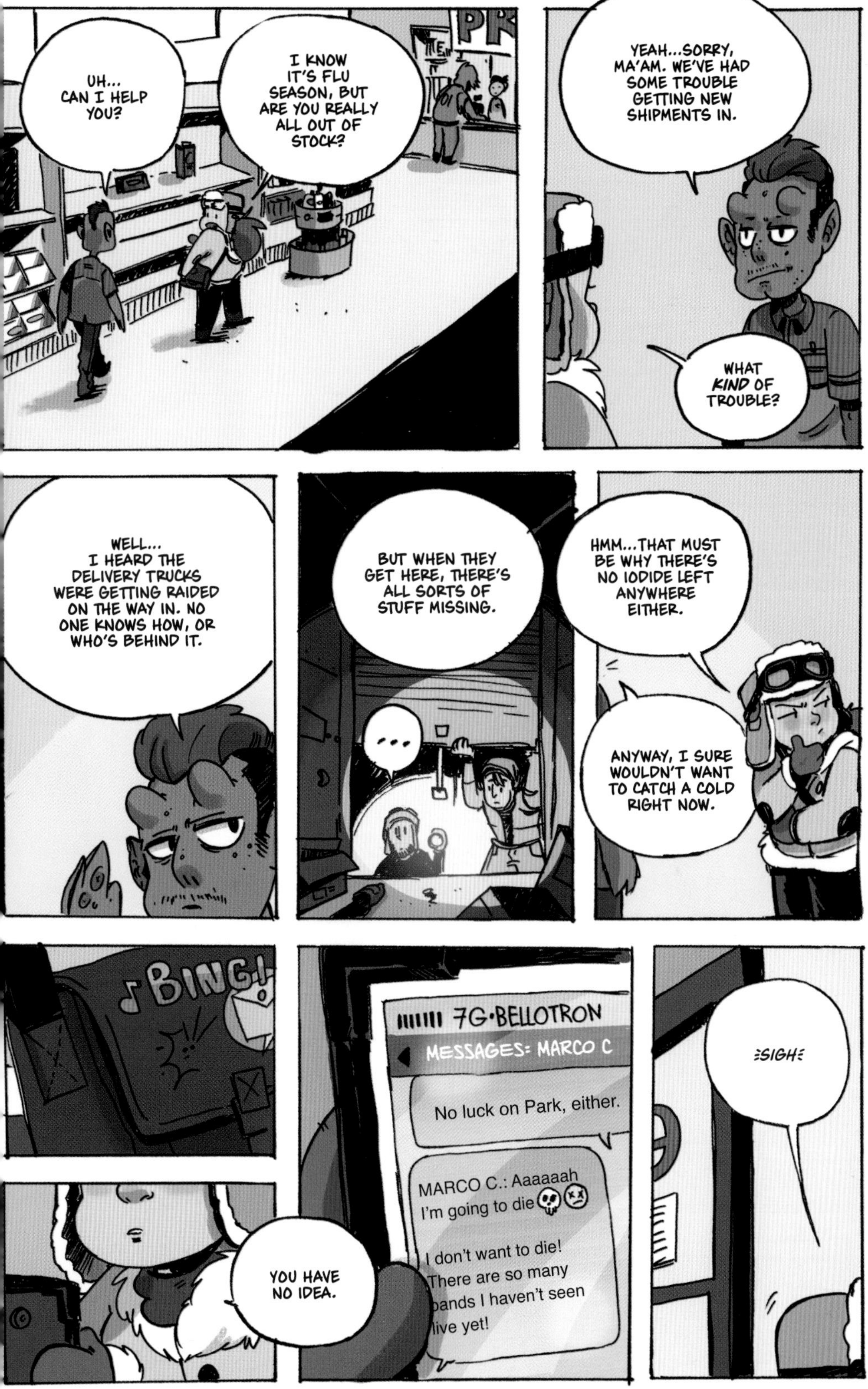
UH... CAN I HELP YOU?
I KNOW IT'S FLU SEASON, BUT ARE YOU REALLY ALL OUT OF STOCK?
YEAH...SORRY, MA'AM. WE'VE HAD SOME TROUBLE GETTING NEW SHIPMENTS IN.
WHAT KIND OF TROUBLE?
WELL... I HEARD THE DELIVERY TRUCKS WERE GETTING RAIDED ON THE WAY IN. NO ONE KNOWS HOW, OR WHO'S BEHIND IT.
BUT WHEN THEY GET HERE, THERE'S ALL SORTS OF STUFF MISSING.
...
HMM...THAT MUST BE WHY THERE'S NO IODIDE LEFT ANYWHERE EITHER.
ANYWAY, I SURE WOULDN'T WANT TO CATCH A COLD RIGHT NOW.
BING!
7G•BELLOTRON
MESSAGES: MARCO C
No luck on Park, either.
MARCO C.: Aaaaaah I'm going to die
I don't want to die! There are so many bands I haven't seen live yet!
YOU HAVE NO IDEA.
SIGH

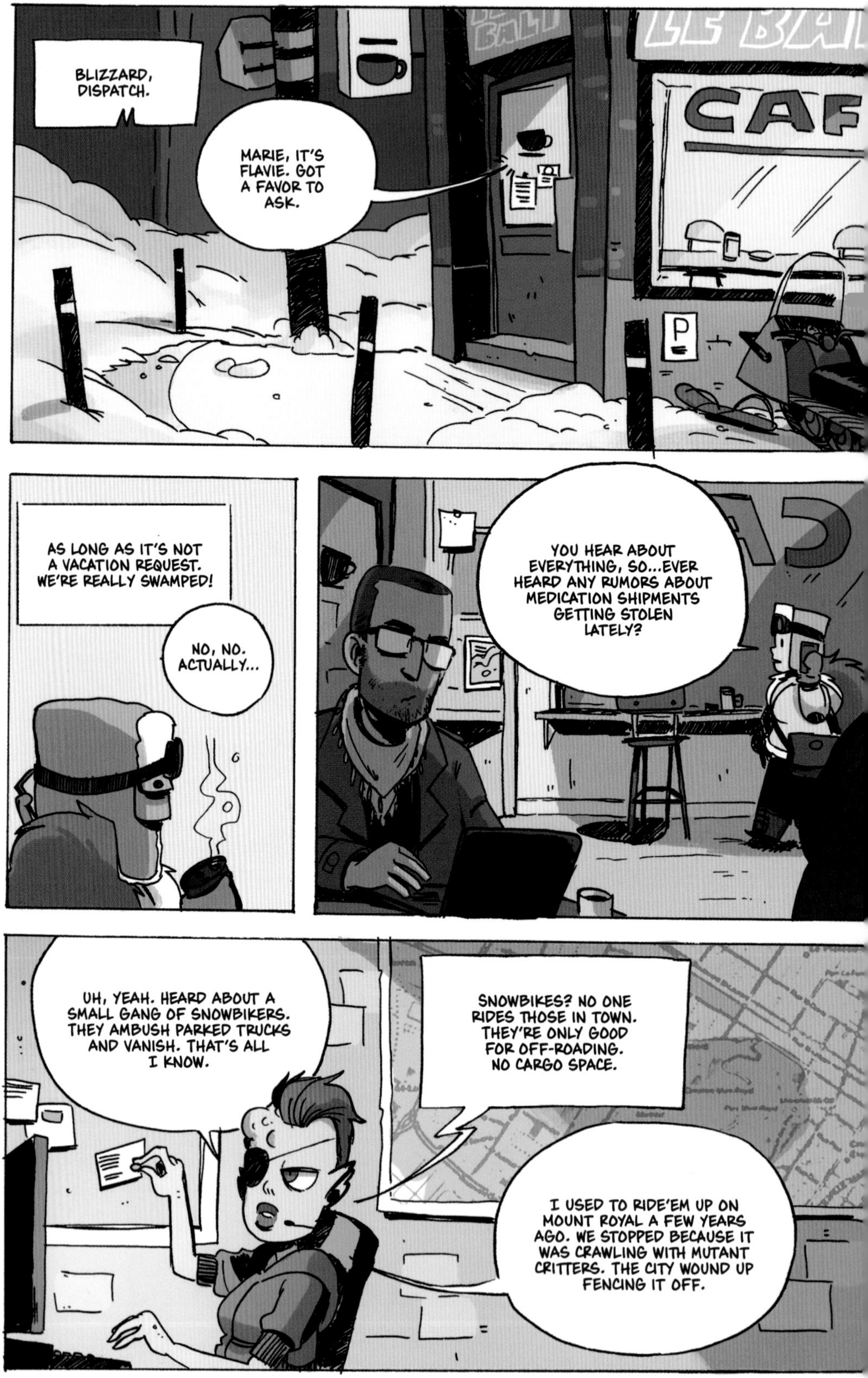
BLIZZARD, DISPATCH.
MARIE, IT'S FLAVIE. GOT A FAVOR TO ASK.
AS LONG AS IT'S NOT A VACATION REQUEST. WE'RE REALLY SWAMPED!
NO, NO. ACTUALLY...
YOU HEAR ABOUT EVERYTHING, SO...EVER HEARD ANY RUMORS ABOUT MEDICATION SHIPMENTS GETTING STOLEN LATELY?
UH, YEAH. HEARD ABOUT A SMALL GANG OF SNOWBIKERS. THEY AMBUSH PARKED TRUCKS AND VANISH. THAT'S ALL I KNOW.
SNOWBIKES? NO ONE RIDES THOSE IN TOWN. THEY'RE ONLY GOOD FOR OFF-ROADING. NO CARGO SPACE.
I USED TO RIDE'EM UP ON MOUNT ROYAL A FEW YEARS AGO. WE STOPPED BECAUSE IT WAS CRAWLING WITH MUTANT CRITTERS. THE CITY WOUND UP FENCING IT OFF.

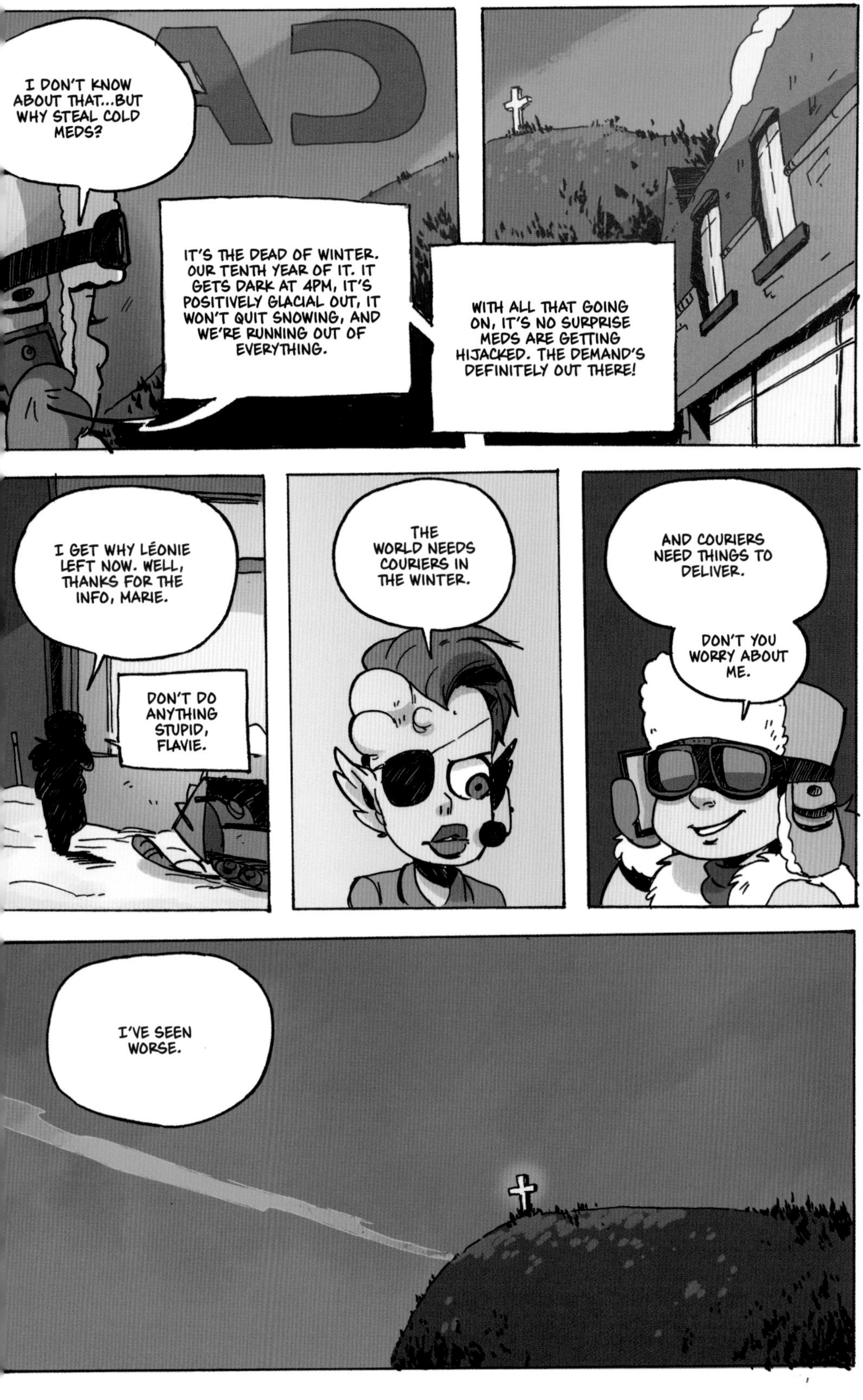
I DON'T KNOW ABOUT THAT...BUT WHY STEAL COLD MEDS?
IT'S THE DEAD OF WINTER. OUR TENTH YEAR OF IT. IT GETS DARK AT 4PM, IT'S POSITIVELY GLACIAL OUT, IT WON'T QUIT SNOWING, AND WE'RE RUNNING OUT OF EVERYTHING.
WITH ALL THAT GOING ON, IT'S NO SURPRISE MEDS ARE GETTING HIJACKED. THE DEMAND'S DEFINITELY OUT THERE!
I GET WHY LÉONIE LEFT NOW. WELL, THANKS FOR THE INFO, MARIE.
DON'T DO ANYTHING STUPID, FLAVIE.
THE WORLD NEEDS COURIERS IN THE WINTER.
AND COURIERS NEED THINGS TO DELIVER.
DON'T YOU WORRY ABOUT ME.
I'VE SEEN WORSE.

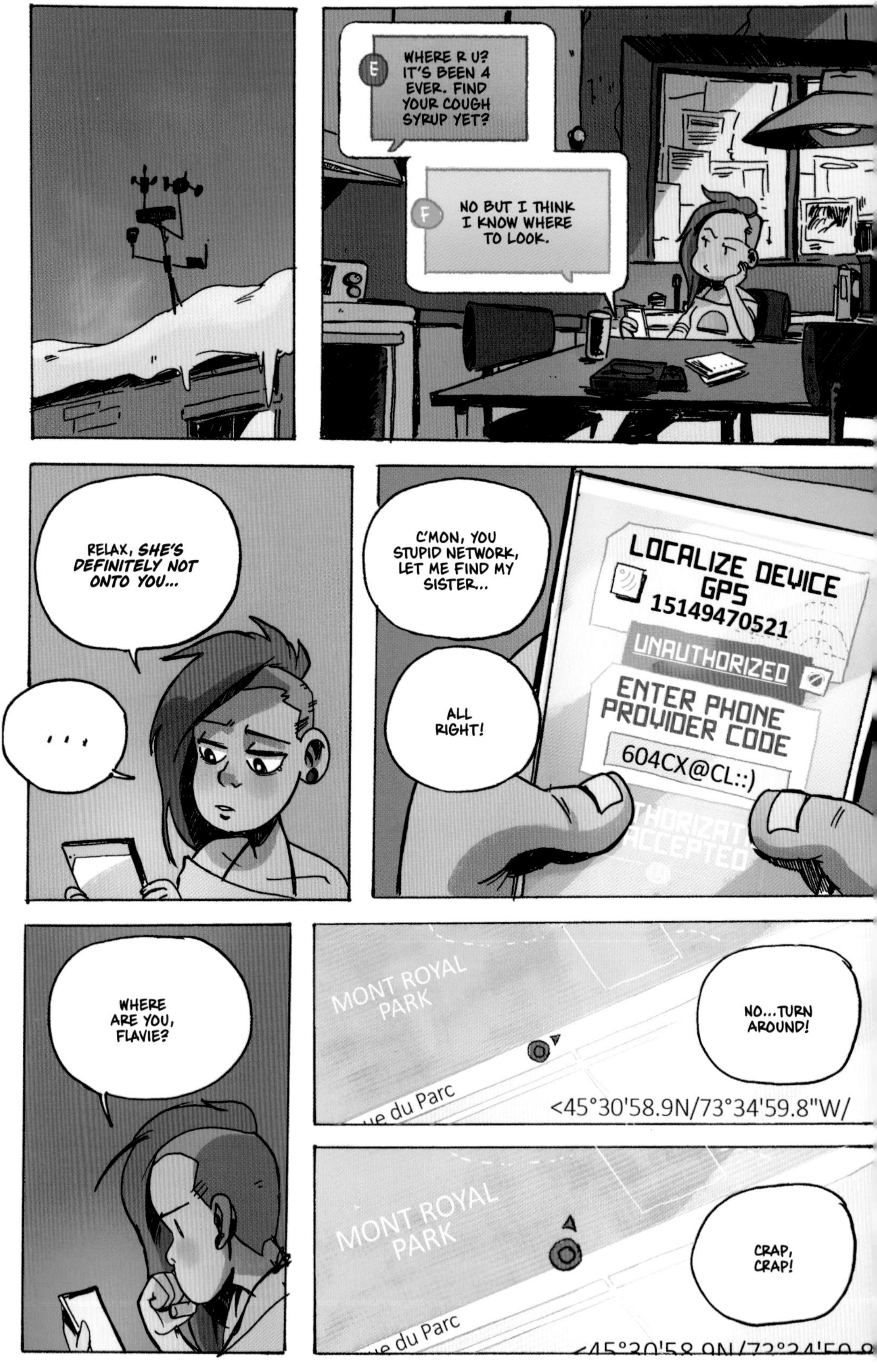
WHERE R U? IT'S BEEN 4 EVER. FIND YOUR COUGH SYRUP YET?
NO BUT I THINK I KNOW WHERE TO LOOK.
RELAX, SHE'S DEFINITELY NOT ONTO YOU...
...
C'MON, YOU STUPID NETWORK, LET ME FIND MY SISTER...
ALL RIGHT!
LOCALIZE DEVICE GPS
15149470521
UNAUTHORIZED
ENTER PHONE PROVIDER CODE
604CX@CL::)
WHERE ARE YOU, FLAVIE?
MONT ROYAL PARK
ue du Parc
<45°30'58.9N/73°34'59.8"W/
NO...TURN AROUND!
MONT ROYAL PARK
ue du Parc
CRAP, CRAP!

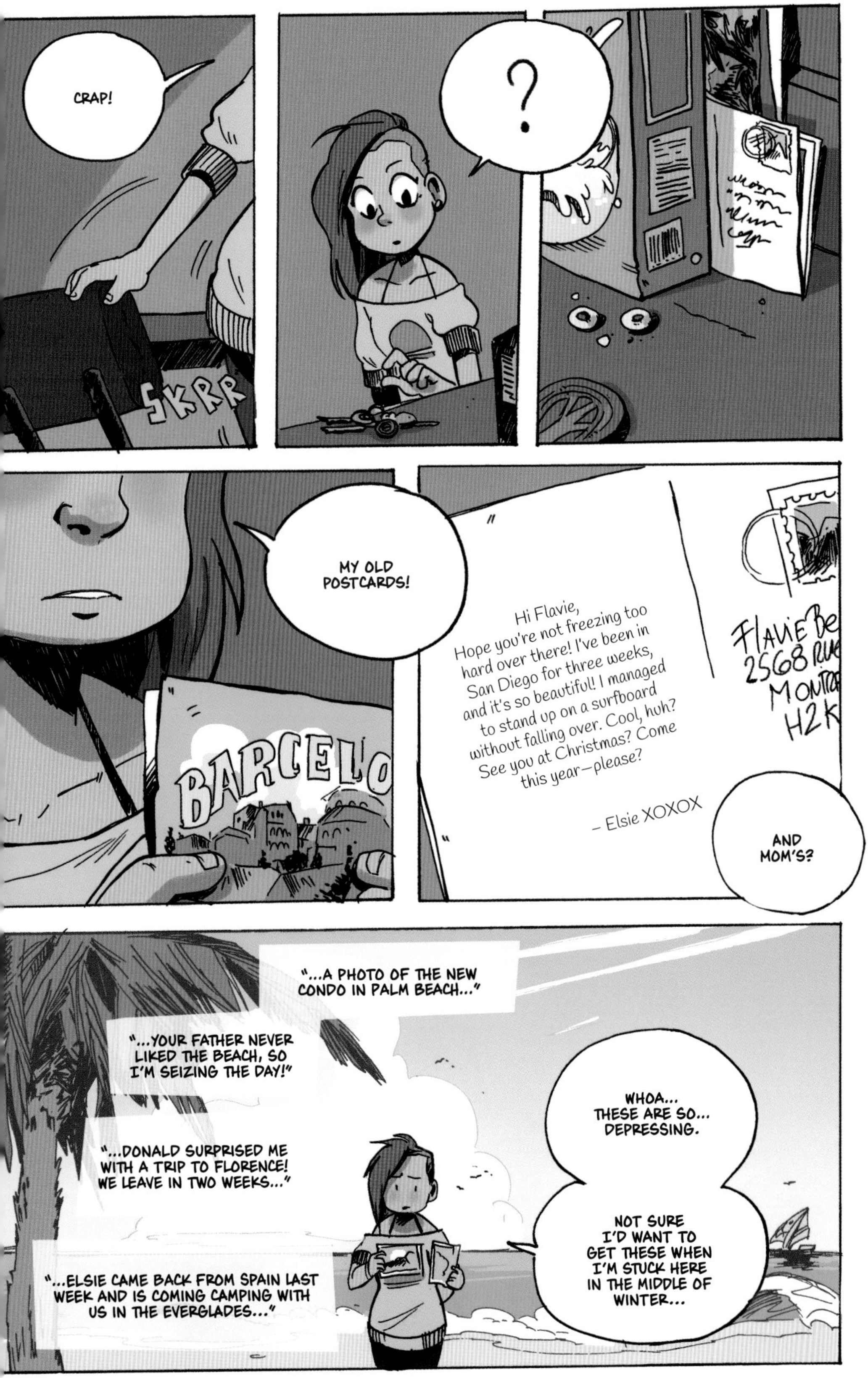
CRAP!
SKRR
?
MY OLD POSTCARDS!
BARCELO
Hi Flavie,
Hope you're not freezing too hard over there! I've been in San Diego for three weeks, and it's so beautiful! I managed to stand up on a surfboard without falling over. Cool, huh? See you at Christmas? Come this year—please?
– Elsie XOXOX
AND MOM'S?
"...A PHOTO OF THE NEW CONDO IN PALM BEACH..."
"...YOUR FATHER NEVER LIKED THE BEACH, SO I'M SEIZING THE DAY!"
"...DONALD SURPRISED ME WITH A TRIP TO FLORENCE! WE LEAVE IN TWO WEEKS..."
"...ELSIE CAME BACK FROM SPAIN LAST WEEK AND IS COMING CAMPING WITH US IN THE EVERGLADES..."
WHOA... THESE ARE SO... DEPRESSING.
NOT SURE I'D WANT TO GET THESE WHEN I'M STUCK HERE IN THE MIDDLE OF WINTER...

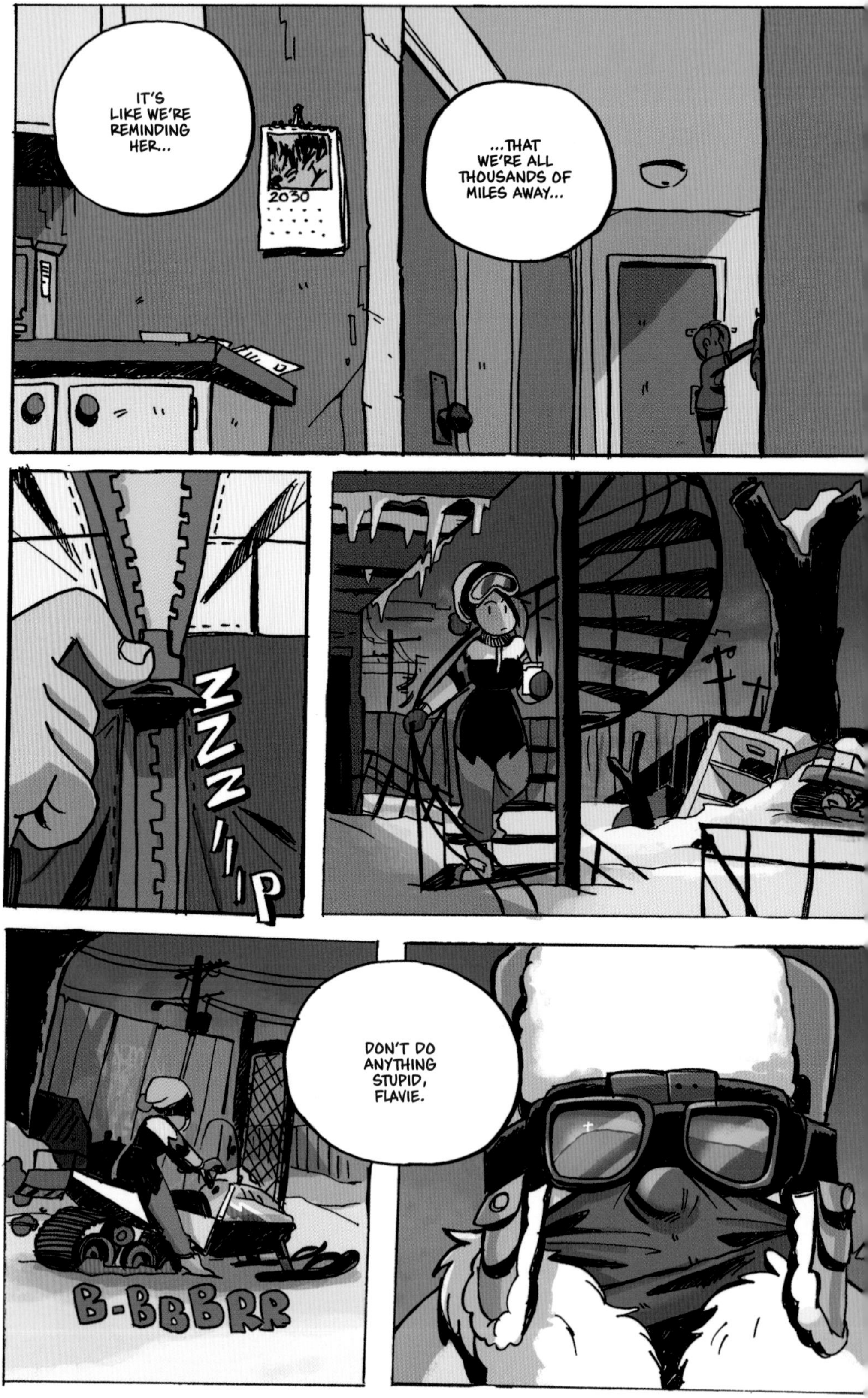
IT'S LIKE WE'RE REMINDING HER...
2030
...THAT WE'RE ALL THOUSANDS OF MILES AWAY...
ZZZIIIP
B-BBBRR
DON'T DO ANYTHING STUPID, FLAVIE.

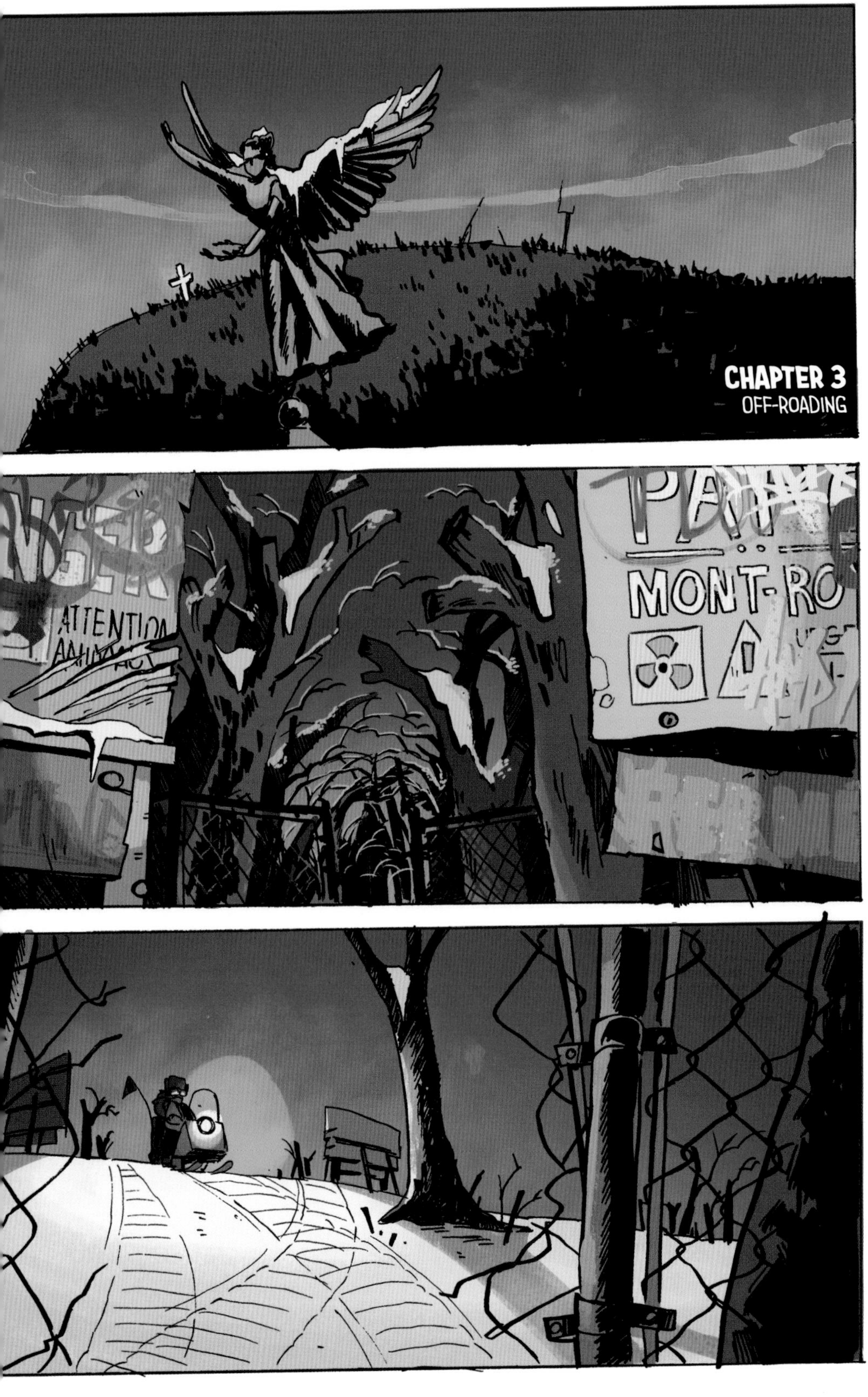
CHAPTER 3
OFF-ROADING
ATTENTION
MONT-RO

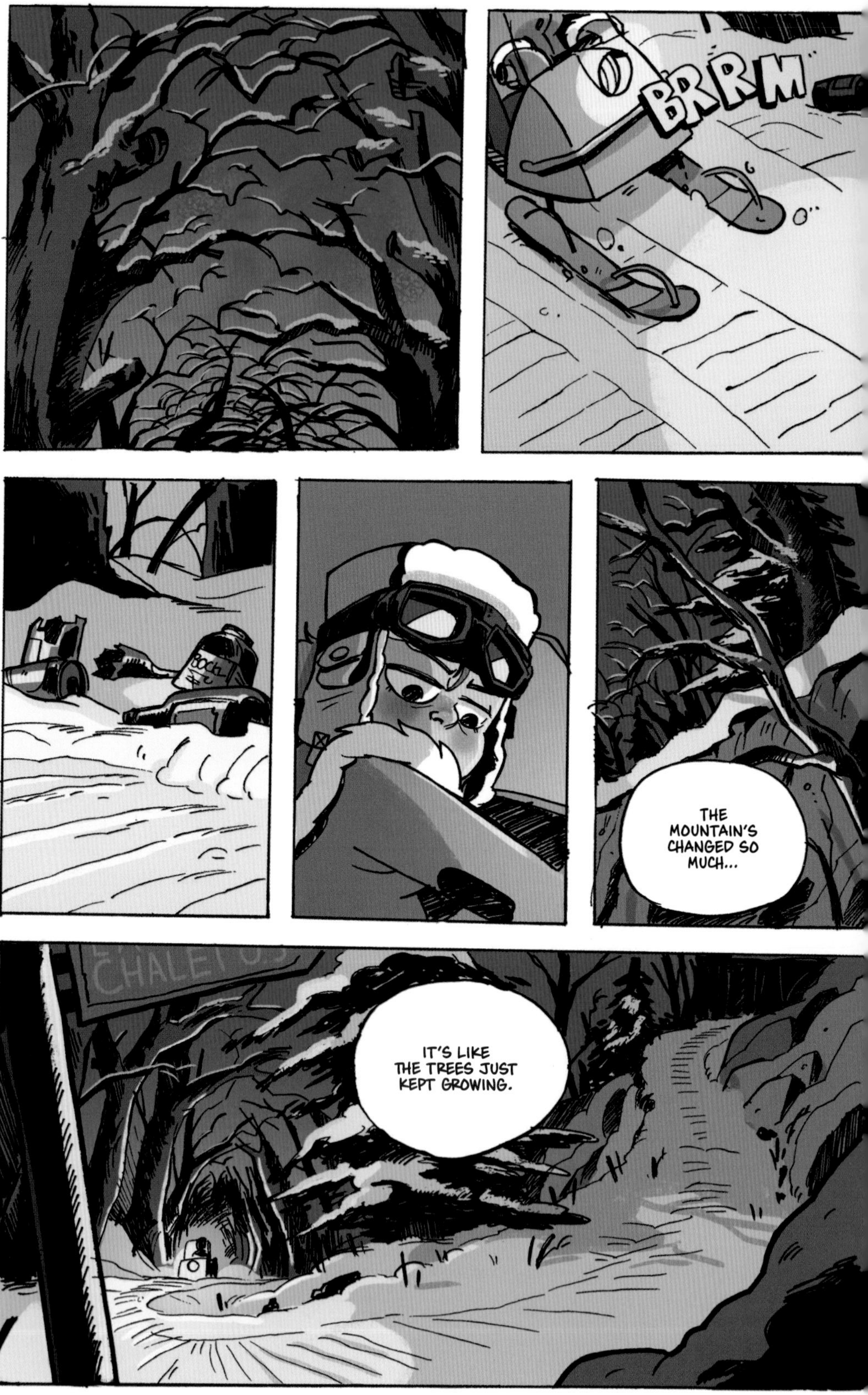
BRRM
THE MOUNTAIN'S CHANGED SO MUCH...
IT'S LIKE THE TREES JUST KEPT GROWING.

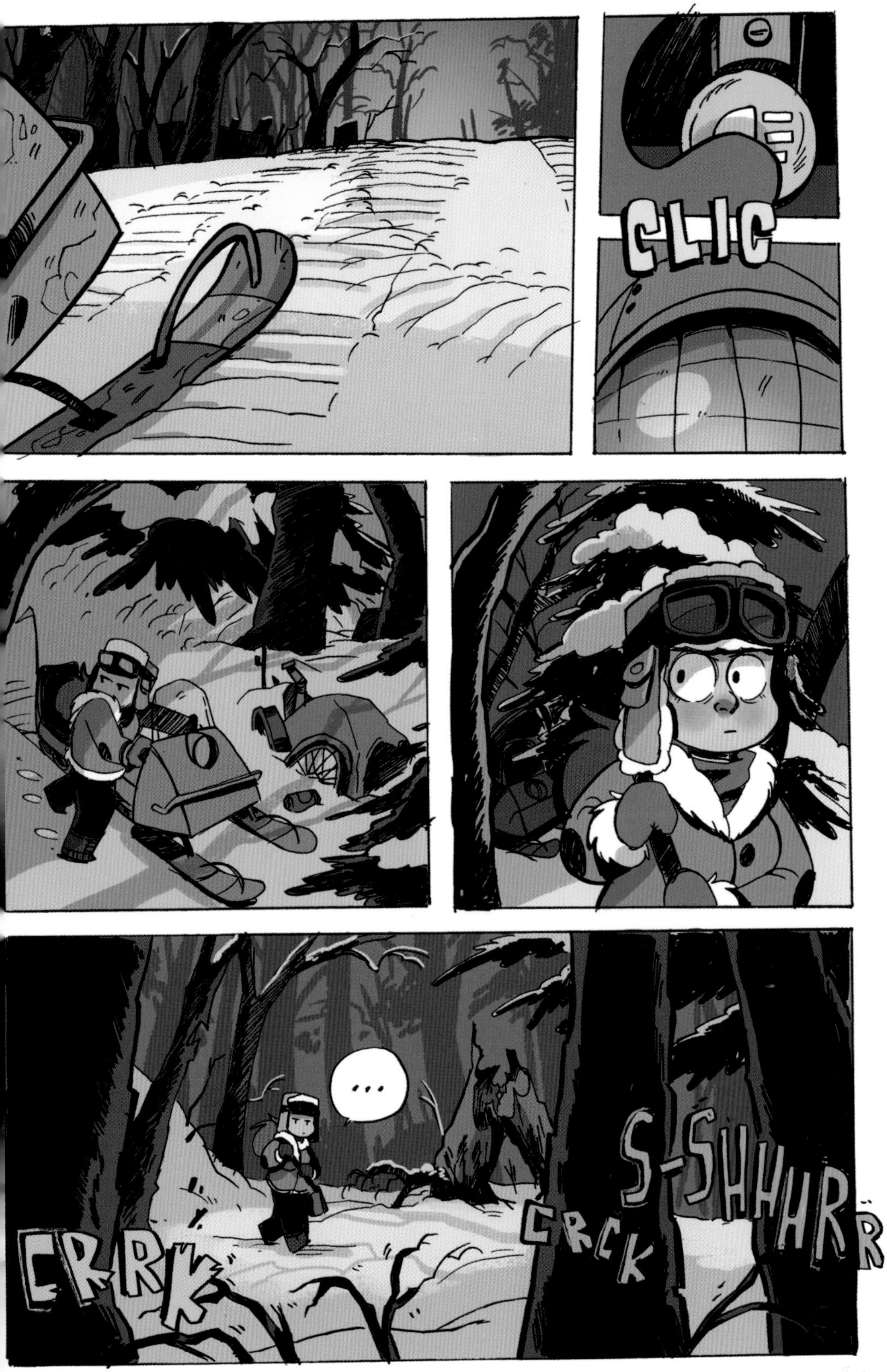
CLIC
...
CRRK
CRCK
S-SHHHRR

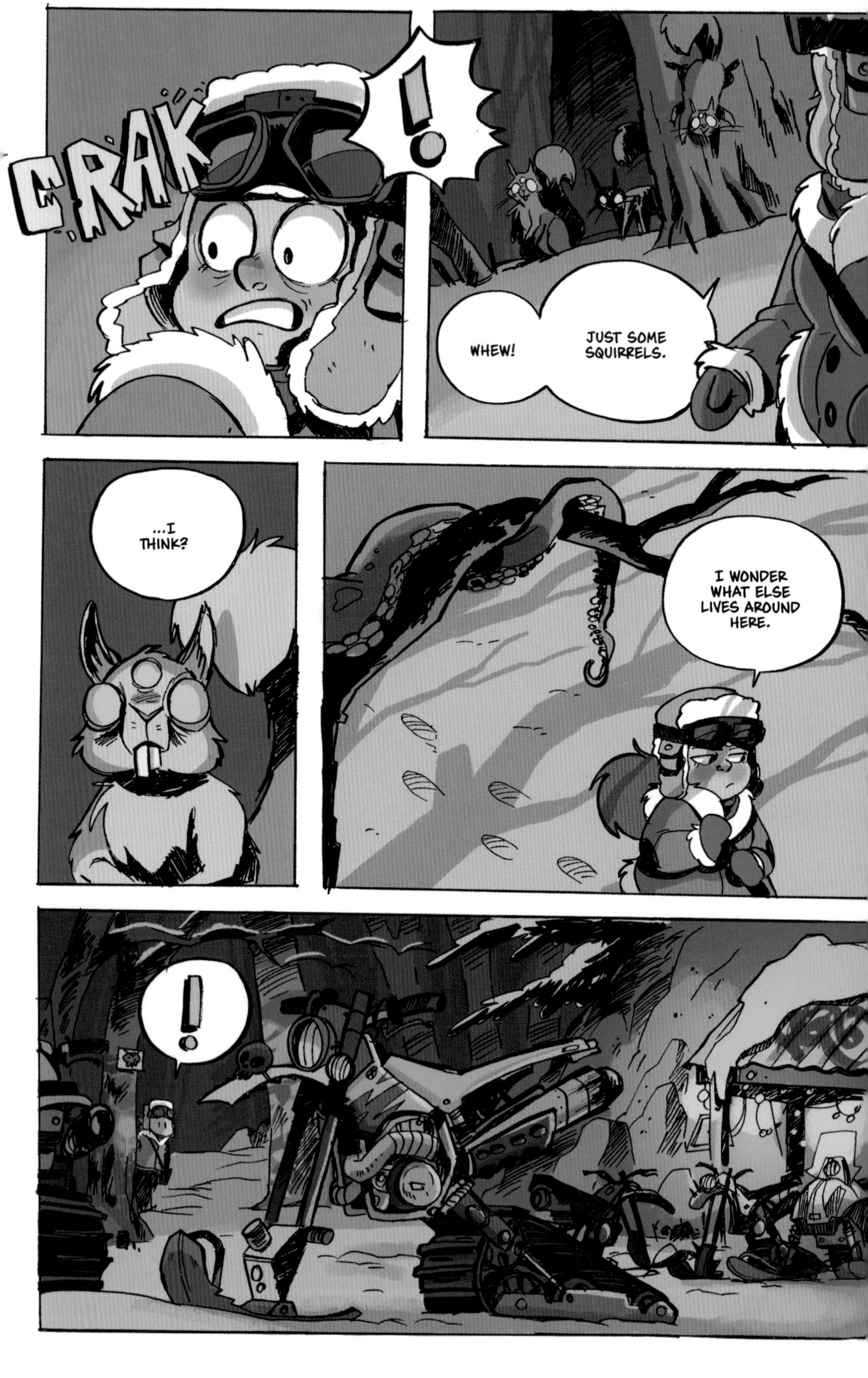
CRAK
!
WHEW!
JUST SOME SQUIRRELS.
...I THINK?
I WONDER WHAT ELSE LIVES AROUND HERE.
!

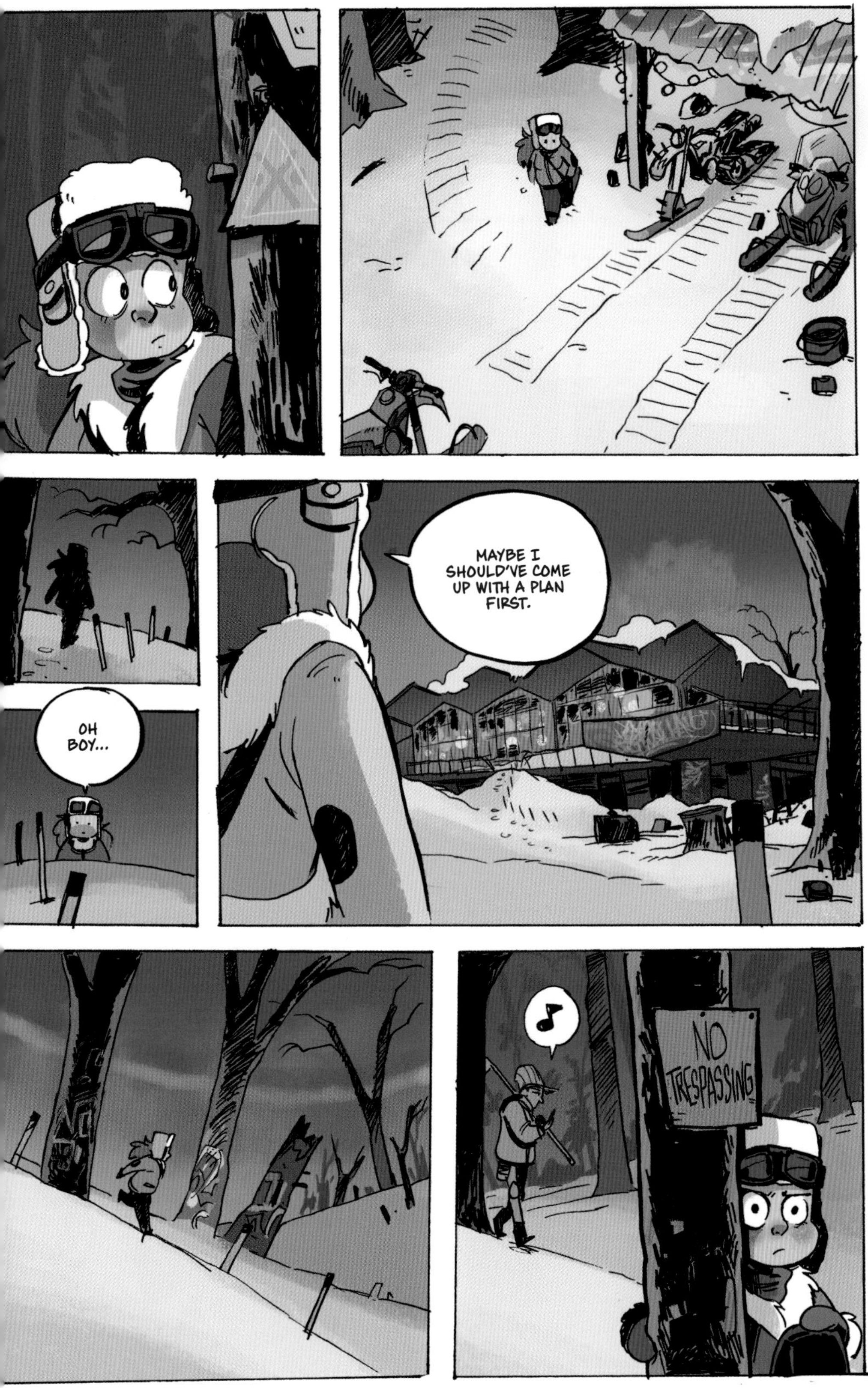
OH BOY...
MAYBE I SHOULD'VE COME UP WITH A PLAN FIRST.
NO TRESPASSING

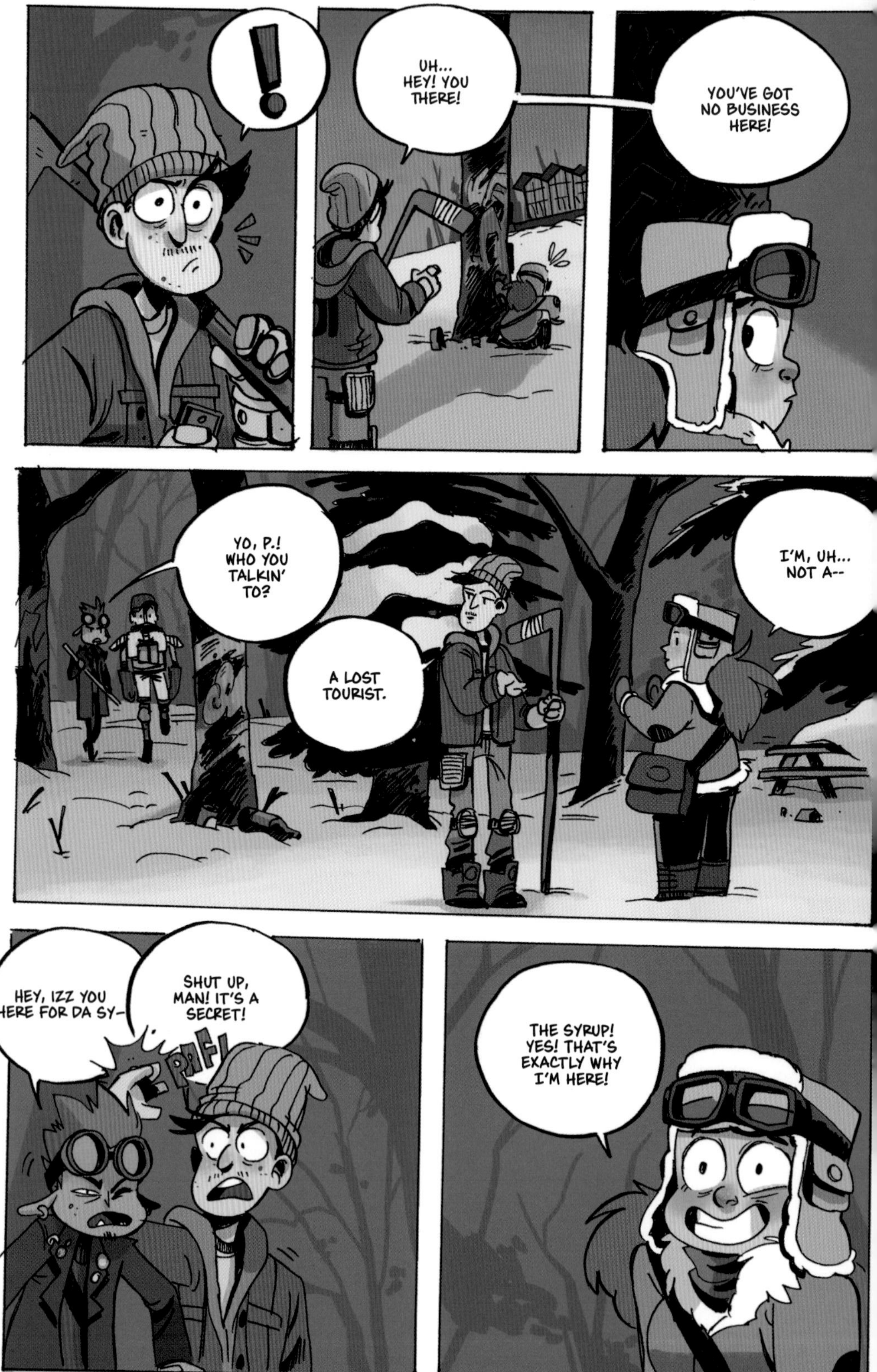
!
UH... HEY! YOU THERE!
YOU'VE GOT NO BUSINESS HERE!
YO, P.! WHO YOU TALKIN' TO?
A LOST TOURIST.
I'M, UH... NOT A--
HEY, IZZ YOU HERE FOR DA SY-
SHUT UP, MAN! IT'S A SECRET!
THE SYRUP! YES! THAT'S EXACTLY WHY I'M HERE!

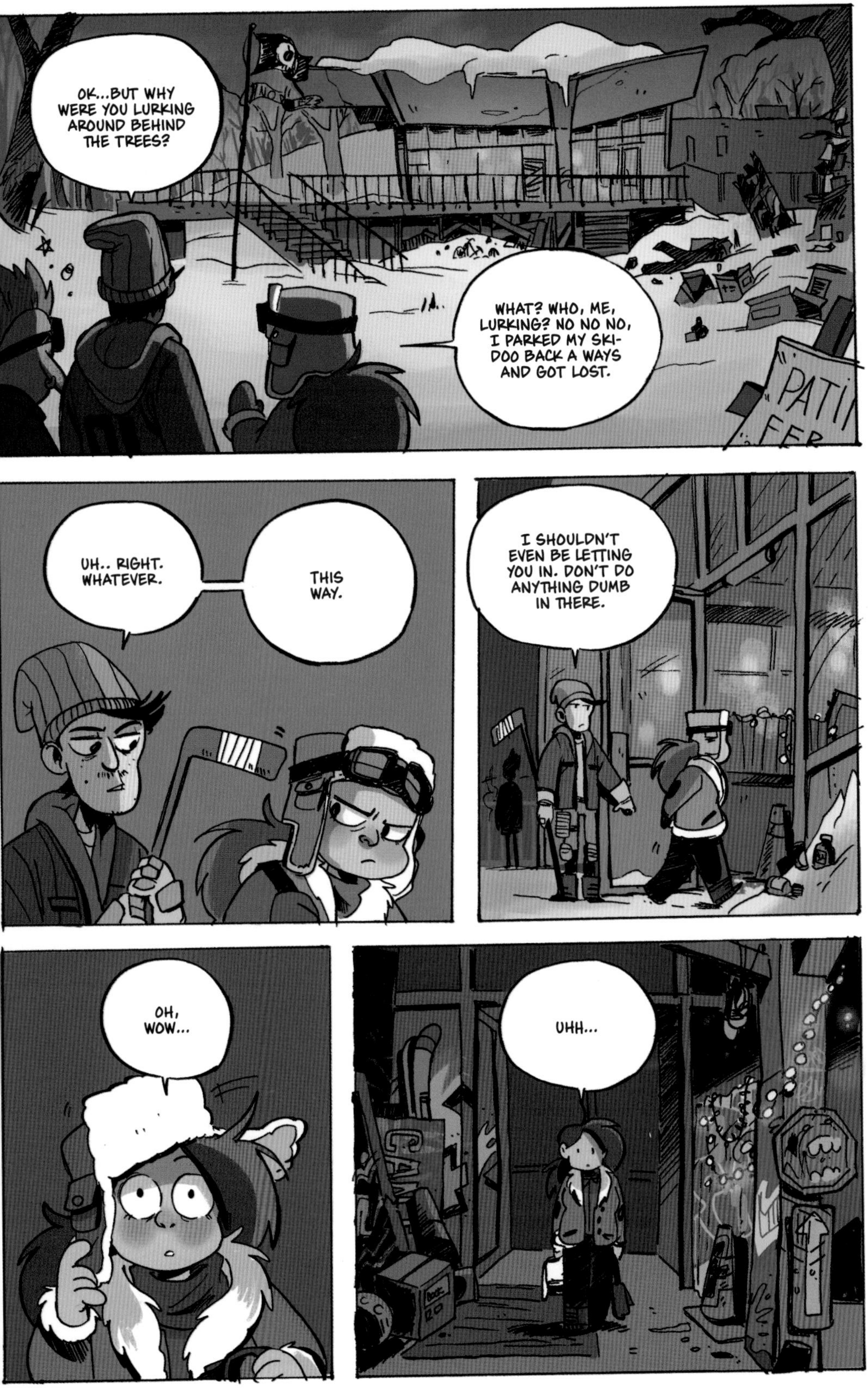
OK...BUT WHY WERE YOU LURKING AROUND BEHIND THE TREES?
WHAT? WHO, ME, LURKING? NO NO NO, I PARKED MY SKI-DOO BACK A WAYS AND GOT LOST.
PATI
UH.. RIGHT. WHATEVER.
THIS WAY.
I SHOULDN'T EVEN BE LETTING YOU IN. DON'T DO ANYTHING DUMB IN THERE.
OH, WOW...
UHH...

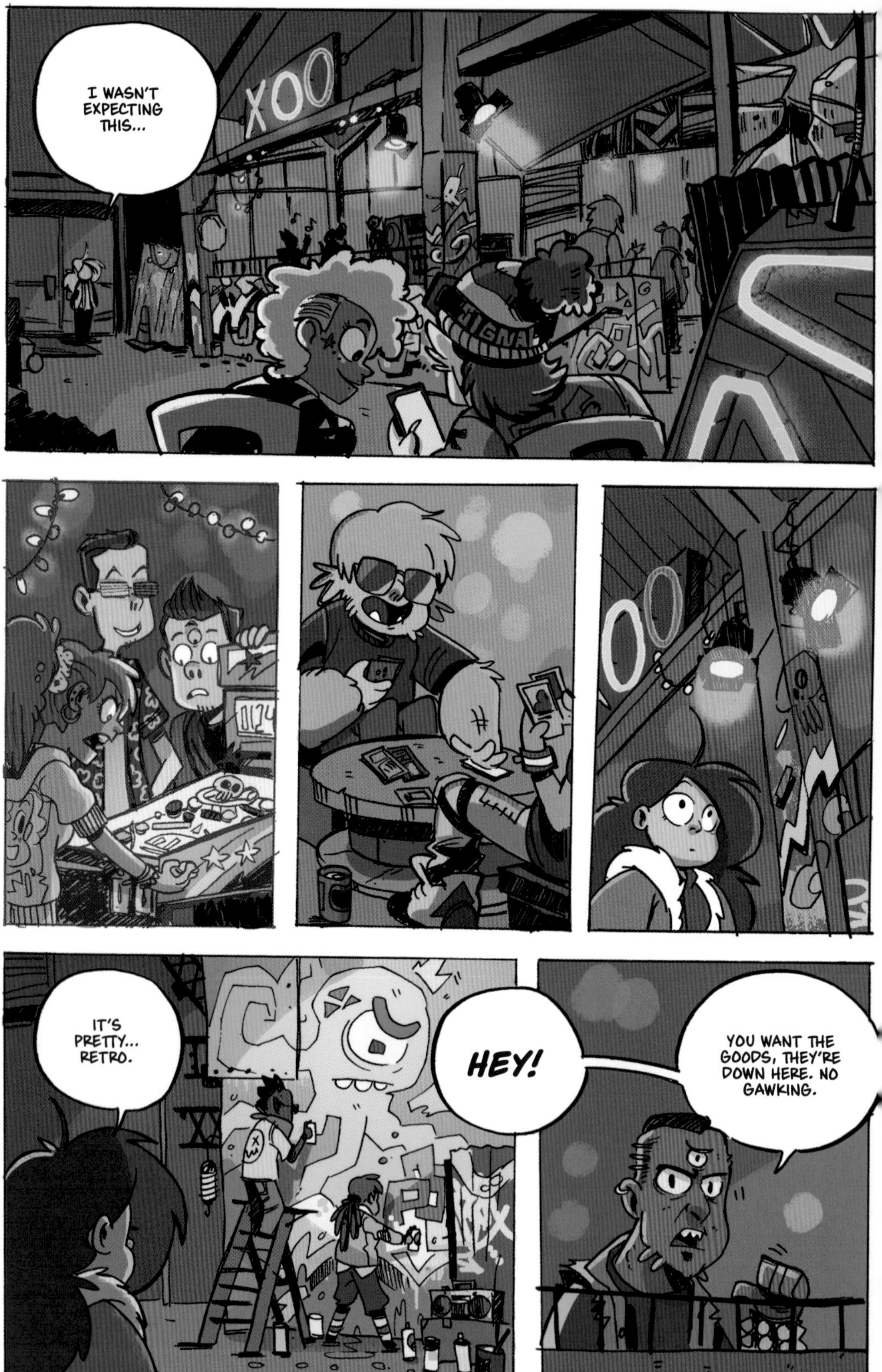
I WASN'T EXPECTING THIS...
IT'S PRETTY... RETRO.
HEY!
YOU WANT THE GOODS, THEY'RE DOWN HERE. NO GAWKING.

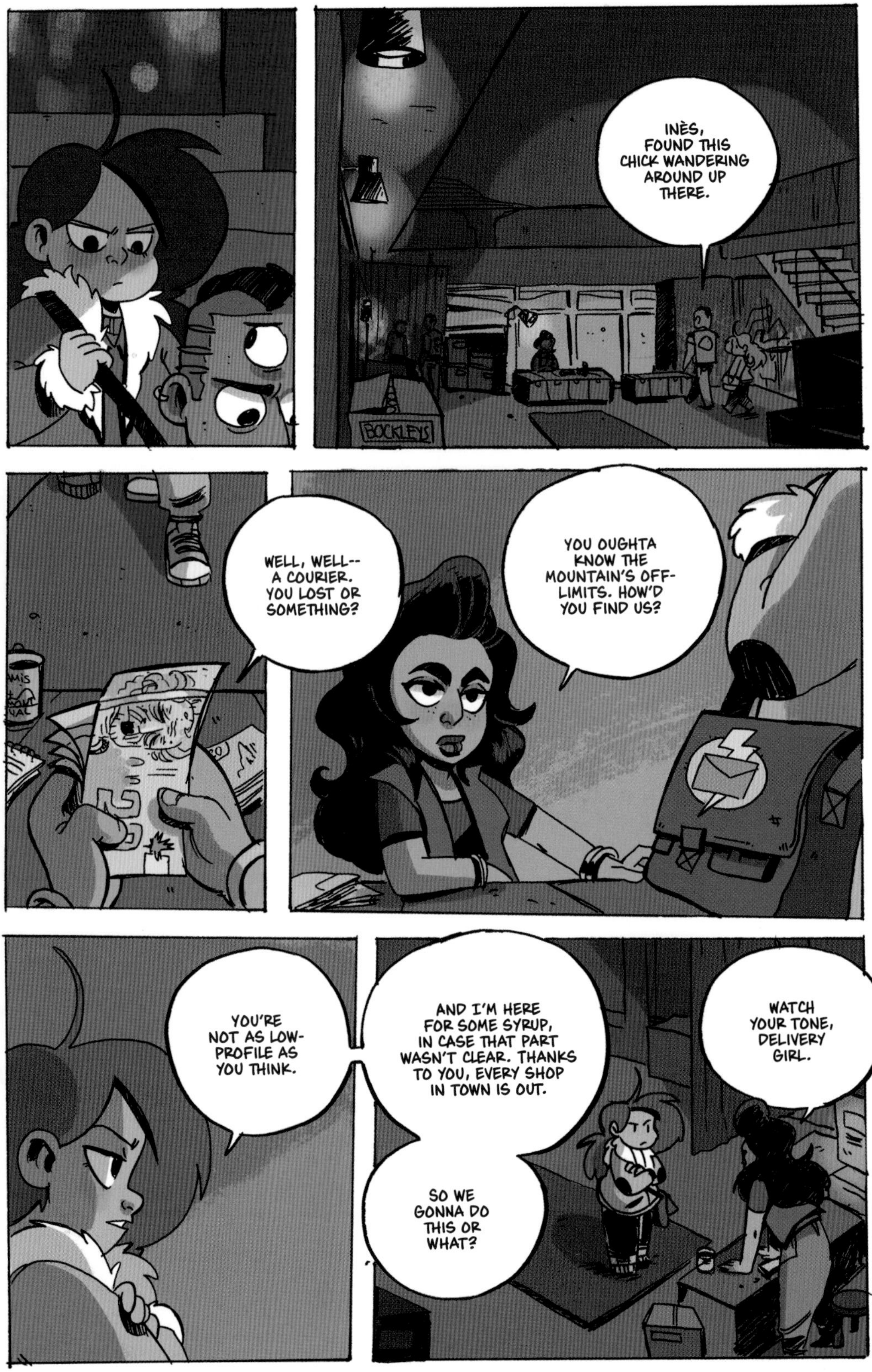
INÈS, FOUND THIS CHICK WANDERING AROUND UP THERE.
BOCKLEYS
WELL, WELL-- A COURIER. YOU LOST OR SOMETHING?
YOU OUGHTA KNOW THE MOUNTAIN'S OFF-LIMITS. HOW'D YOU FIND US?
YOU'RE NOT AS LOW-PROFILE AS YOU THINK.
AND I'M HERE FOR SOME SYRUP, IN CASE THAT PART WASN'T CLEAR. THANKS TO YOU, EVERY SHOP IN TOWN IS OUT.
SO WE GONNA DO THIS OR WHAT?
WATCH YOUR TONE, DELIVERY GIRL.

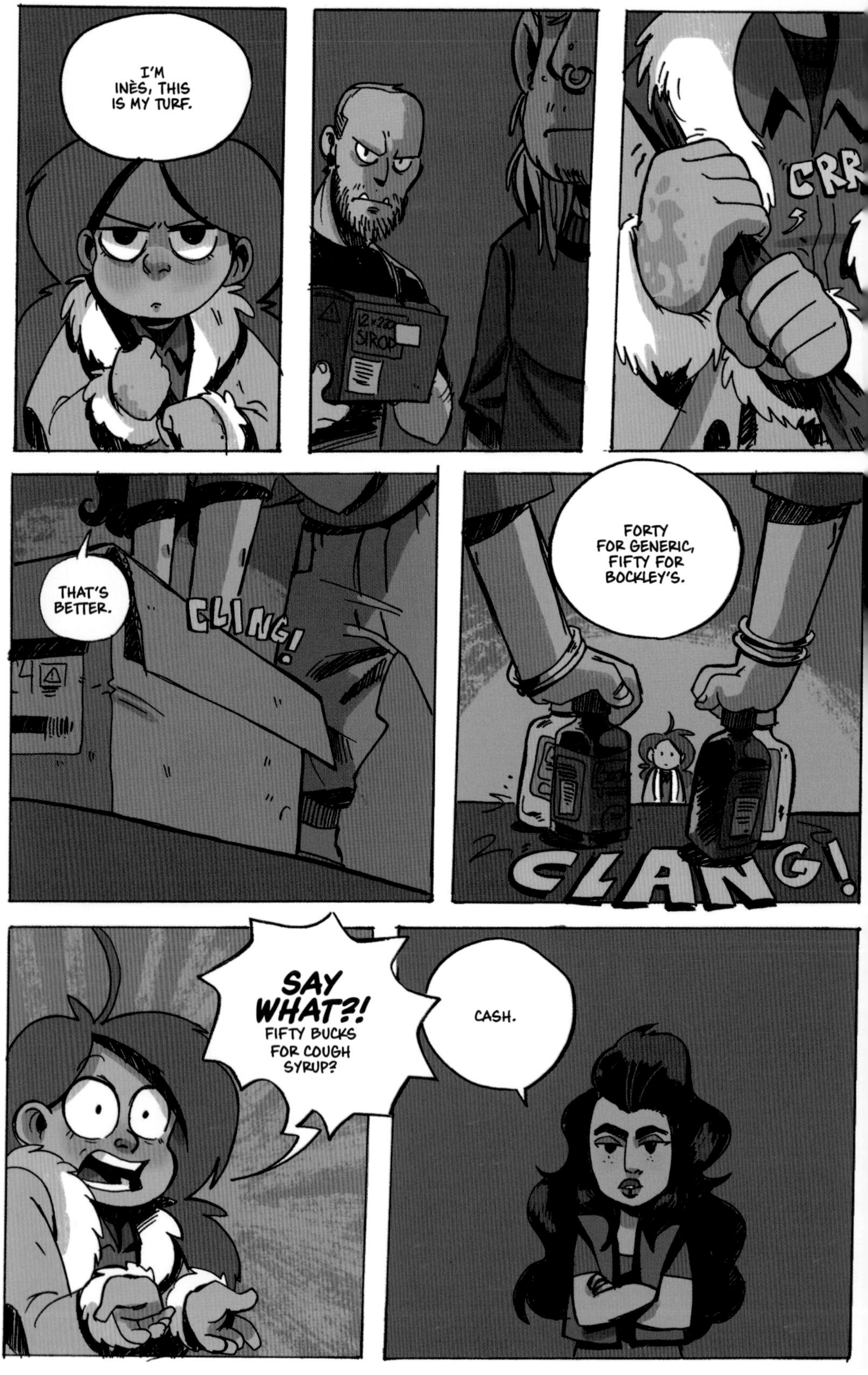
I'M INÈS, THIS IS MY TURF.
12×200 SIROP
CRR
THAT'S BETTER.
CLING!
FORTY FOR GENERIC, FIFTY FOR BOCKLEY'S.
CLANG!
SAY WHAT?! FIFTY BUCKS FOR COUGH SYRUP?
CASH.

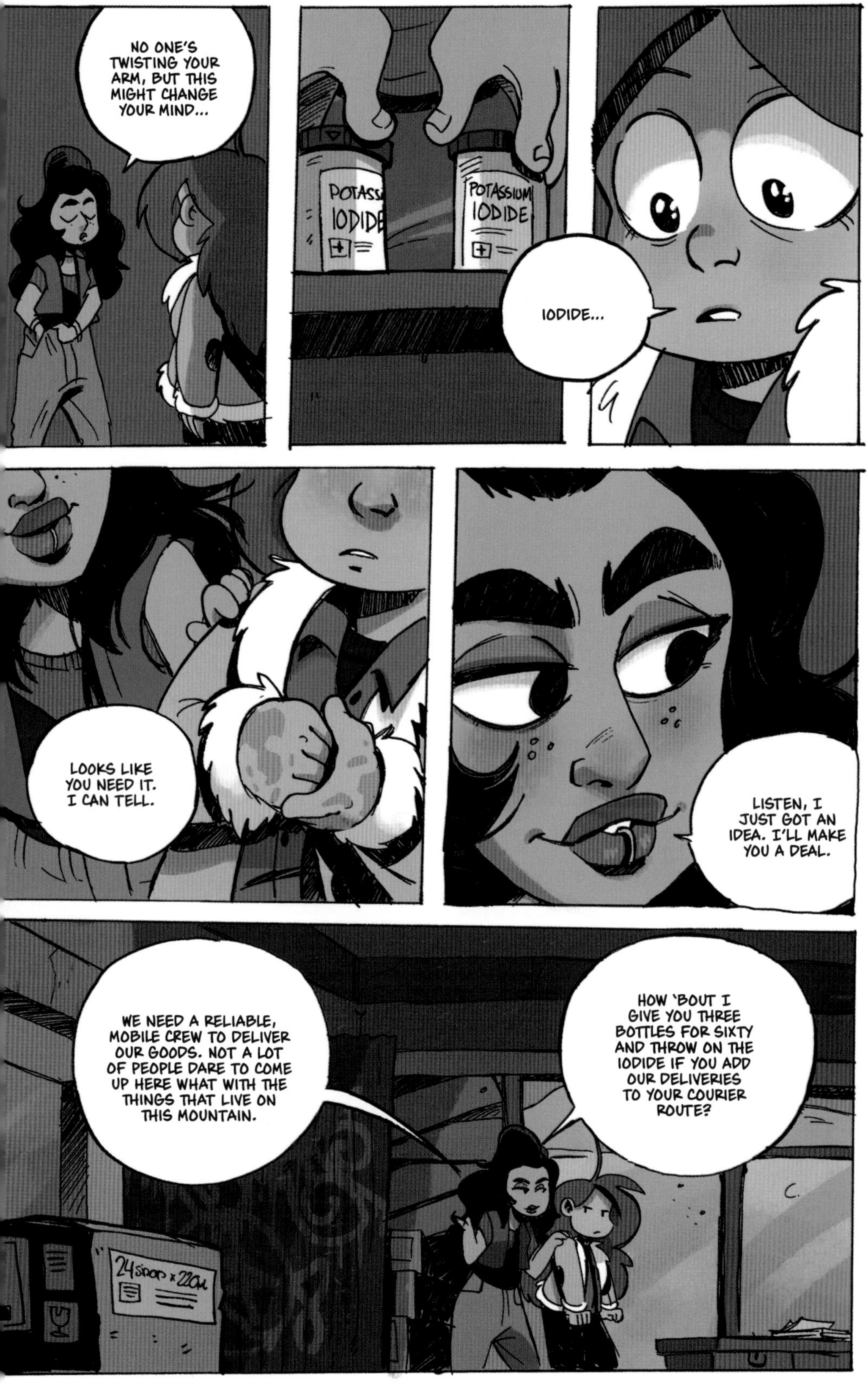
NO ONE'S TWISTING YOUR ARM, BUT THIS MIGHT CHANGE YOUR MIND...
POTASSIUM IODIDE
POTASSIUM IODIDE
IODIDE...
LOOKS LIKE YOU NEED IT. I CAN TELL.
LISTEN, I JUST GOT AN IDEA. I'LL MAKE YOU A DEAL.
WE NEED A RELIABLE, MOBILE CREW TO DELIVER OUR GOODS. NOT A LOT OF PEOPLE DARE TO COME UP HERE WHAT WITH THE THINGS THAT LIVE ON THIS MOUNTAIN.
HOW 'BOUT I GIVE YOU THREE BOTTLES FOR SIXTY AND THROW ON THE IODIDE IF YOU ADD OUR DELIVERIES TO YOUR COURIER ROUTE?

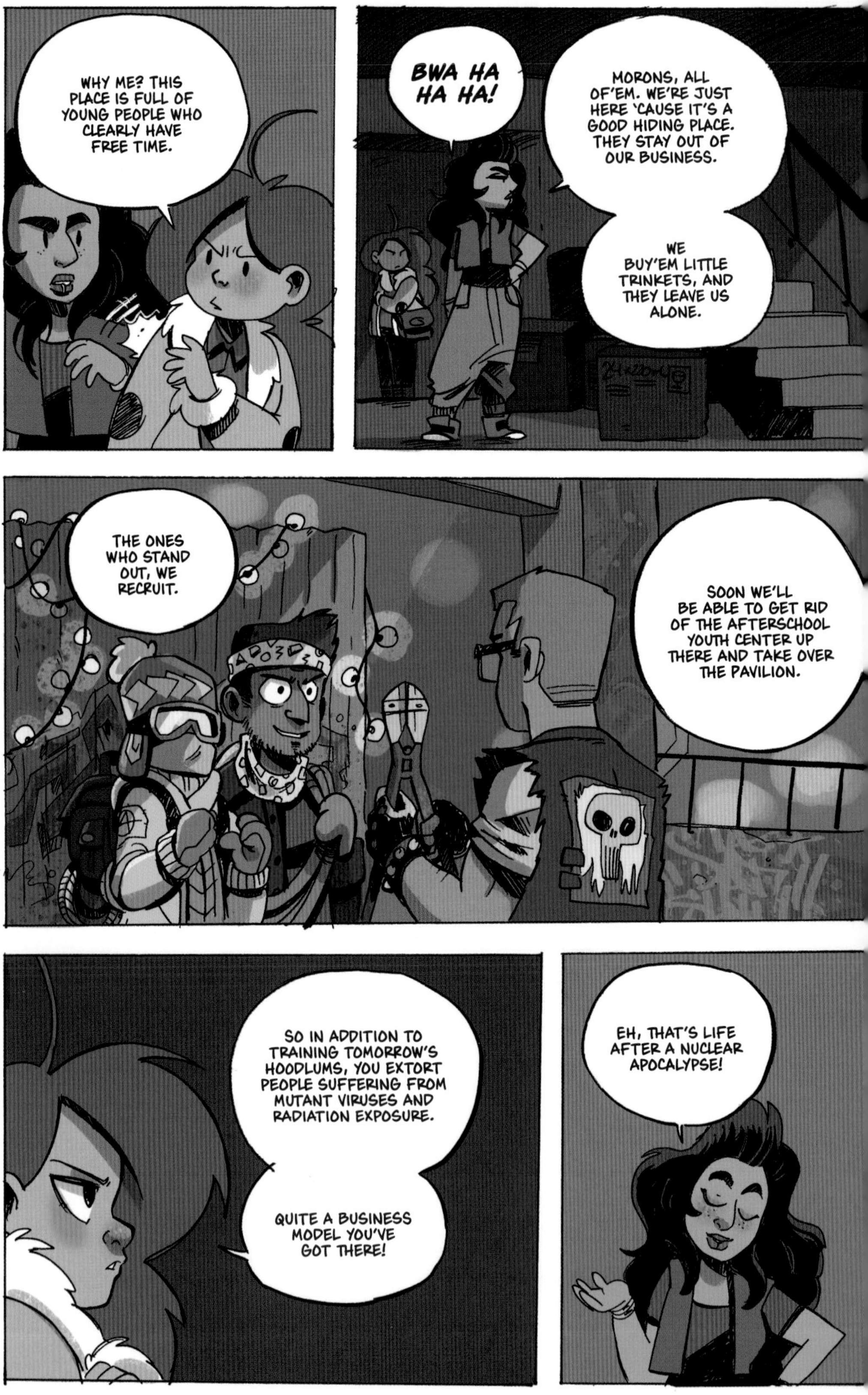
WHY ME? THIS PLACE IS FULL OF YOUNG PEOPLE WHO CLEARLY HAVE FREE TIME.
BWA HA HA HA!
MORONS, ALL OF'EM. WE'RE JUST HERE 'CAUSE IT'S A GOOD HIDING PLACE. THEY STAY OUT OF OUR BUSINESS.
WE BUY'EM LITTLE TRINKETS, AND THEY LEAVE US ALONE.
THE ONES WHO STAND OUT, WE RECRUIT.
SOON WE'LL BE ABLE TO GET RID OF THE AFTERSCHOOL YOUTH CENTER UP THERE AND TAKE OVER THE PAVILION.
SO IN ADDITION TO TRAINING TOMORROW'S HOODLUMS, YOU EXTORT PEOPLE SUFFERING FROM MUTANT VIRUSES AND RADIATION EXPOSURE.
QUITE A BUSINESS MODEL YOU'VE GOT THERE!
EH, THAT'S LIFE AFTER A NUCLEAR APOCALYPSE!

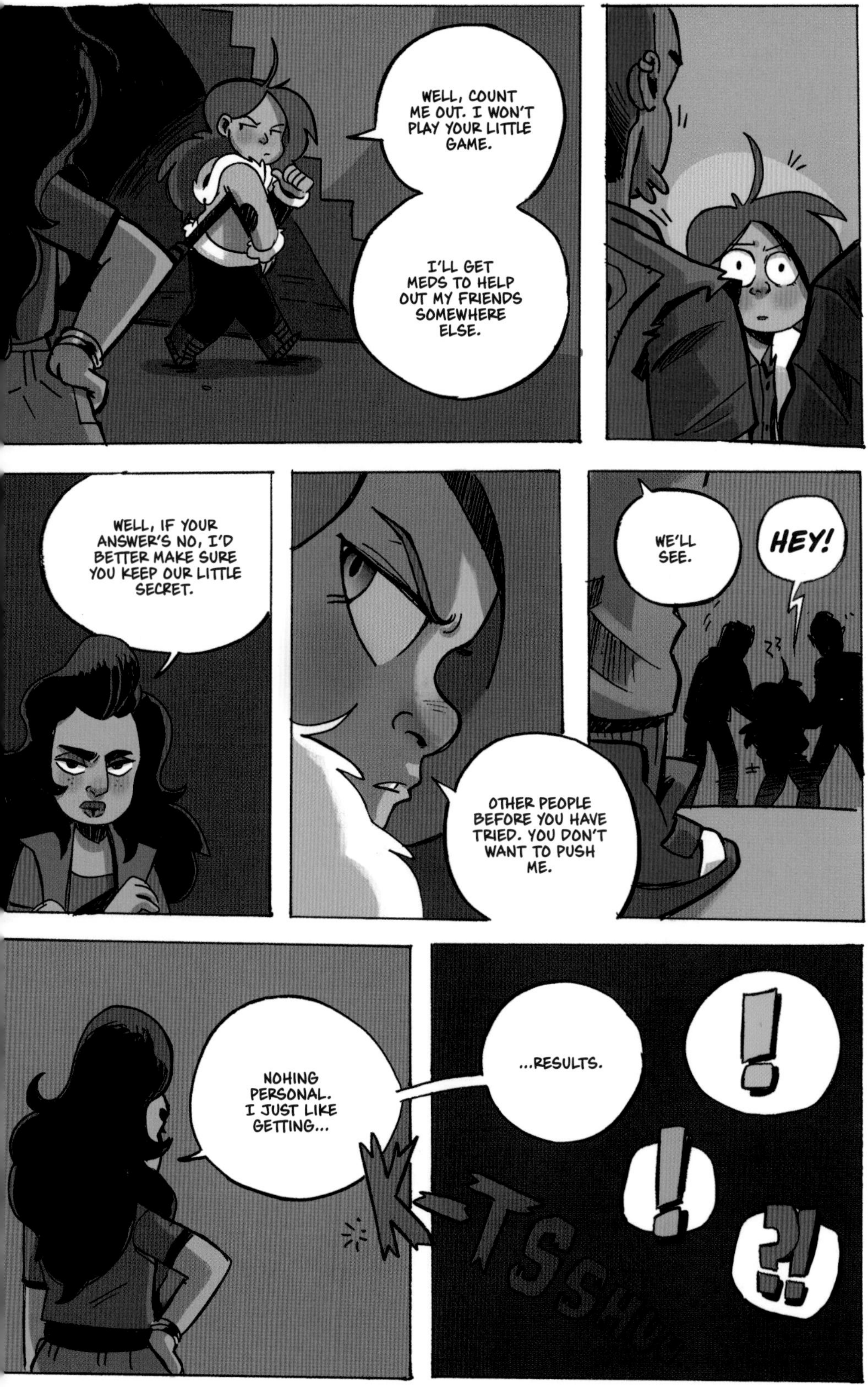
WELL, COUNT ME OUT. I WON'T PLAY YOUR LITTLE GAME.
I'LL GET MEDS TO HELP OUT MY FRIENDS SOMEWHERE ELSE.
WELL, IF YOUR ANSWER'S NO, I'D BETTER MAKE SURE YOU KEEP OUR LITTLE SECRET.
OTHER PEOPLE BEFORE YOU HAVE TRIED. YOU DON'T WANT TO PUSH ME.
WE'LL SEE.
HEY!
NOHING PERSONAL. I JUST LIKE GETTING...
...RESULTS.
!
!
?
TSSH

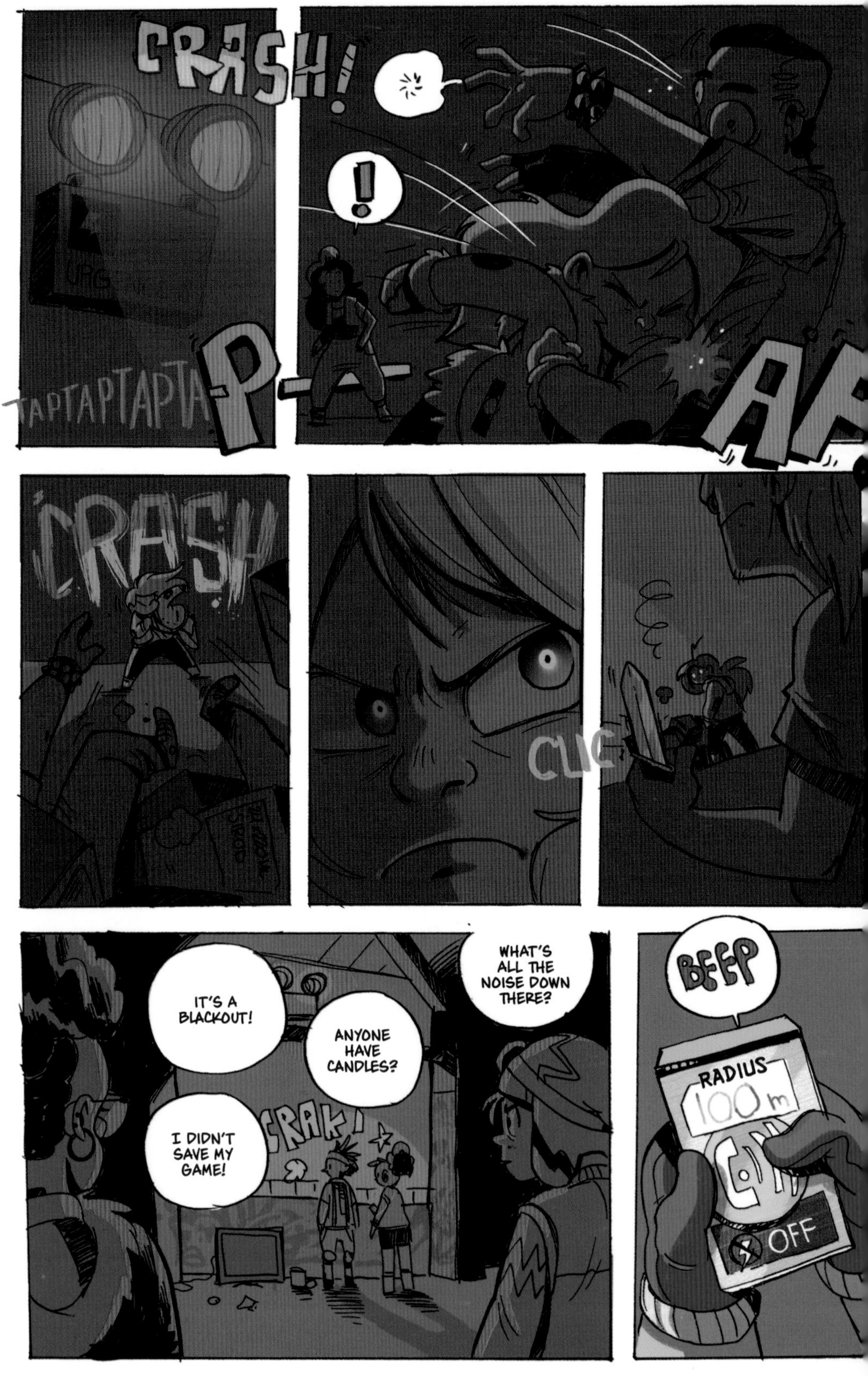
CRASH!
!
TAPTAPTAPTAPTA-P-
AF
CRASH
CLIC
IT'S A BLACKOUT!
WHAT'S ALL THE NOISE DOWN THERE?
ANYONE HAVE CANDLES?
I DIDN'T SAVE MY GAME!
CRAK!
BEEP
RADIUS
100 m
OFF

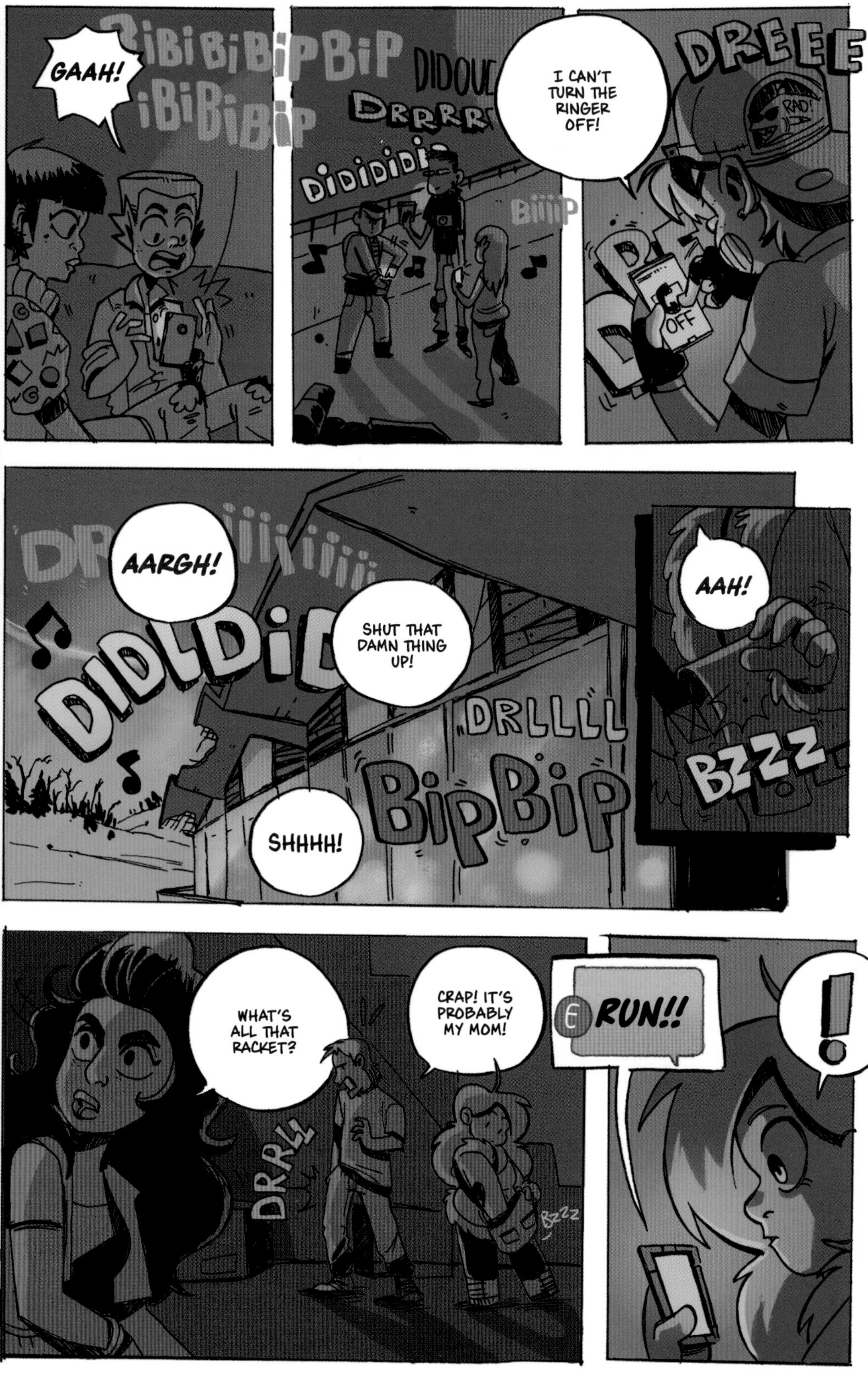
GAAH!
BIBIBIBIPBIP
iBiBiBiBiP
DIDOUD
DRRRRR
DIDIDIDI
BIIIIP
I CAN'T TURN THE RINGER OFF!
DREEE
RAD!
OFF
DRIIIIII
AARGH!
DIDLDID
SHUT THAT DAMN THING UP!
DRLLLL
BIPBIP
SHHHH!
AAH!
BZZZ
WHAT'S ALL THAT RACKET?
DRRLL
CRAP! IT'S PROBABLY MY MOM!
BZZZ
E
RUN!!
!

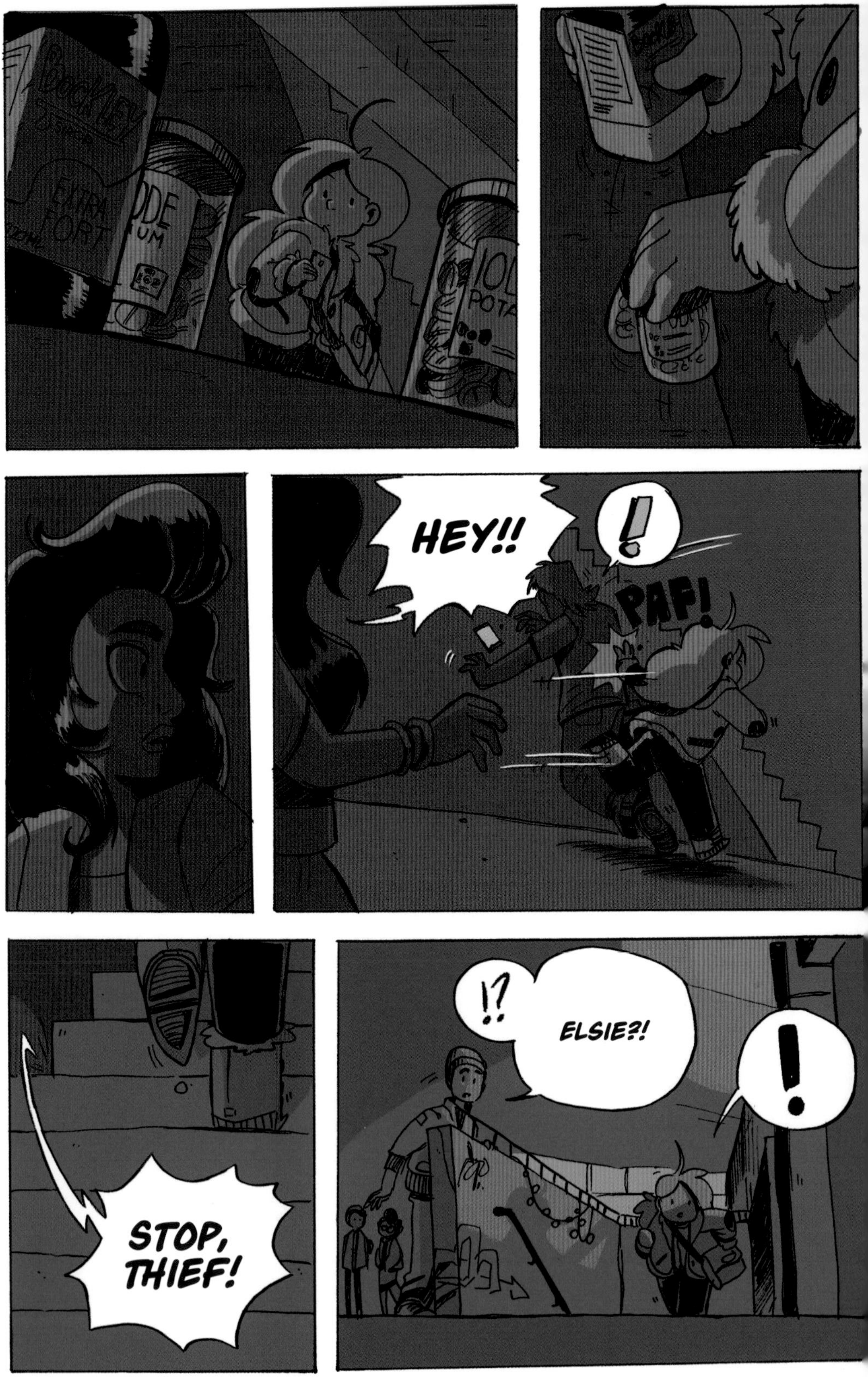
HEY!!
!
PAF!
STOP, THIEF!
!?
ELSIE?!
!

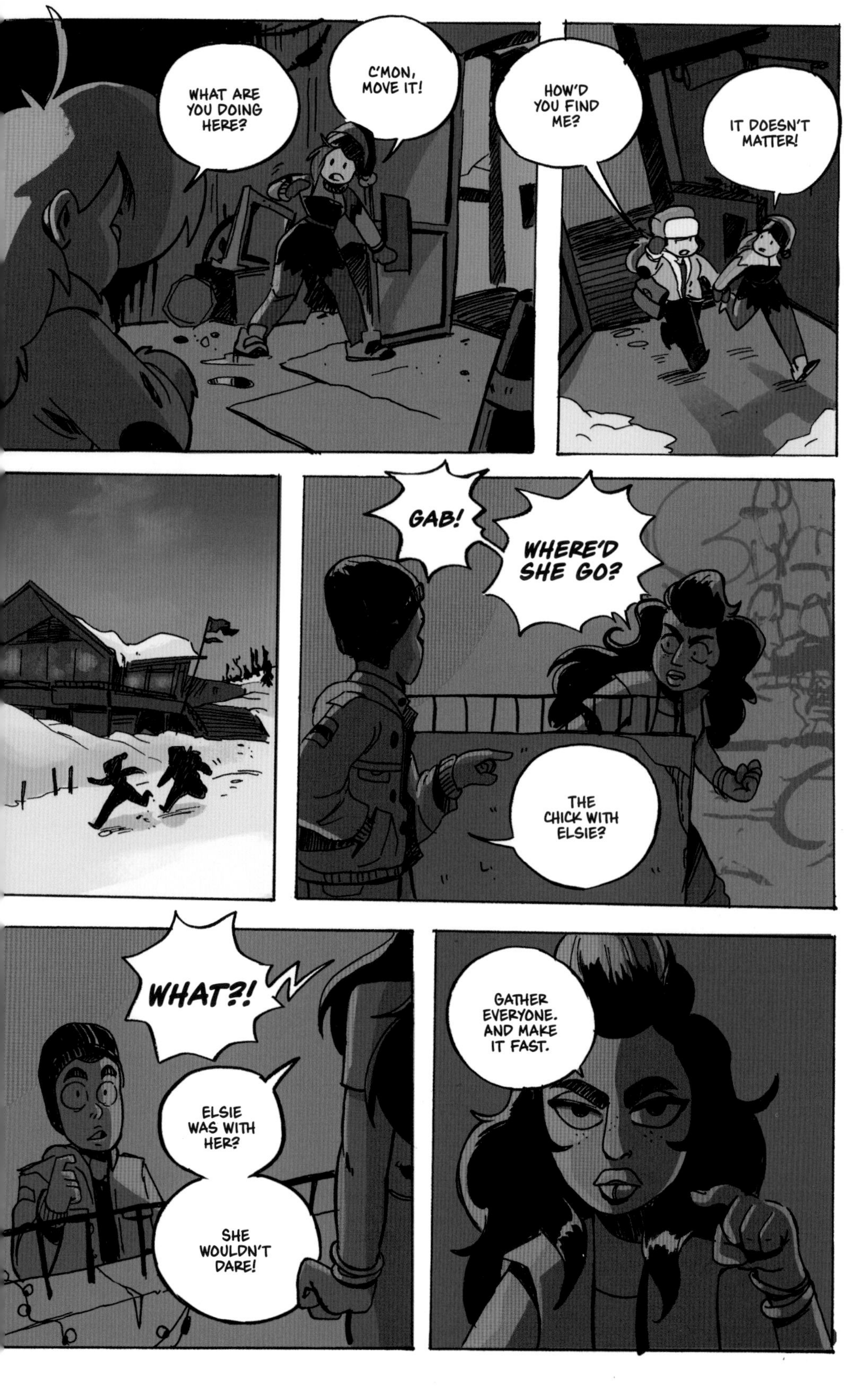
WHAT ARE YOU DOING HERE?
C'MON, MOVE IT!
HOW'D YOU FIND ME?
IT DOESN'T MATTER!
GAB!
WHERE'D SHE GO?
THE CHICK WITH ELSIE?
WHAT?!
ELSIE WAS WITH HER?
SHE WOULDN'T DARE!
GATHER EVERYONE. AND MAKE IT FAST.

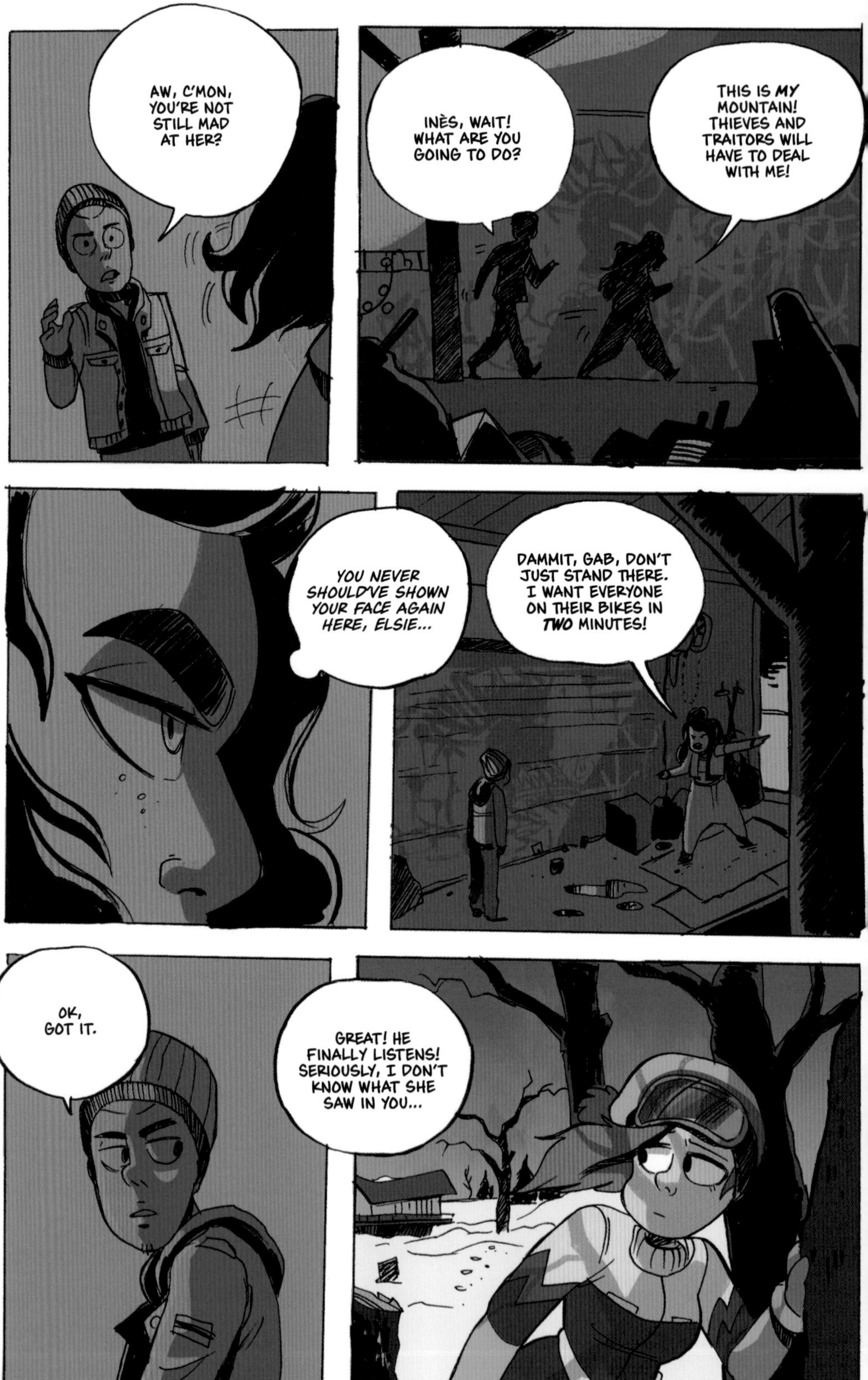
AW, C'MON, YOU'RE NOT STILL MAD AT HER?
INÈS, WAIT! WHAT ARE YOU GOING TO DO?
THIS IS *MY* MOUNTAIN! THIEVES AND TRAITORS WILL HAVE TO DEAL WITH ME!
YOU NEVER SHOULD'VE SHOWN YOUR FACE AGAIN HERE, ELSIE...
DAMMIT, GAB, DON'T JUST STAND THERE. I WANT EVERYONE ON THEIR BIKES IN *TWO* MINUTES!
OK, GOT IT.
GREAT! HE FINALLY LISTENS! SERIOUSLY, I DON'T KNOW WHAT SHE SAW IN YOU...

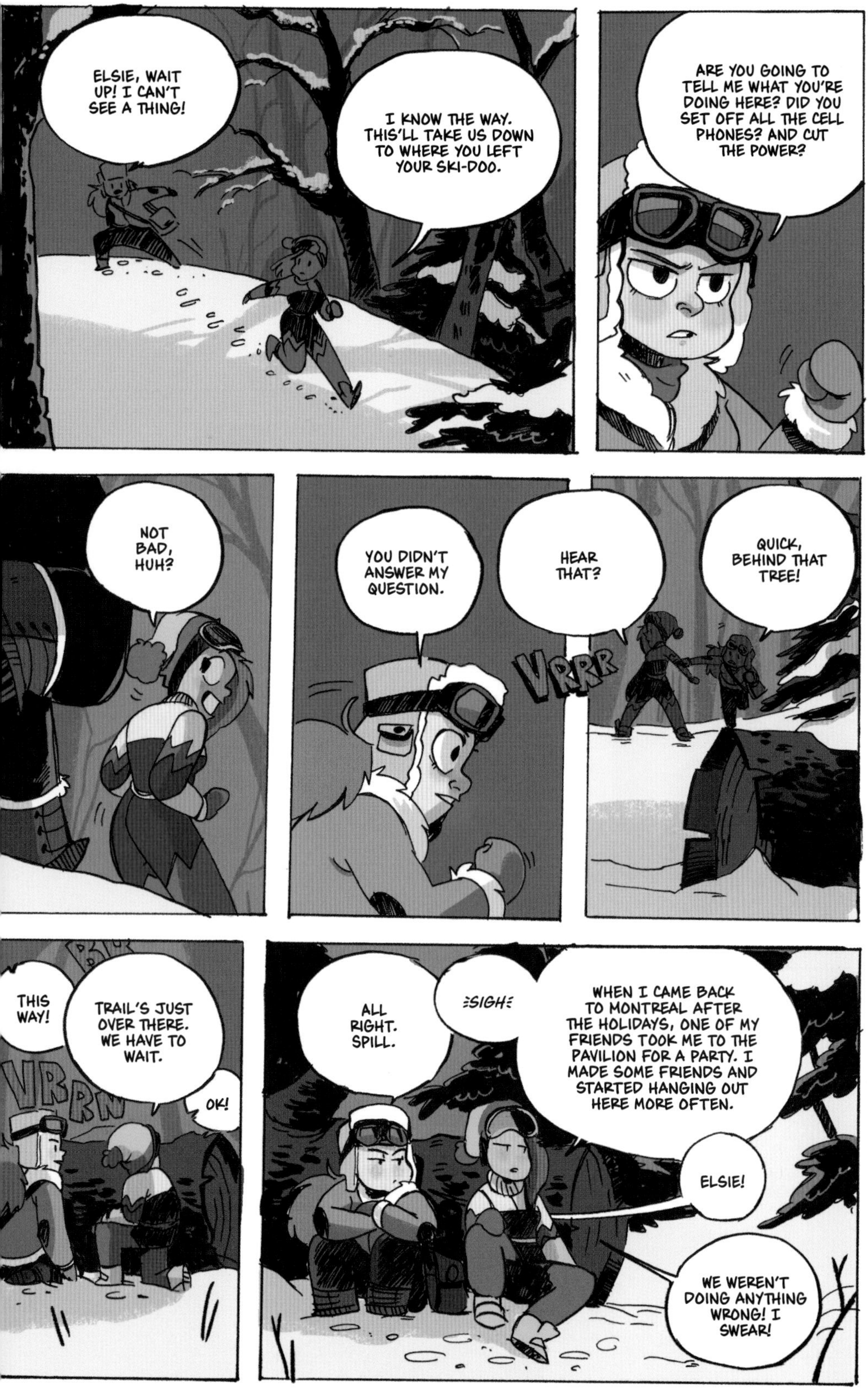

ELSIE, WAIT UP! I CAN'T SEE A THING!
I KNOW THE WAY. THIS'LL TAKE US DOWN TO WHERE YOU LEFT YOUR SKI-DOO.
ARE YOU GOING TO TELL ME WHAT YOU'RE DOING HERE? DID YOU SET OFF ALL THE CELL PHONES? AND CUT THE POWER?
NOT BAD, HUH?
YOU DIDN'T ANSWER MY QUESTION.
VRRR
HEAR THAT?
QUICK, BEHIND THAT TREE!
THIS WAY!
TRAIL'S JUST OVER THERE. WE HAVE TO WAIT.
VRRN
OK!
ALL RIGHT. SPILL.
SIGH
WHEN I CAME BACK TO MONTREAL AFTER THE HOLIDAYS, ONE OF MY FRIENDS TOOK ME TO THE PAVILION FOR A PARTY. I MADE SOME FRIENDS AND STARTED HANGING OUT HERE MORE OFTEN.
ELSIE!
WE WEREN'T DOING ANYTHING WRONG! I SWEAR!

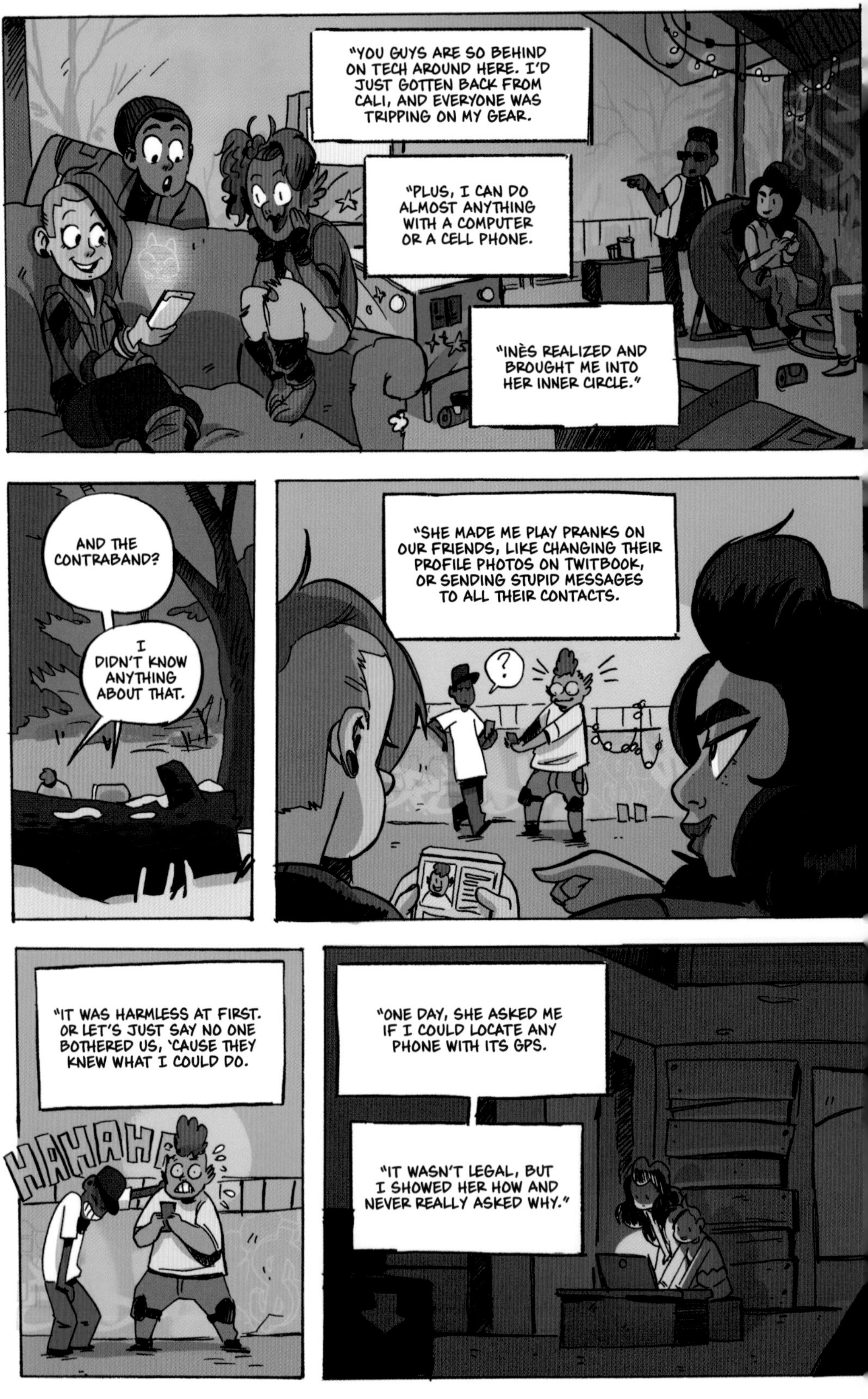
"YOU GUYS ARE SO BEHIND ON TECH AROUND HERE. I'D JUST GOTTEN BACK FROM CALI, AND EVERYONE WAS TRIPPING ON MY GEAR.
"PLUS, I CAN DO ALMOST ANYTHING WITH A COMPUTER OR A CELL PHONE.
"INÈS REALIZED AND BROUGHT ME INTO HER INNER CIRCLE."
AND THE CONTRABAND?
I DIDN'T KNOW ANYTHING ABOUT THAT.
"SHE MADE ME PLAY PRANKS ON OUR FRIENDS, LIKE CHANGING THEIR PROFILE PHOTOS ON TWITBOOK, OR SENDING STUPID MESSAGES TO ALL THEIR CONTACTS.
?
"IT WAS HARMLESS AT FIRST. OR LET'S JUST SAY NO ONE BOTHERED US, 'CAUSE THEY KNEW WHAT I COULD DO.
HAHAHA
"ONE DAY, SHE ASKED ME IF I COULD LOCATE ANY PHONE WITH ITS GPS.
"IT WASN'T LEGAL, BUT I SHOWED HER HOW AND NEVER REALLY ASKED WHY."

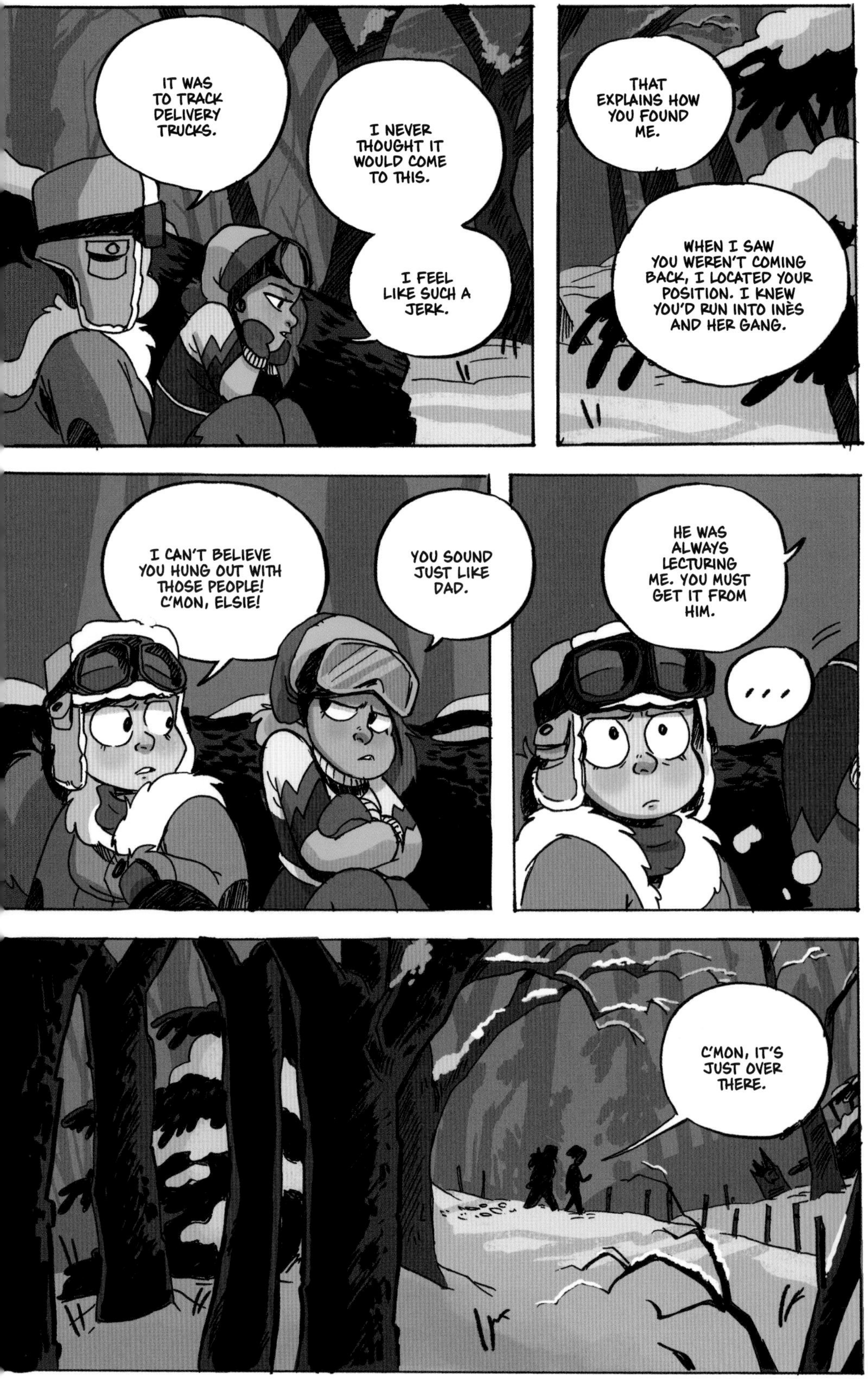
IT WAS TO TRACK DELIVERY TRUCKS.
I NEVER THOUGHT IT WOULD COME TO THIS.
I FEEL LIKE SUCH A JERK.
THAT EXPLAINS HOW YOU FOUND ME.
WHEN I SAW YOU WEREN'T COMING BACK, I LOCATED YOUR POSITION. I KNEW YOU'D RUN INTO INÈS AND HER GANG.
I CAN'T BELIEVE YOU HUNG OUT WITH THOSE PEOPLE! C'MON, ELSIE!
YOU SOUND JUST LIKE DAD.
HE WAS ALWAYS LECTURING ME. YOU MUST GET IT FROM HIM.
...
C'MON, IT'S JUST OVER THERE.

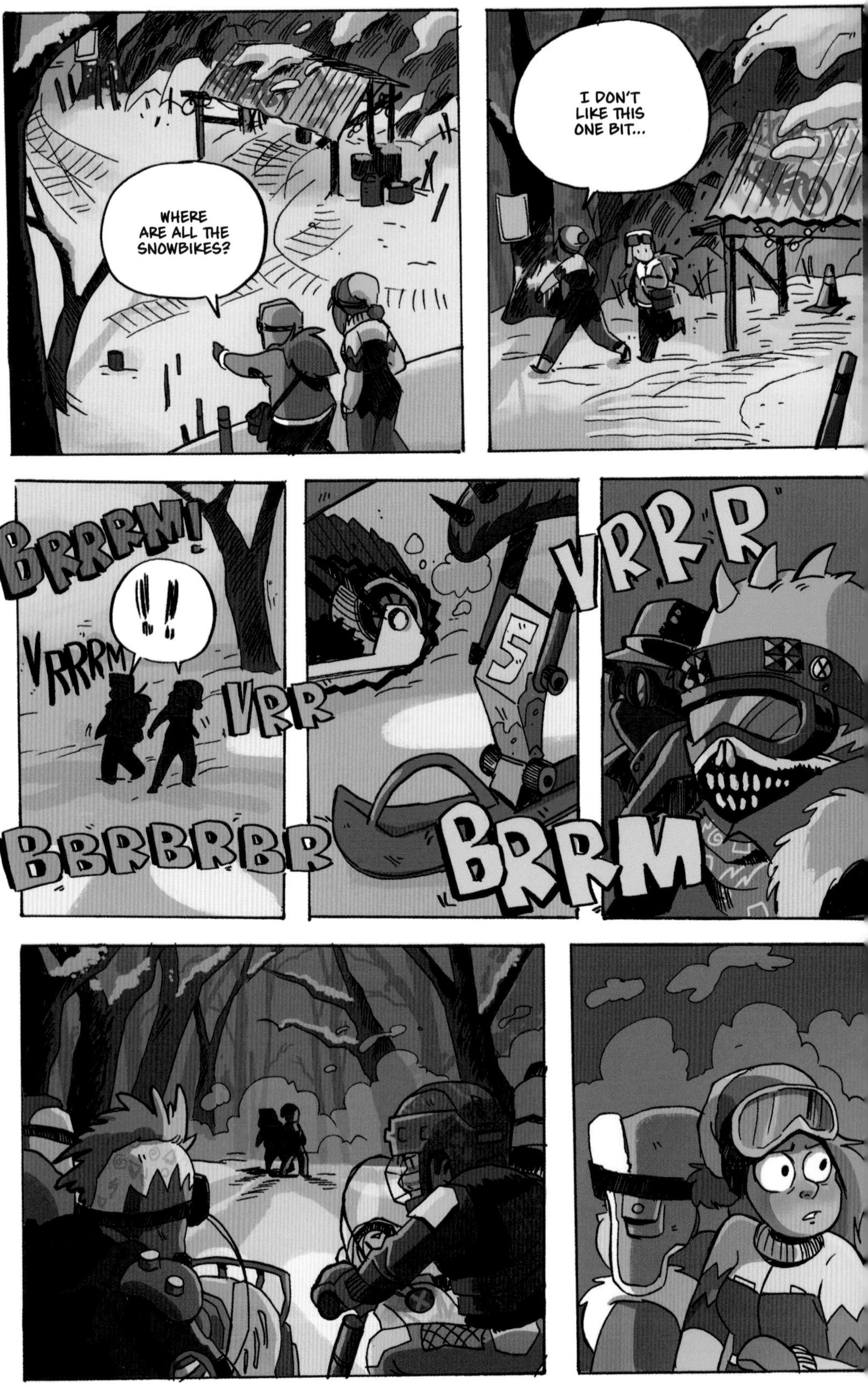
WHERE ARE ALL THE SNOWBIKES?
I DON'T LIKE THIS ONE BIT...
BRRRM!
!!
VRRRM
VRR
BBRBRBR
VRRR
BRRM

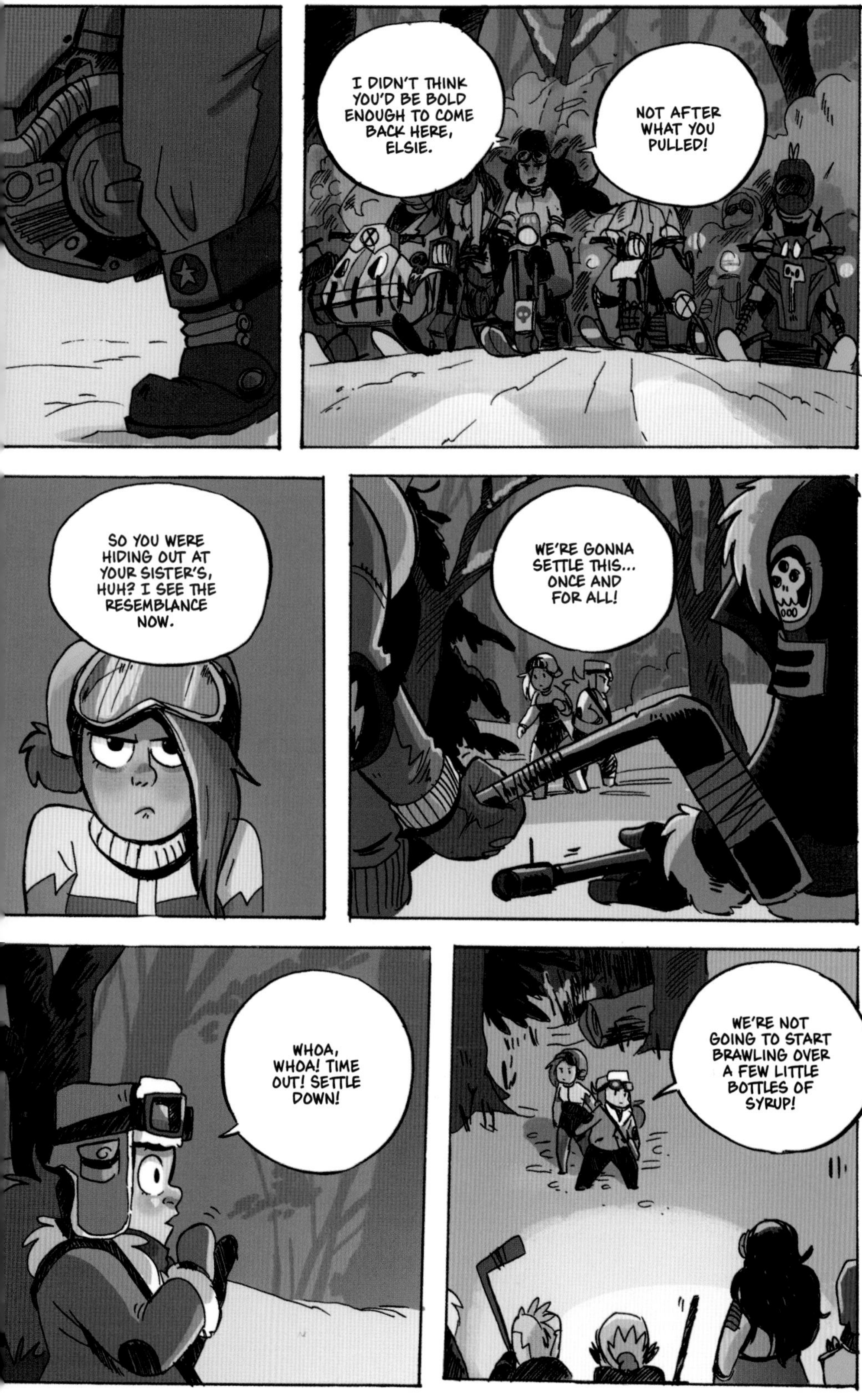
I DIDN'T THINK YOU'D BE BOLD ENOUGH TO COME BACK HERE, ELSIE.
NOT AFTER WHAT YOU PULLED!
SO YOU WERE HIDING OUT AT YOUR SISTER'S, HUH? I SEE THE RESEMBLANCE NOW.
WE'RE GONNA SETTLE THIS... ONCE AND FOR ALL!
WHOA, WHOA! TIME OUT! SETTLE DOWN!
WE'RE NOT GOING TO START BRAWLING OVER A FEW LITTLE BOTTLES OF SYRUP!

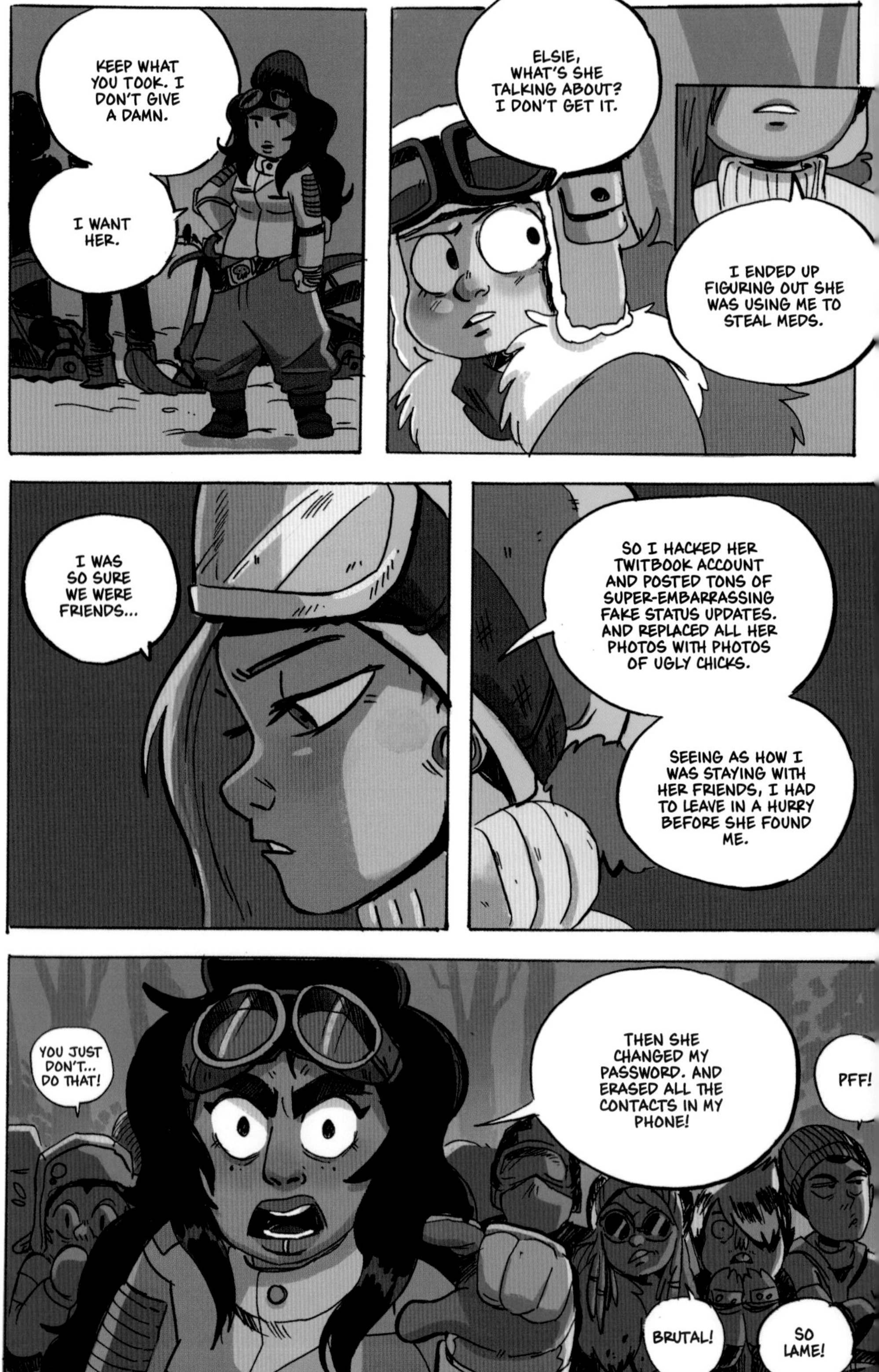
KEEP WHAT YOU TOOK. I DON'T GIVE A DAMN.
I WANT HER.
ELSIE, WHAT'S SHE TALKING ABOUT? I DON'T GET IT.
I ENDED UP FIGURING OUT SHE WAS USING ME TO STEAL MEDS.
I WAS SO SURE WE WERE FRIENDS...
SO I HACKED HER TWITBOOK ACCOUNT AND POSTED TONS OF SUPER-EMBARRASSING FAKE STATUS UPDATES. AND REPLACED ALL HER PHOTOS WITH PHOTOS OF UGLY CHICKS.
SEEING AS HOW I WAS STAYING WITH HER FRIENDS, I HAD TO LEAVE IN A HURRY BEFORE SHE FOUND ME.
YOU JUST DON'T... DO THAT!
THEN SHE CHANGED MY PASSWORD. AND ERASED ALL THE CONTACTS IN MY PHONE!
PFF!
BRUTAL!
SO LAME!

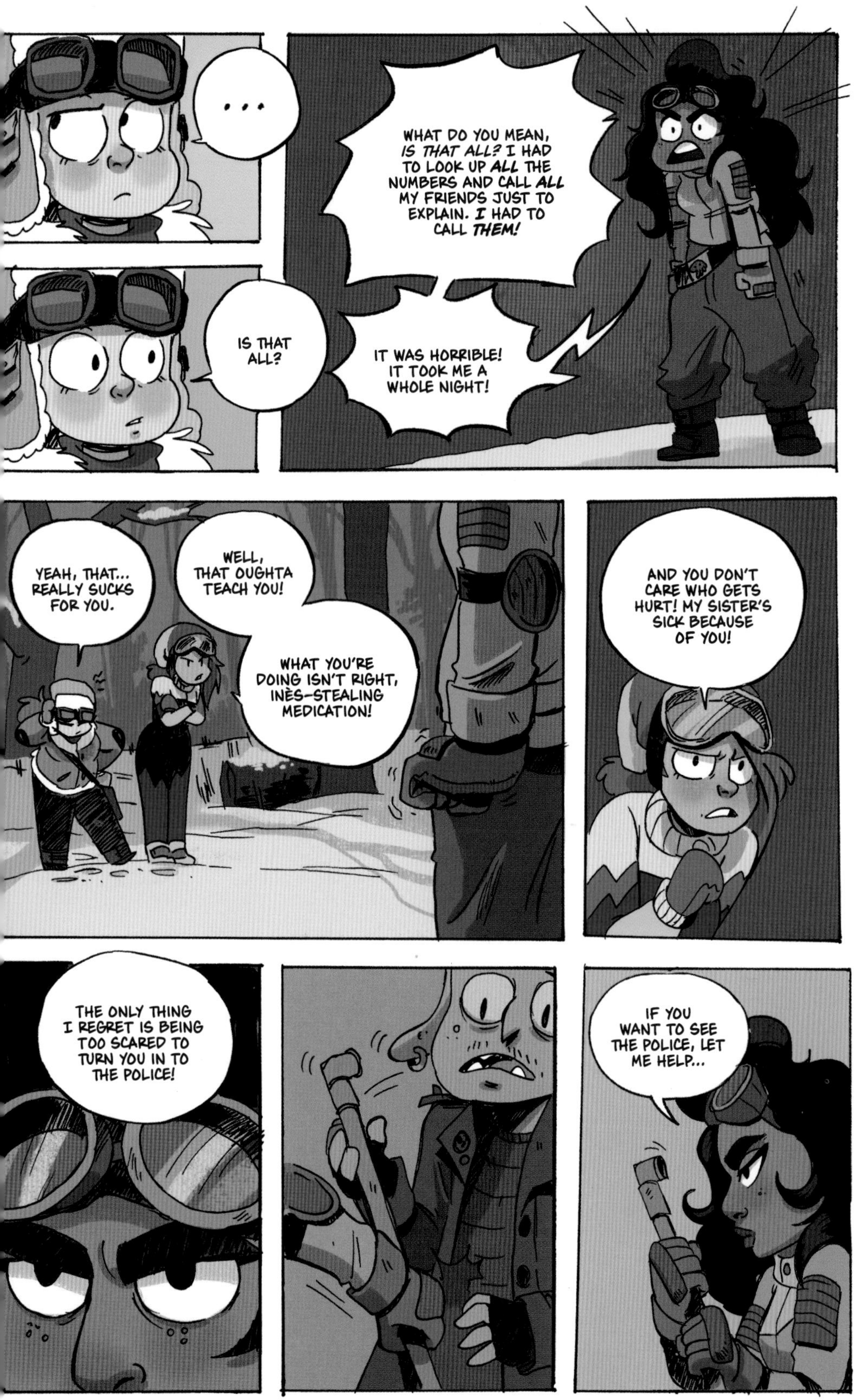
...
IS THAT ALL?
WHAT DO YOU MEAN, IS THAT ALL? I HAD TO LOOK UP ALL THE NUMBERS AND CALL ALL MY FRIENDS JUST TO EXPLAIN. I HAD TO CALL THEM!
IT WAS HORRIBLE! IT TOOK ME A WHOLE NIGHT!
YEAH, THAT... REALLY SUCKS FOR YOU.
WELL, THAT OUGHTA TEACH YOU!
WHAT YOU'RE DOING ISN'T RIGHT, INÈS—STEALING MEDICATION!
AND YOU DON'T CARE WHO GETS HURT! MY SISTER'S SICK BECAUSE OF YOU!
THE ONLY THING I REGRET IS BEING TOO SCARED TO TURN YOU IN TO THE POLICE!
IF YOU WANT TO SEE THE POLICE, LET ME HELP...

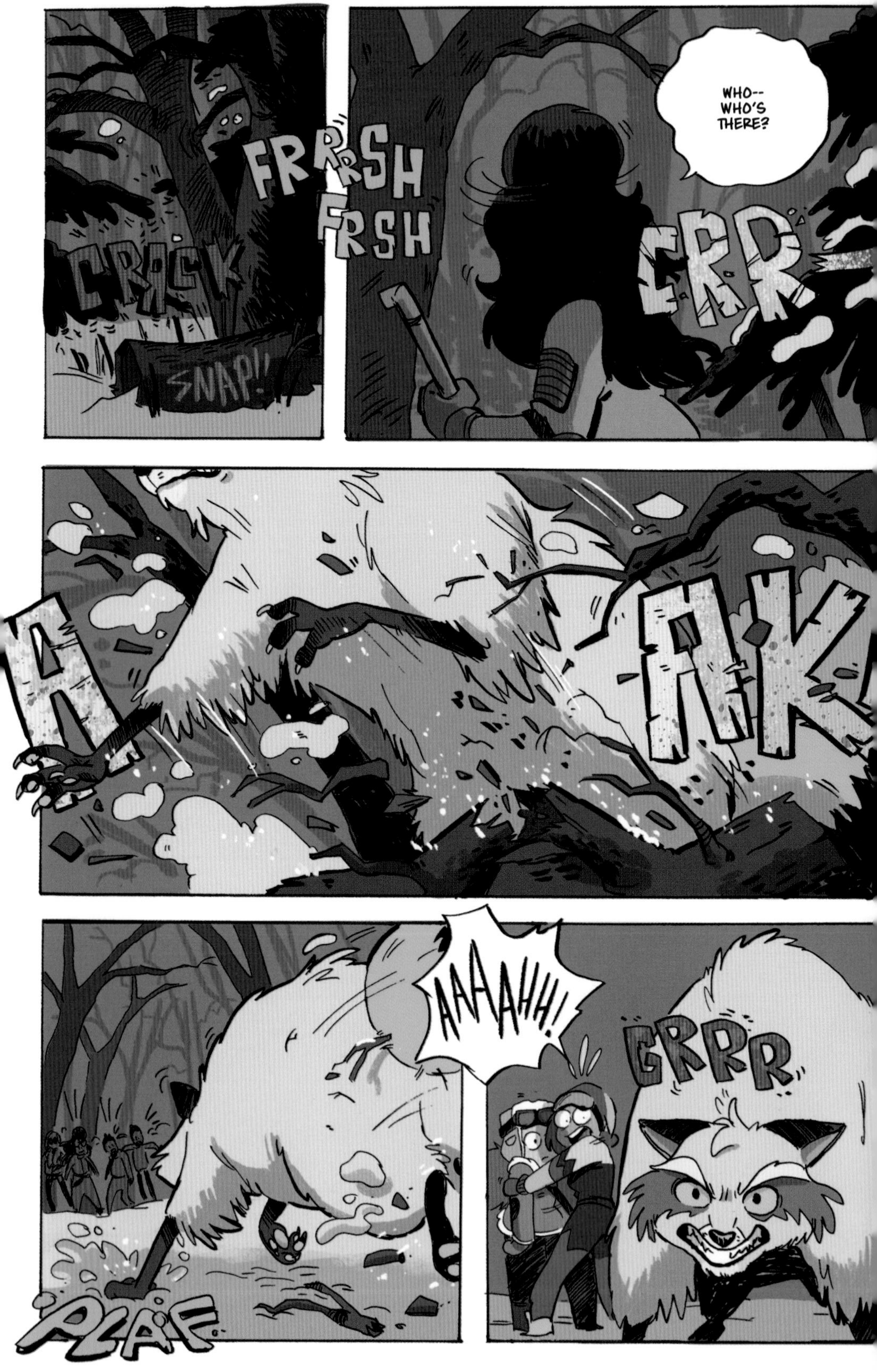

CRACK
SNAP!!
FRRRSH
FRSH
WHO--
WHO'S
THERE?
CRR
A
AK
AAAAHH!
GRRR
PLAF

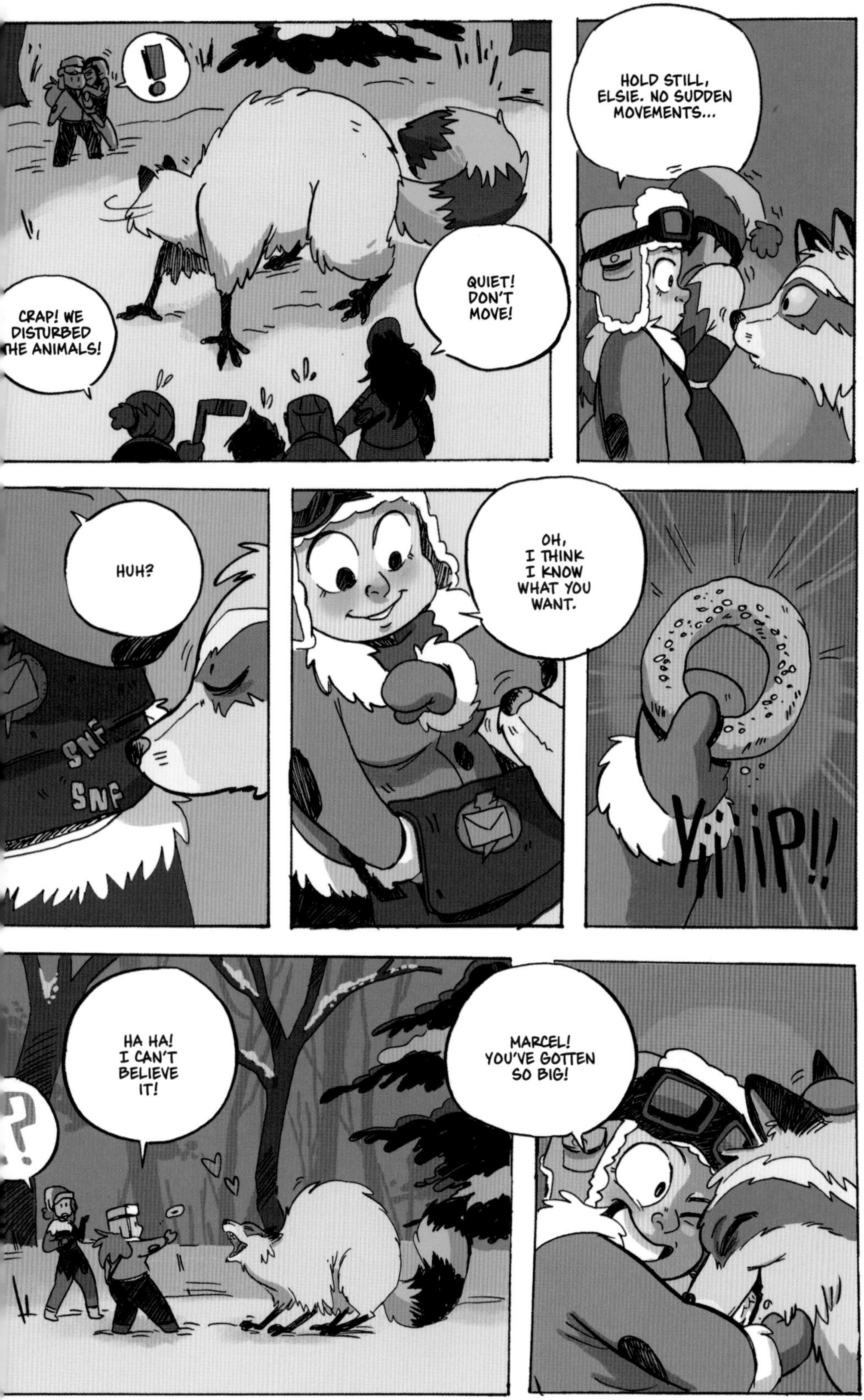
!
CRAP! WE DISTURBED THE ANIMALS!
QUIET! DON'T MOVE!
HOLD STILL, ELSIE. NO SUDDEN MOVEMENTS...
HUH?
SNF
SNF
OH, I THINK I KNOW WHAT YOU WANT.
YIIIP!!
?
HA HA! I CAN'T BELIEVE IT!
MARCEL! YOU'VE GOTTEN SO BIG!

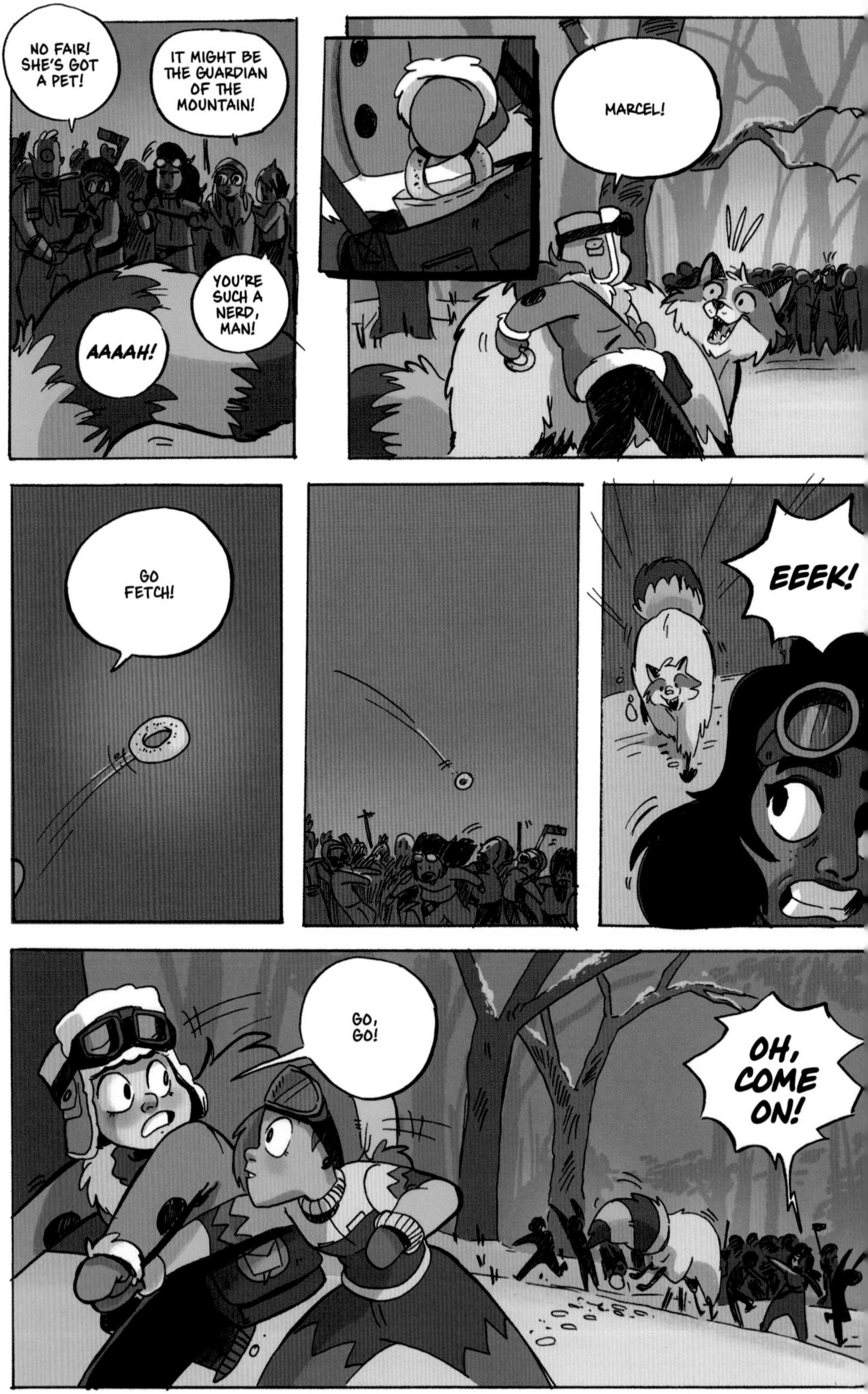
NO FAIR! SHE'S GOT A PET!
IT MIGHT BE THE GUARDIAN OF THE MOUNTAIN!
YOU'RE SUCH A NERD, MAN!
AAAAH!
MARCEL!
GO FETCH!
EEEK!
GO, GO!
OH, COME ON!

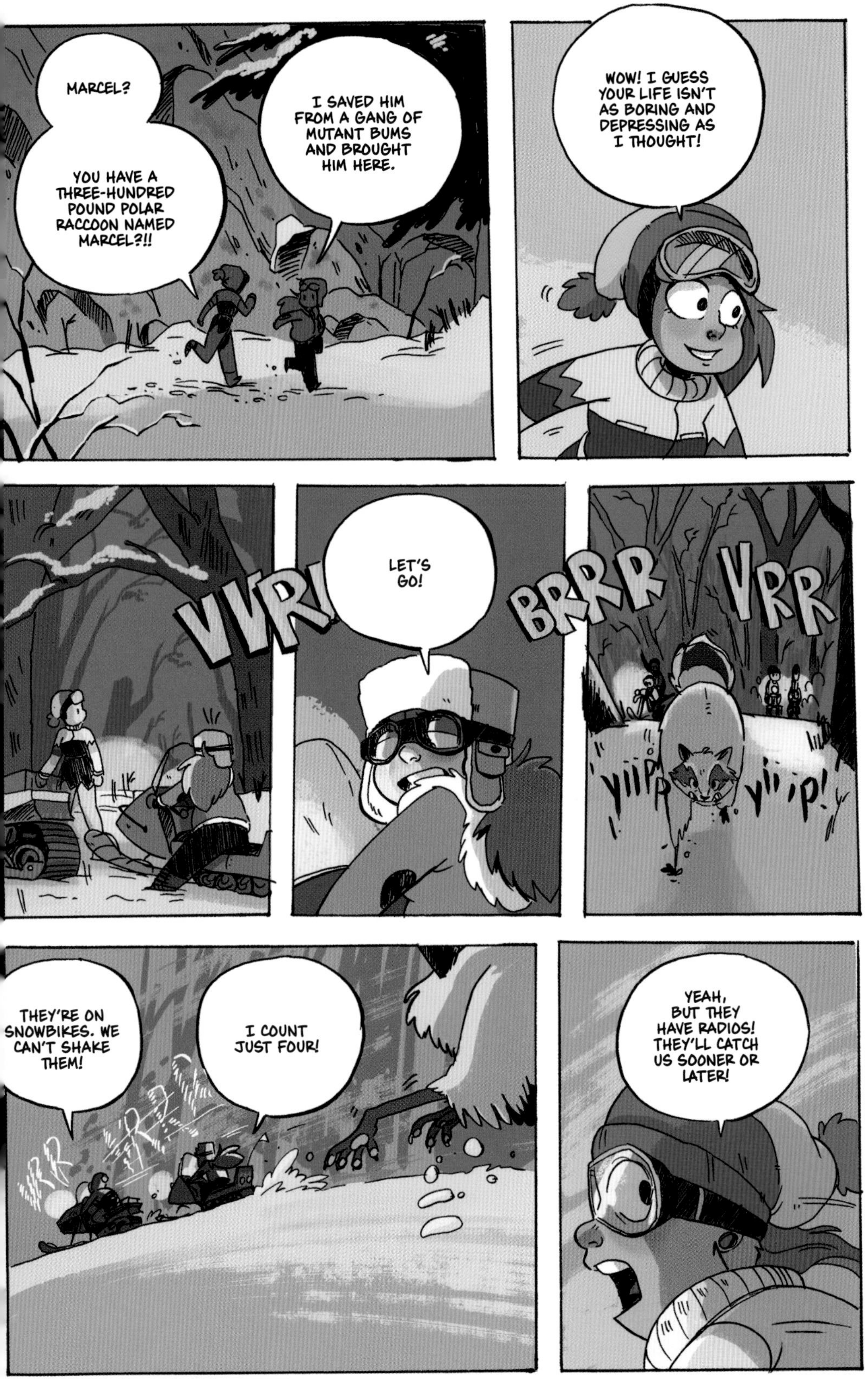
MARCEL?
YOU HAVE A THREE-HUNDRED POUND POLAR RACCOON NAMED MARCEL?!!
I SAVED HIM FROM A GANG OF MUTANT BUMS AND BROUGHT HIM HERE.
WOW! I GUESS YOUR LIFE ISN'T AS BORING AND DEPRESSING AS I THOUGHT!
VVR
LET'S GO!
BRRR
VRR
YIIP
YIIP!
THEY'RE ON SNOWBIKES. WE CAN'T SHAKE THEM!
I COUNT JUST FOUR!
YEAH, BUT THEY HAVE RADIOS! THEY'LL CATCH US SOONER OR LATER!

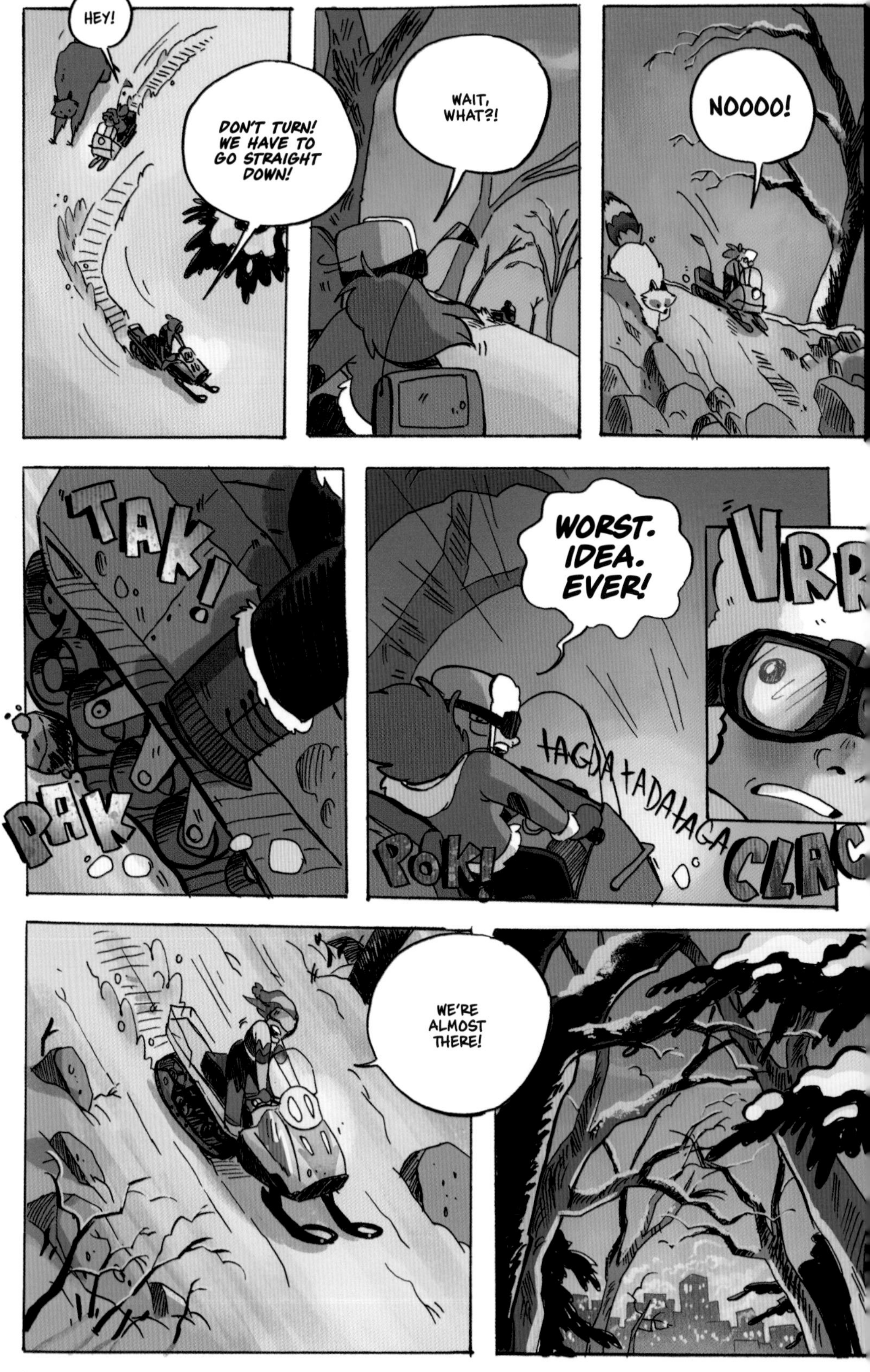
HEY!
DON'T TURN! WE HAVE TO GO STRAIGHT DOWN!
WAIT, WHAT?!
NOOOO!
TAK!
PAK
WORST. IDEA. EVER!
TAGDA TADATAGA
POK!
CLAC
VRR
WE'RE ALMOST THERE!

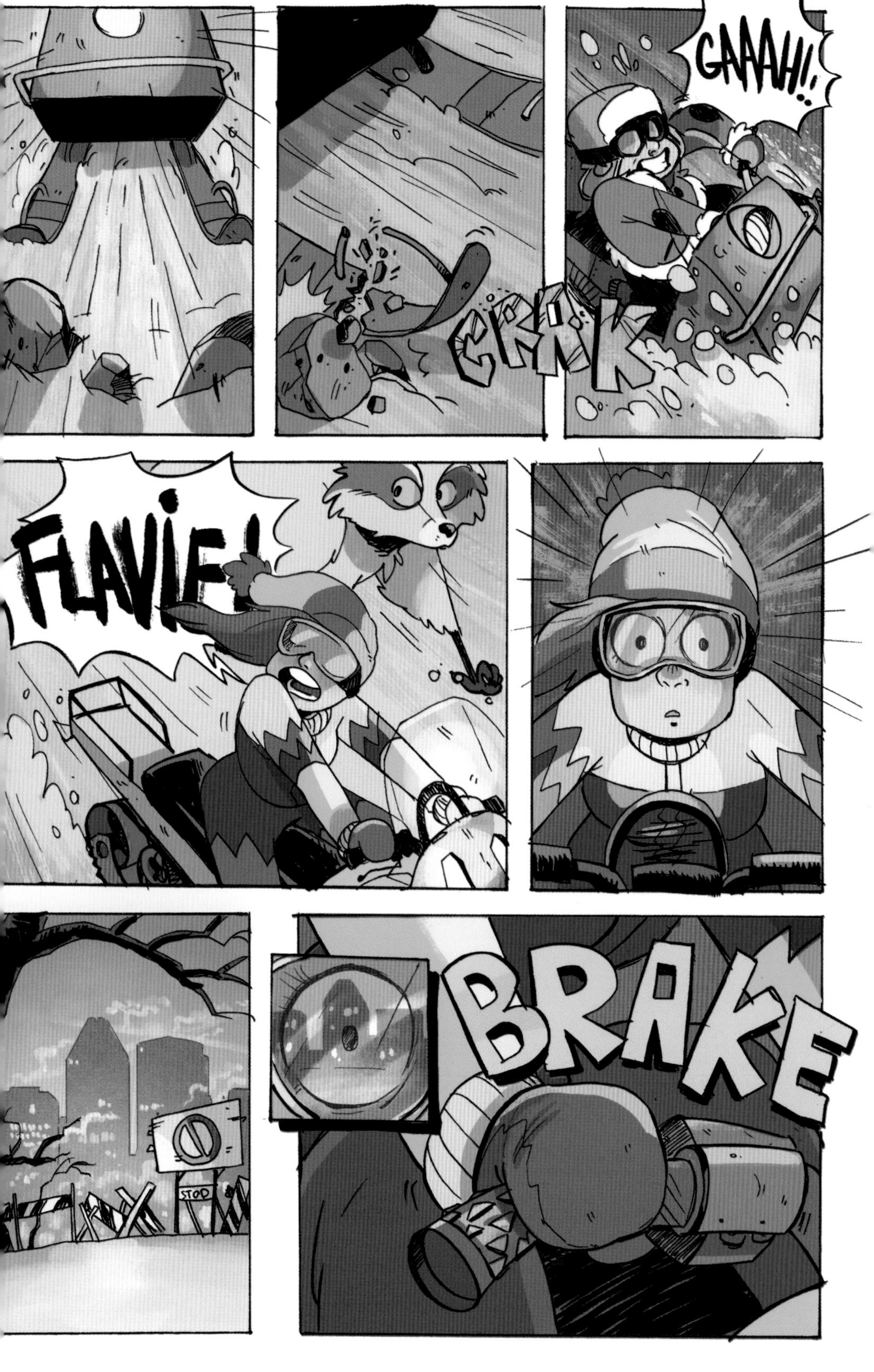
GAAAH!!
CRRK
FLAVIE!
STOP
BRAKE

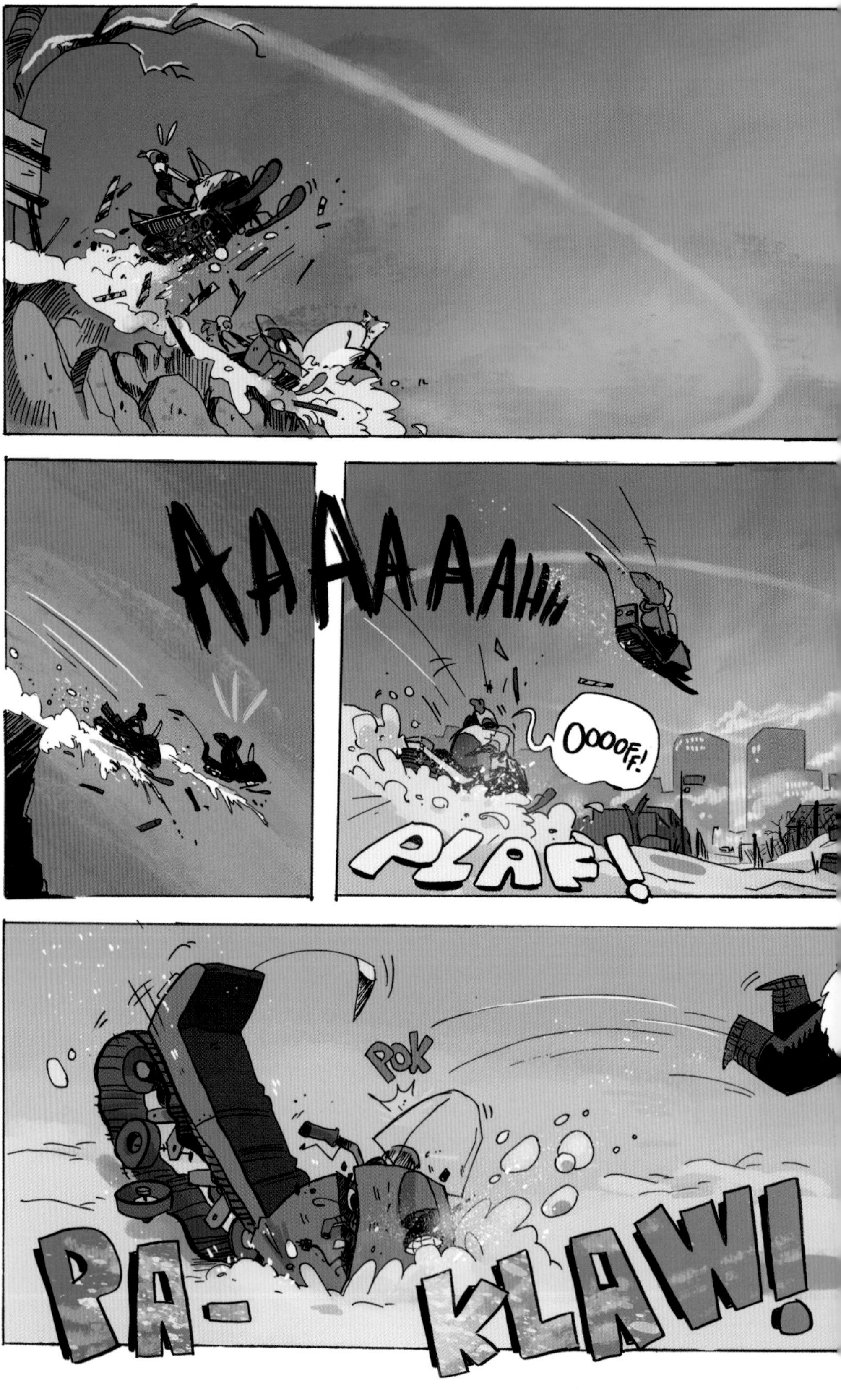
AAAAAAHH
OOOOFF!
PLAF!
POK
PA-
KLAW!

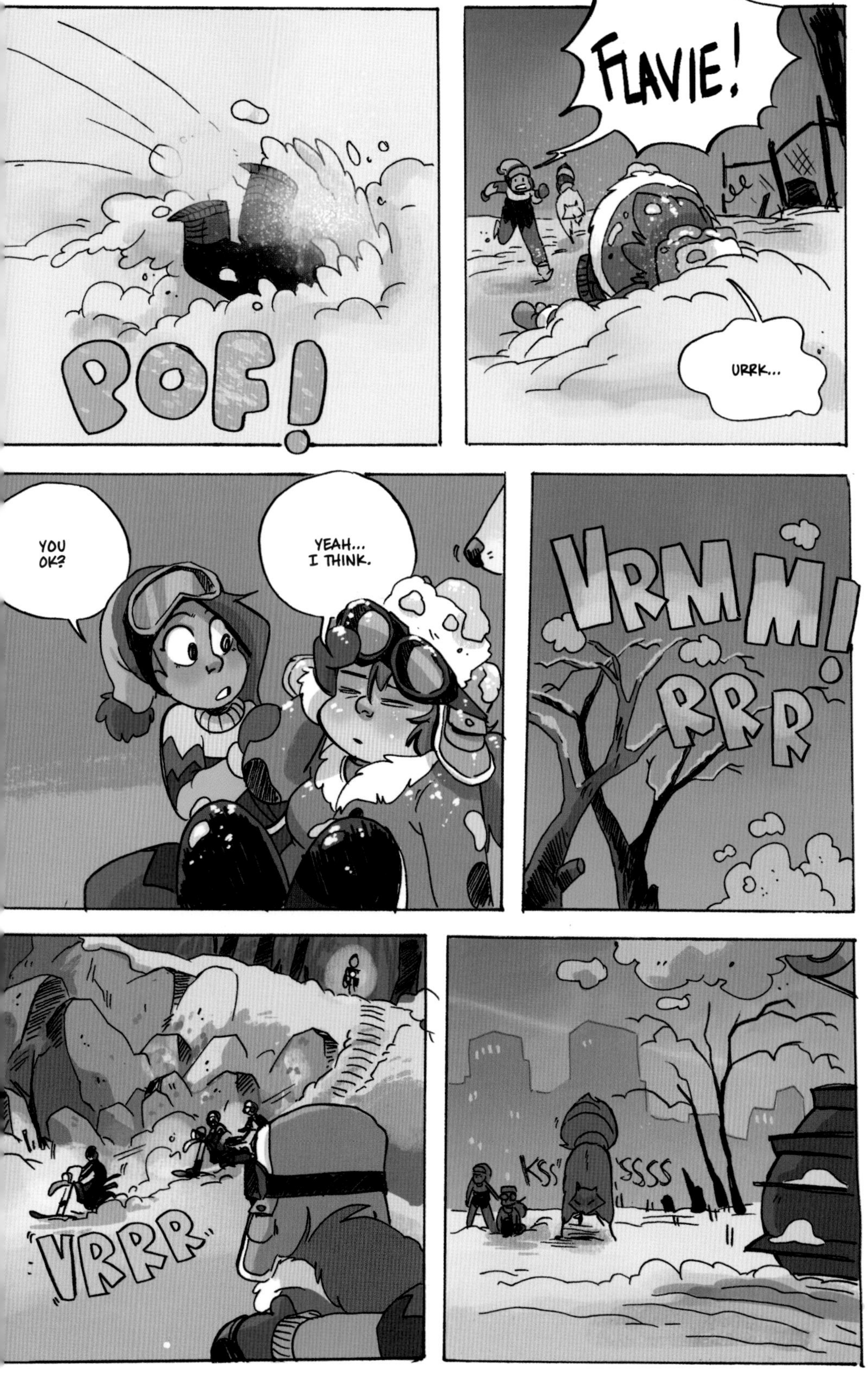
POF!
FLAVIE!
URRK...
YOU OK?
YEAH... I THINK.
VRMM!
RRR
VRRR
KSS
SSSS

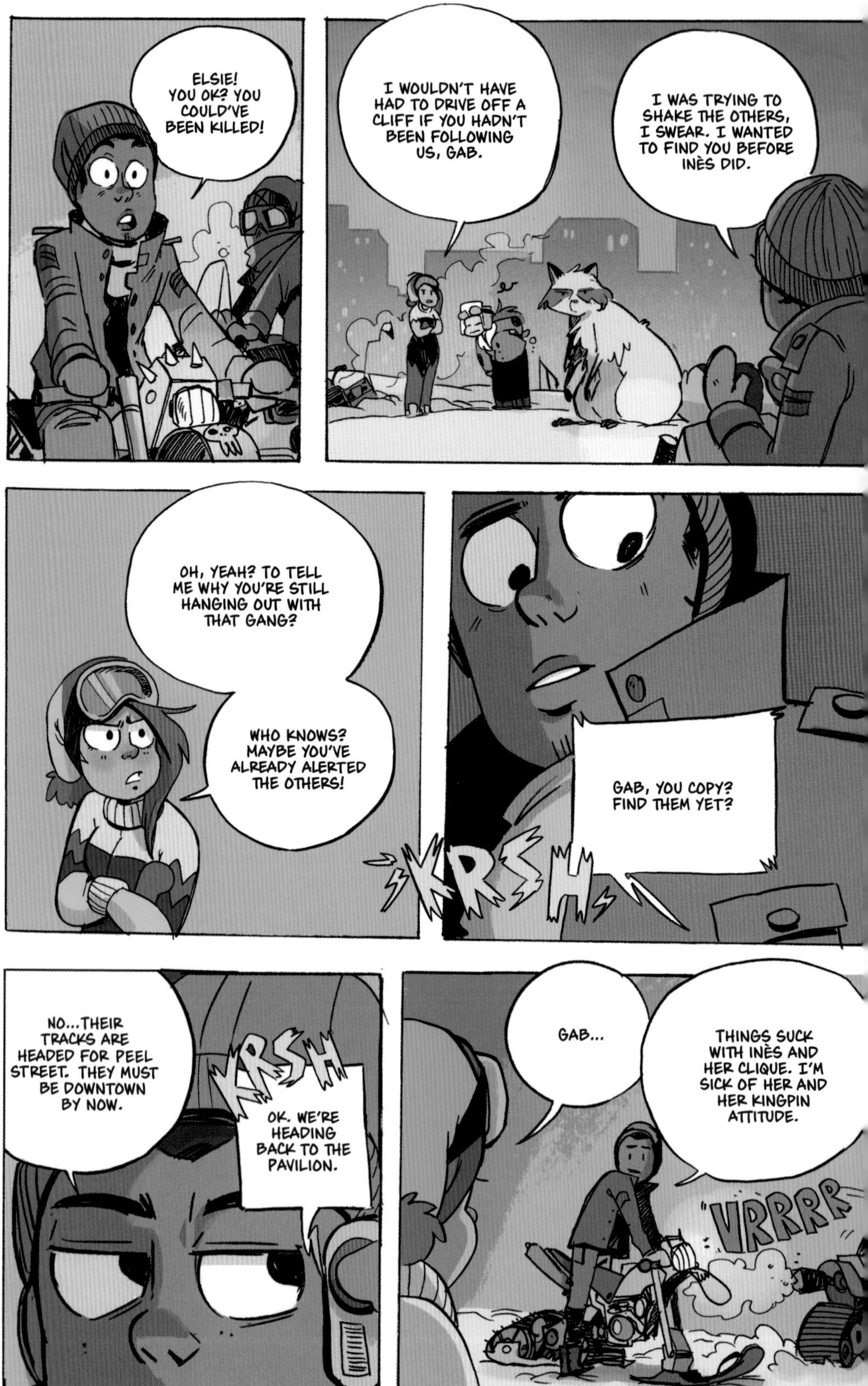
ELSIE! YOU OK? YOU COULD'VE BEEN KILLED!
I WOULDN'T HAVE HAD TO DRIVE OFF A CLIFF IF YOU HADN'T BEEN FOLLOWING US, GAB.
I WAS TRYING TO SHAKE THE OTHERS, I SWEAR. I WANTED TO FIND YOU BEFORE INÈS DID.
OH, YEAH? TO TELL ME WHY YOU'RE STILL HANGING OUT WITH THAT GANG?
WHO KNOWS? MAYBE YOU'VE ALREADY ALERTED THE OTHERS!
GAB, YOU COPY? FIND THEM YET?
KRSH
NO...THEIR TRACKS ARE HEADED FOR PEEL STREET. THEY MUST BE DOWNTOWN BY NOW.
KRSH
OK. WE'RE HEADING BACK TO THE PAVILION.
GAB...
THINGS SUCK WITH INÈS AND HER CLIQUE. I'M SICK OF HER AND HER KINGPIN ATTITUDE.
VRRRR

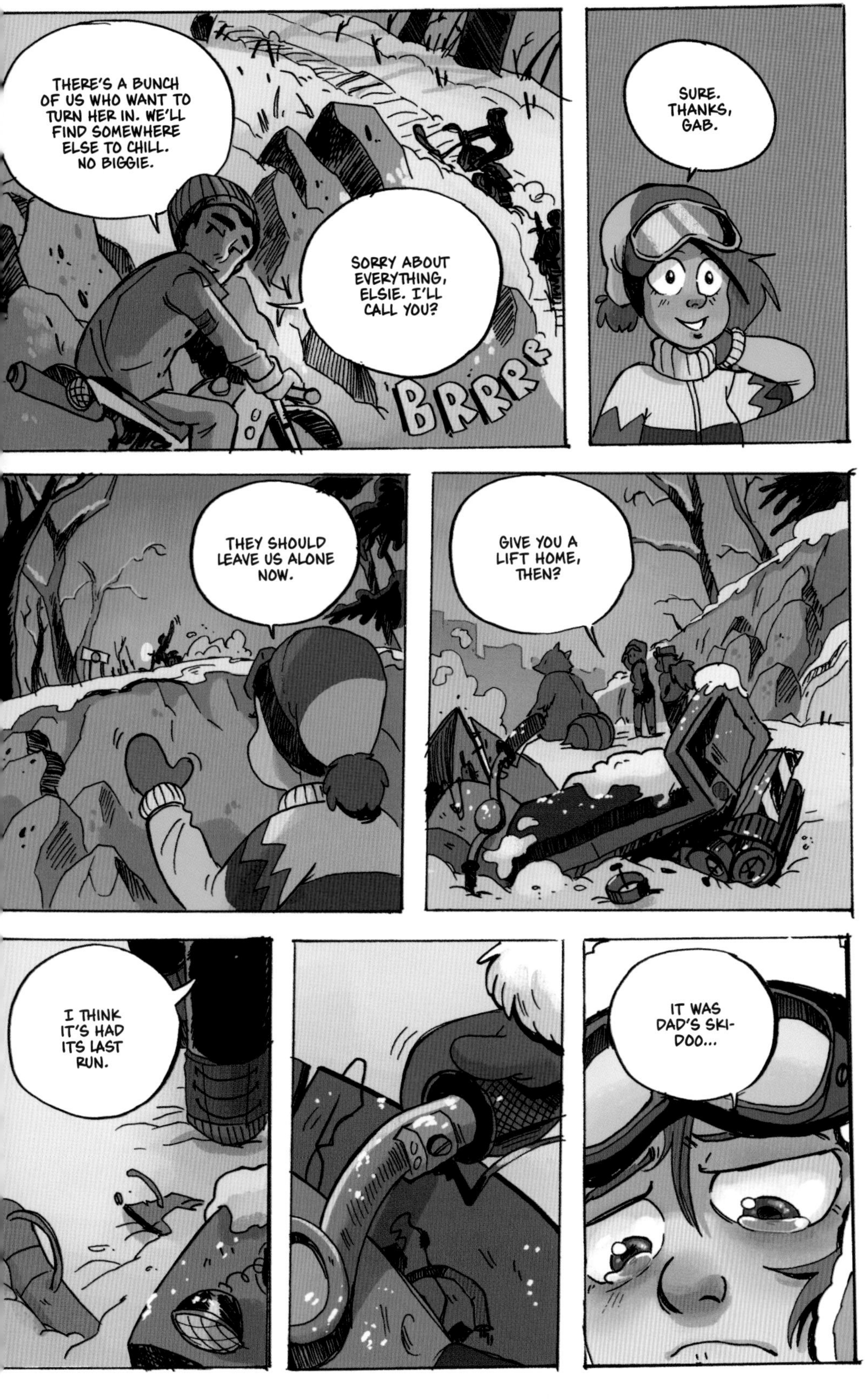
THERE'S A BUNCH OF US WHO WANT TO TURN HER IN. WE'LL FIND SOMEWHERE ELSE TO CHILL. NO BIGGIE.
SORRY ABOUT EVERYTHING, ELSIE. I'LL CALL YOU?
BRRRR
SURE. THANKS, GAB.
THEY SHOULD LEAVE US ALONE NOW.
GIVE YOU A LIFT HOME, THEN?
I THINK IT'S HAD ITS LAST RUN.
IT WAS DAD'S SKI-DOO...

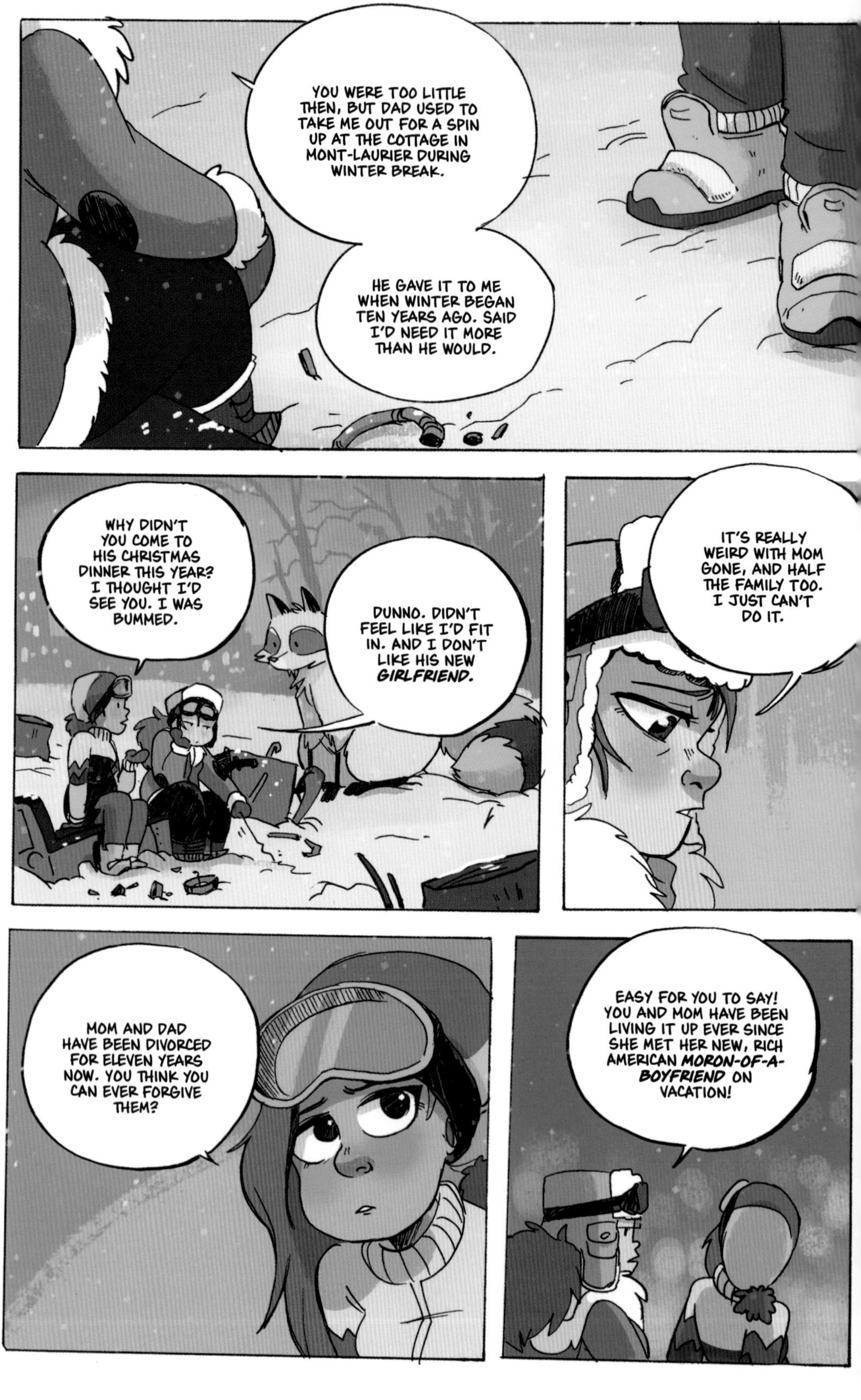
YOU WERE TOO LITTLE THEN, BUT DAD USED TO TAKE ME OUT FOR A SPIN UP AT THE COTTAGE IN MONT-LAURIER DURING WINTER BREAK.
HE GAVE IT TO ME WHEN WINTER BEGAN TEN YEARS AGO. SAID I'D NEED IT MORE THAN HE WOULD.
WHY DIDN'T YOU COME TO HIS CHRISTMAS DINNER THIS YEAR? I THOUGHT I'D SEE YOU. I WAS BUMMED.
DUNNO. DIDN'T FEEL LIKE I'D FIT IN. AND I DON'T LIKE HIS NEW ***GIRLFRIEND.***
IT'S REALLY WEIRD WITH MOM GONE, AND HALF THE FAMILY TOO. I JUST CAN'T DO IT.
MOM AND DAD HAVE BEEN DIVORCED FOR ELEVEN YEARS NOW. YOU THINK YOU CAN EVER FORGIVE THEM?
EASY FOR YOU TO SAY! YOU AND MOM HAVE BEEN LIVING IT UP EVER SINCE SHE MET HER NEW, RICH AMERICAN ***MORON-OF-A-BOYFRIEND*** ON VACATION!

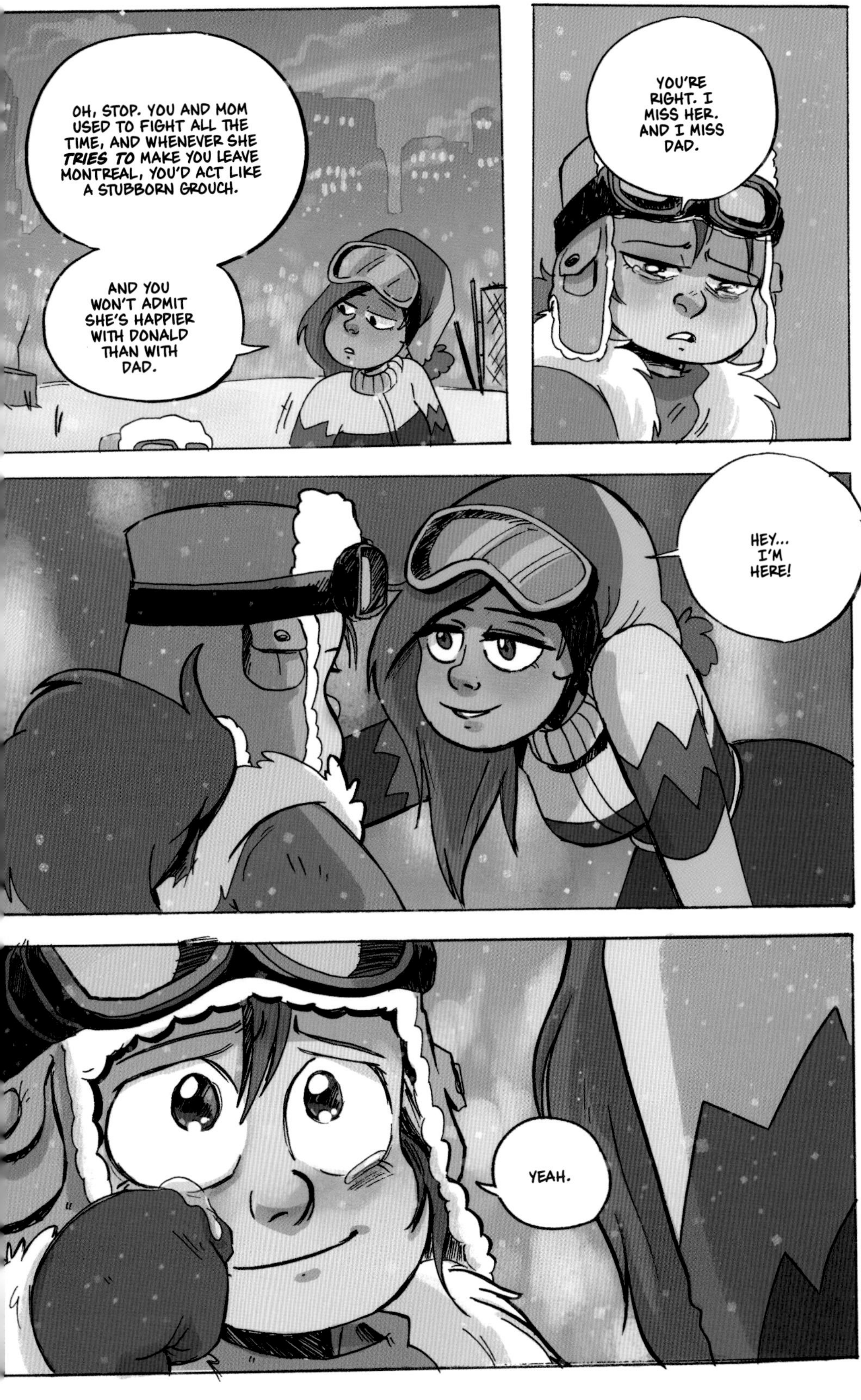
OH, STOP. YOU AND MOM USED TO FIGHT ALL THE TIME, AND WHENEVER SHE *TRIES TO* MAKE YOU LEAVE MONTREAL, YOU'D ACT LIKE A STUBBORN GROUCH.
AND YOU WON'T ADMIT SHE'S HAPPIER WITH DONALD THAN WITH DAD.
YOU'RE RIGHT. I MISS HER. AND I MISS DAD.
HEY... I'M HERE!
YEAH.

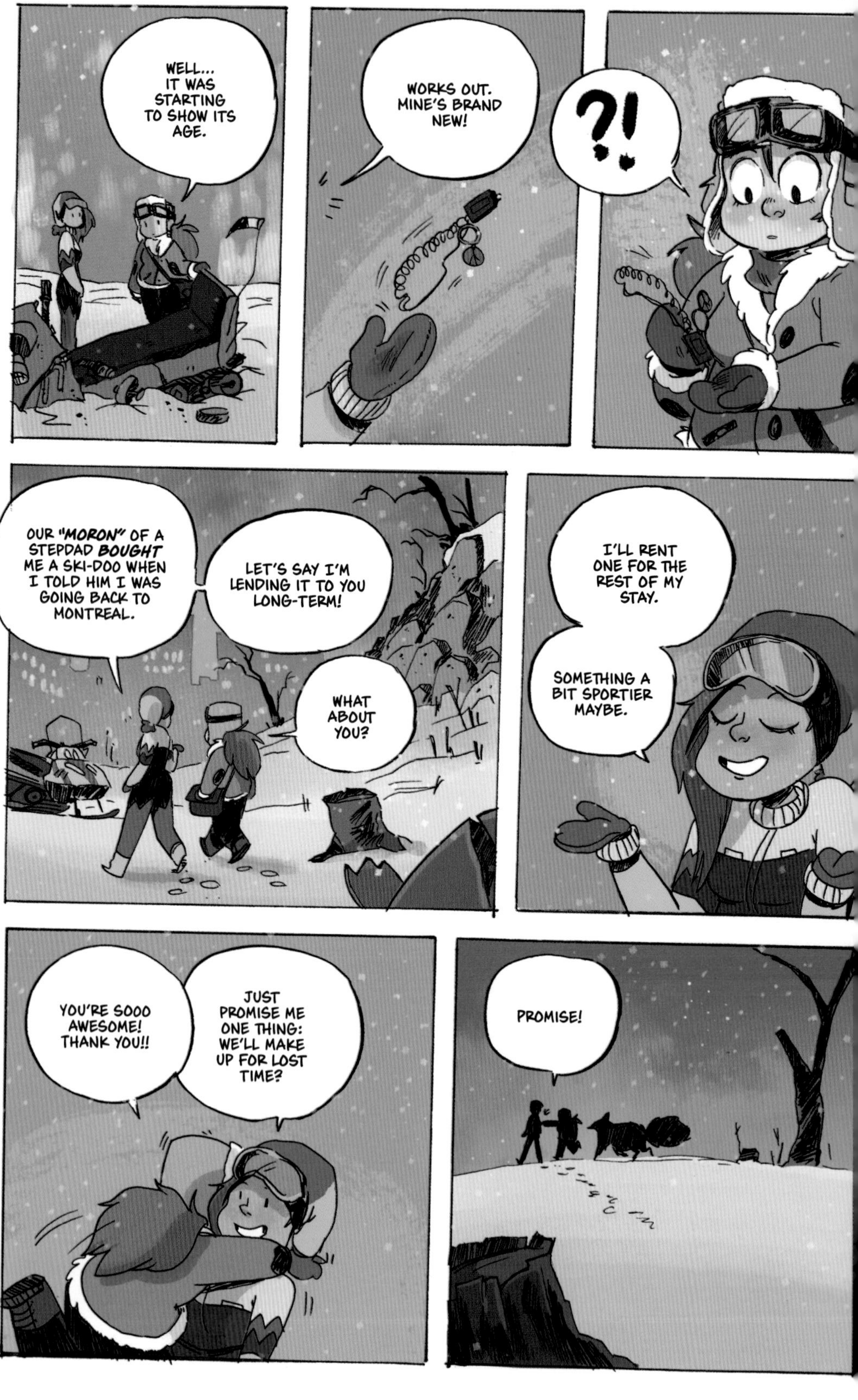
WELL... IT WAS STARTING TO SHOW ITS AGE.
WORKS OUT. MINE'S BRAND NEW!
?!
OUR "*MORON*" OF A STEPDAD ***BOUGHT*** ME A SKI-DOO WHEN I TOLD HIM I WAS GOING BACK TO MONTREAL.
LET'S SAY I'M LENDING IT TO YOU LONG-TERM!
WHAT ABOUT YOU?
I'LL RENT ONE FOR THE REST OF MY STAY.
SOMETHING A BIT SPORTIER MAYBE.
YOU'RE SOOO AWESOME! THANK YOU!!
JUST PROMISE ME ONE THING: WE'LL MAKE UP FOR LOST TIME?
PROMISE!

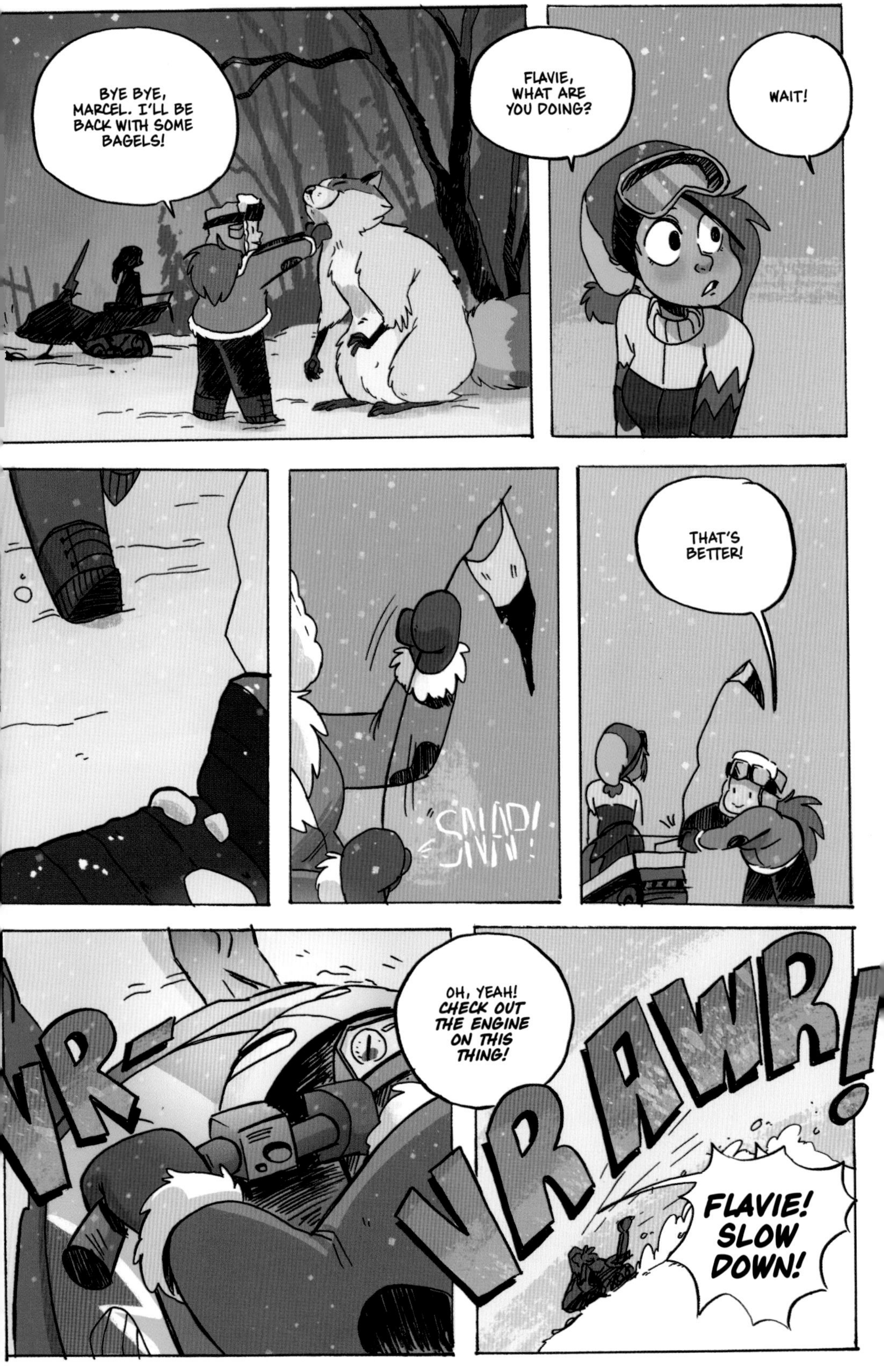
BYE BYE, MARCEL. I'LL BE BACK WITH SOME BAGELS!
FLAVIE, WHAT ARE YOU DOING?
WAIT!
SNAP!
THAT'S BETTER!
VR-
OH, YEAH! CHECK OUT THE ENGINE ON THIS THING!
VRAWR!
FLAVIE! SLOW DOWN!

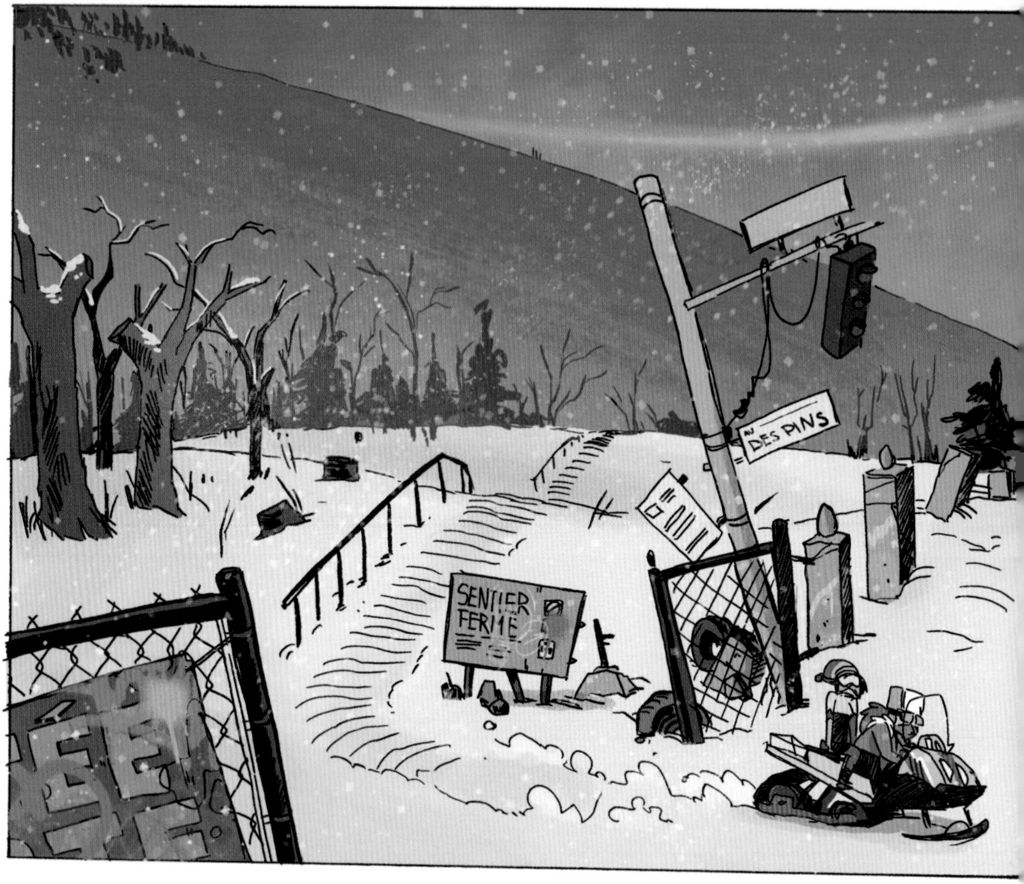

AV DES PINS
SENTIER FERMÉ

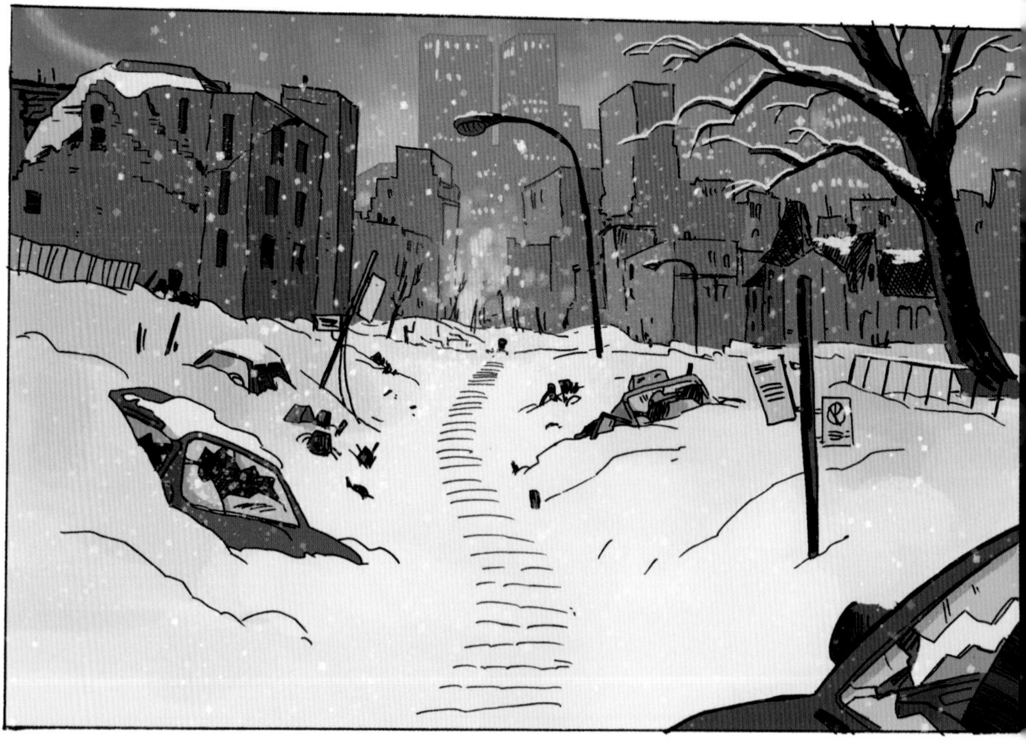

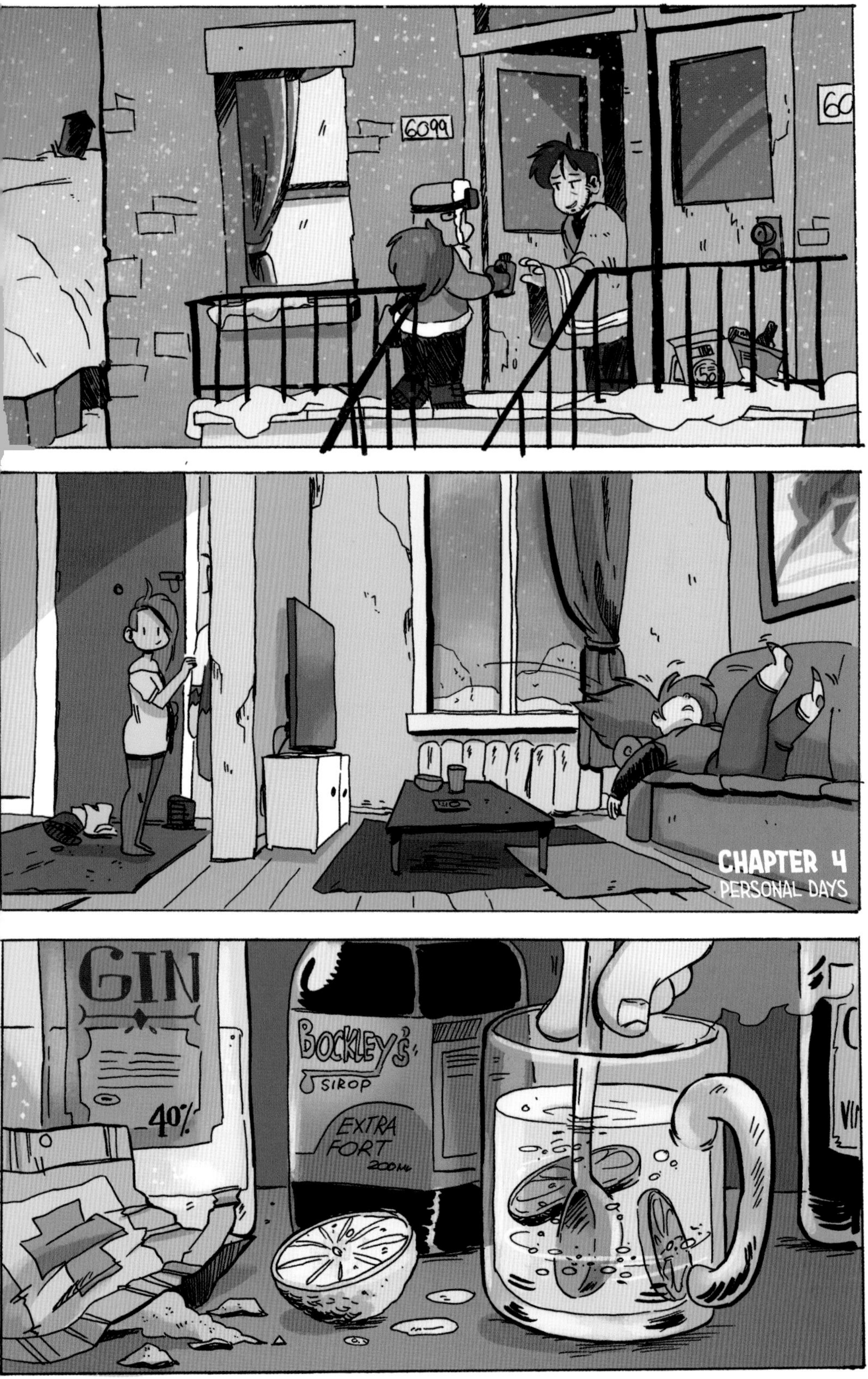
6099
60
CHAPTER 4
PERSONAL DAYS
GIN
40%
BOCKLEY'S
SIROP
EXTRA
FORT
200ML

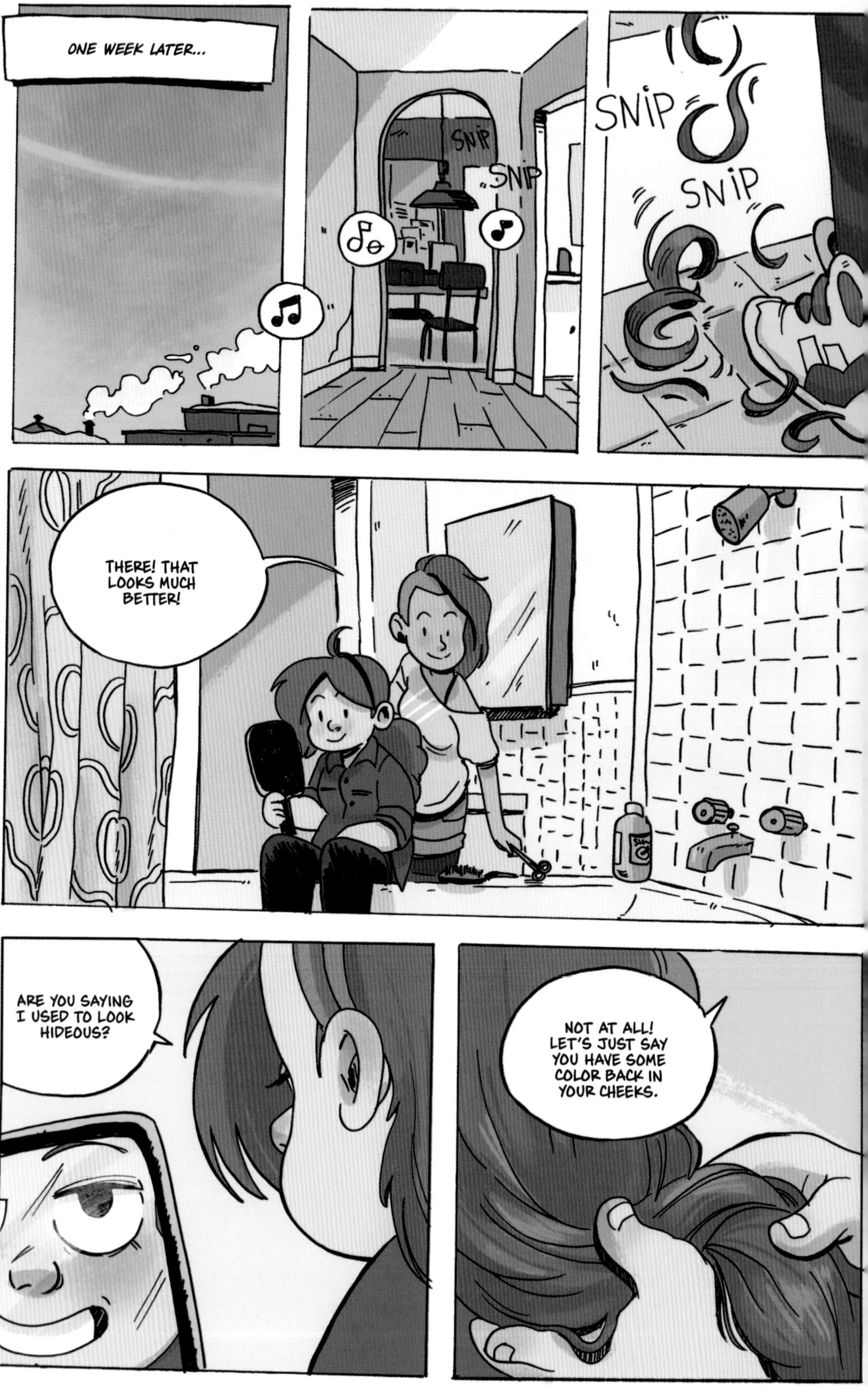
ONE WEEK LATER...
SNIP
SNIP
SNIP
SNIP
THERE! THAT LOOKS MUCH BETTER!
ARE YOU SAYING I USED TO LOOK HIDEOUS?
NOT AT ALL! LET'S JUST SAY YOU HAVE SOME COLOR BACK IN YOUR CHEEKS.

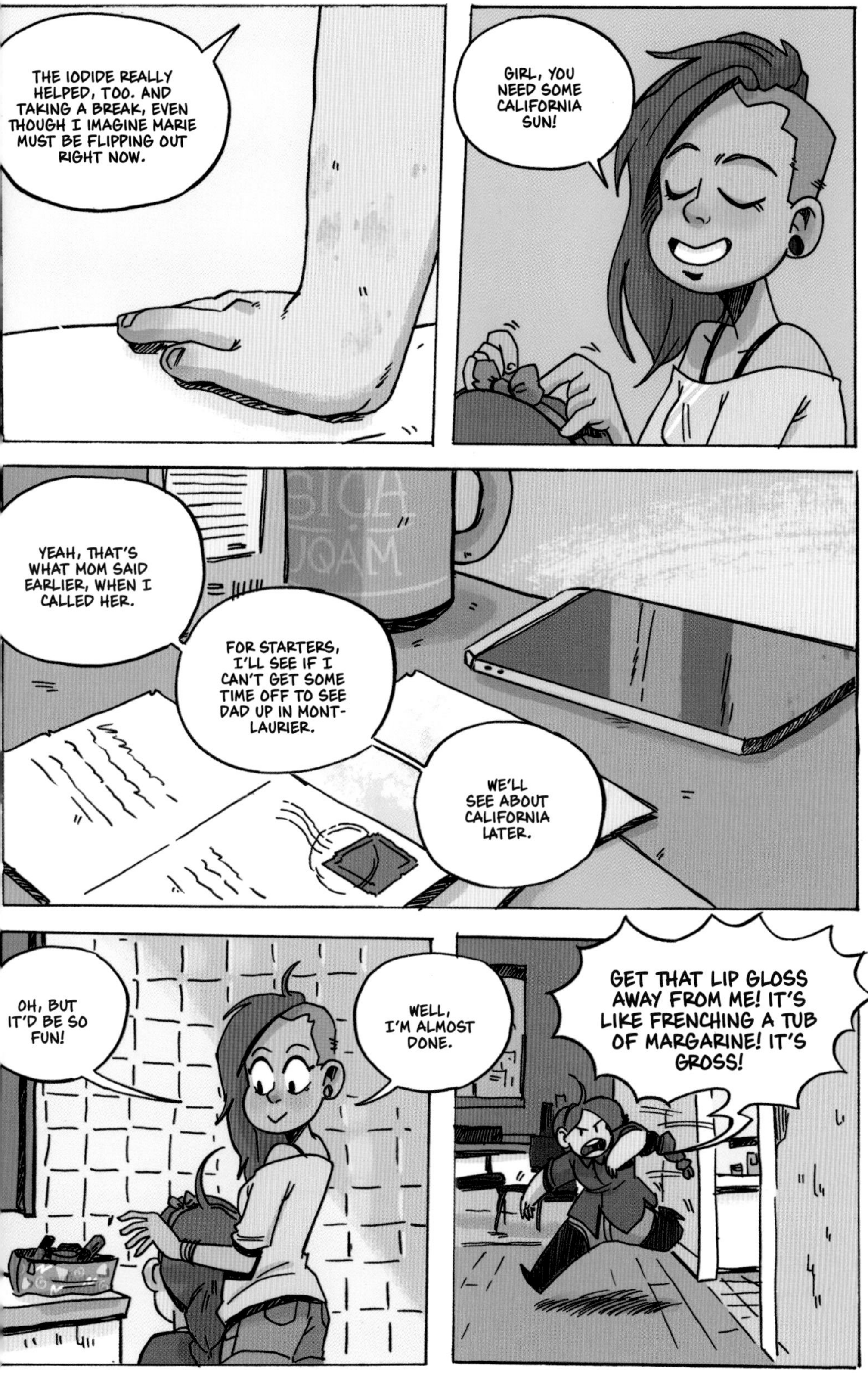
THE IODIDE REALLY HELPED, TOO. AND TAKING A BREAK, EVEN THOUGH I IMAGINE MARIE MUST BE FLIPPING OUT RIGHT NOW.
GIRL, YOU NEED SOME CALIFORNIA SUN!
YEAH, THAT'S WHAT MOM SAID EARLIER, WHEN I CALLED HER.
FOR STARTERS, I'LL SEE IF I CAN'T GET SOME TIME OFF TO SEE DAD UP IN MONT-LAURIER.
WE'LL SEE ABOUT CALIFORNIA LATER.
OH, BUT IT'D BE SO FUN!
WELL, I'M ALMOST DONE.
GET THAT LIP GLOSS AWAY FROM ME! IT'S LIKE FRENCHING A TUB OF MARGARINE! IT'S GROSS!

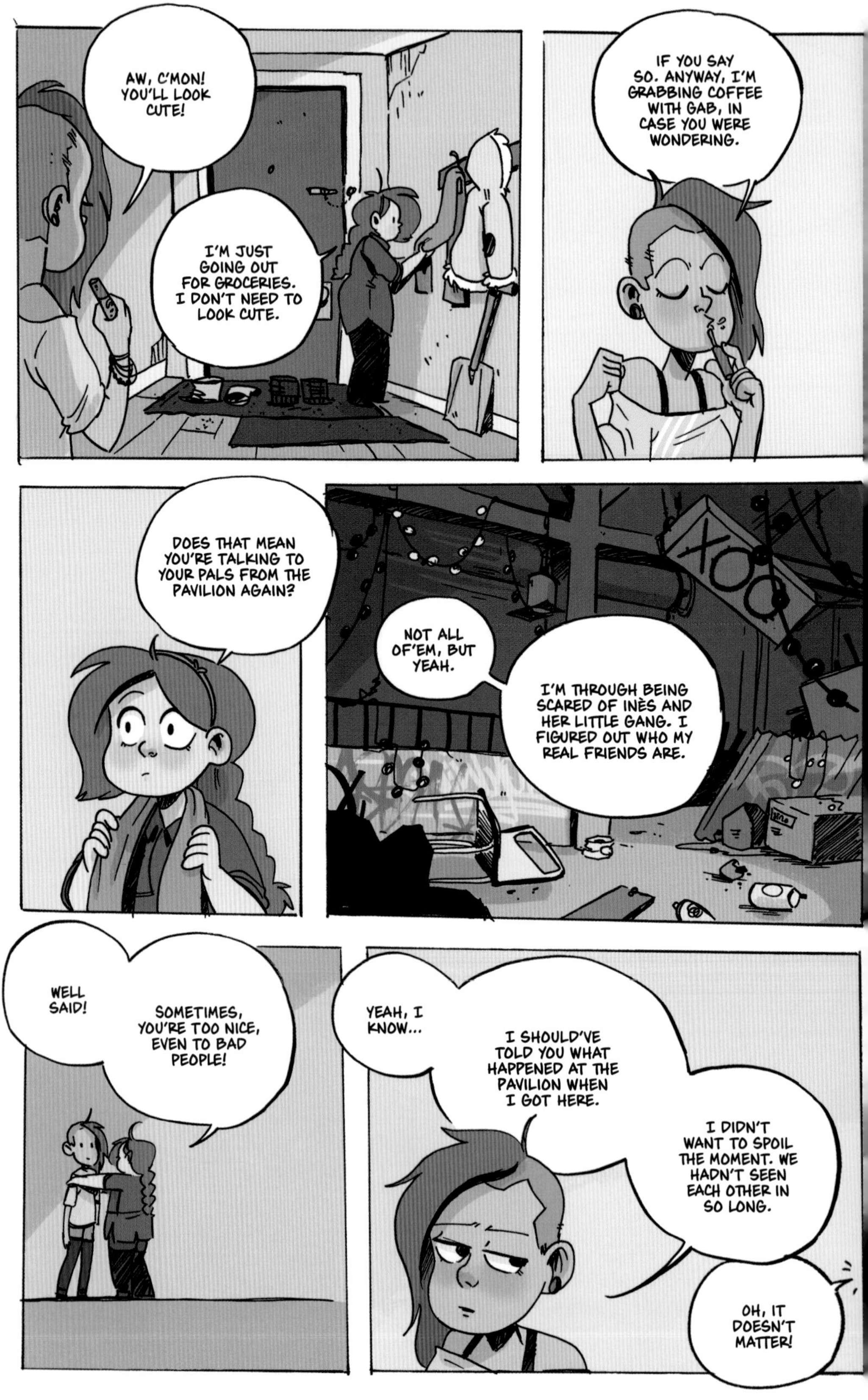
AW, C'MON! YOU'LL LOOK CUTE!
I'M JUST GOING OUT FOR GROCERIES. I DON'T NEED TO LOOK CUTE.
IF YOU SAY SO. ANYWAY, I'M GRABBING COFFEE WITH GAB, IN CASE YOU WERE WONDERING.
DOES THAT MEAN YOU'RE TALKING TO YOUR PALS FROM THE PAVILION AGAIN?
NOT ALL OF'EM, BUT YEAH.
I'M THROUGH BEING SCARED OF INÈS AND HER LITTLE GANG. I FIGURED OUT WHO MY REAL FRIENDS ARE.
WELL SAID!
SOMETIMES, YOU'RE TOO NICE, EVEN TO BAD PEOPLE!
YEAH, I KNOW...
I SHOULD'VE TOLD YOU WHAT HAPPENED AT THE PAVILION WHEN I GOT HERE.
I DIDN'T WANT TO SPOIL THE MOMENT. WE HADN'T SEEN EACH OTHER IN SO LONG.
OH, IT DOESN'T MATTER!

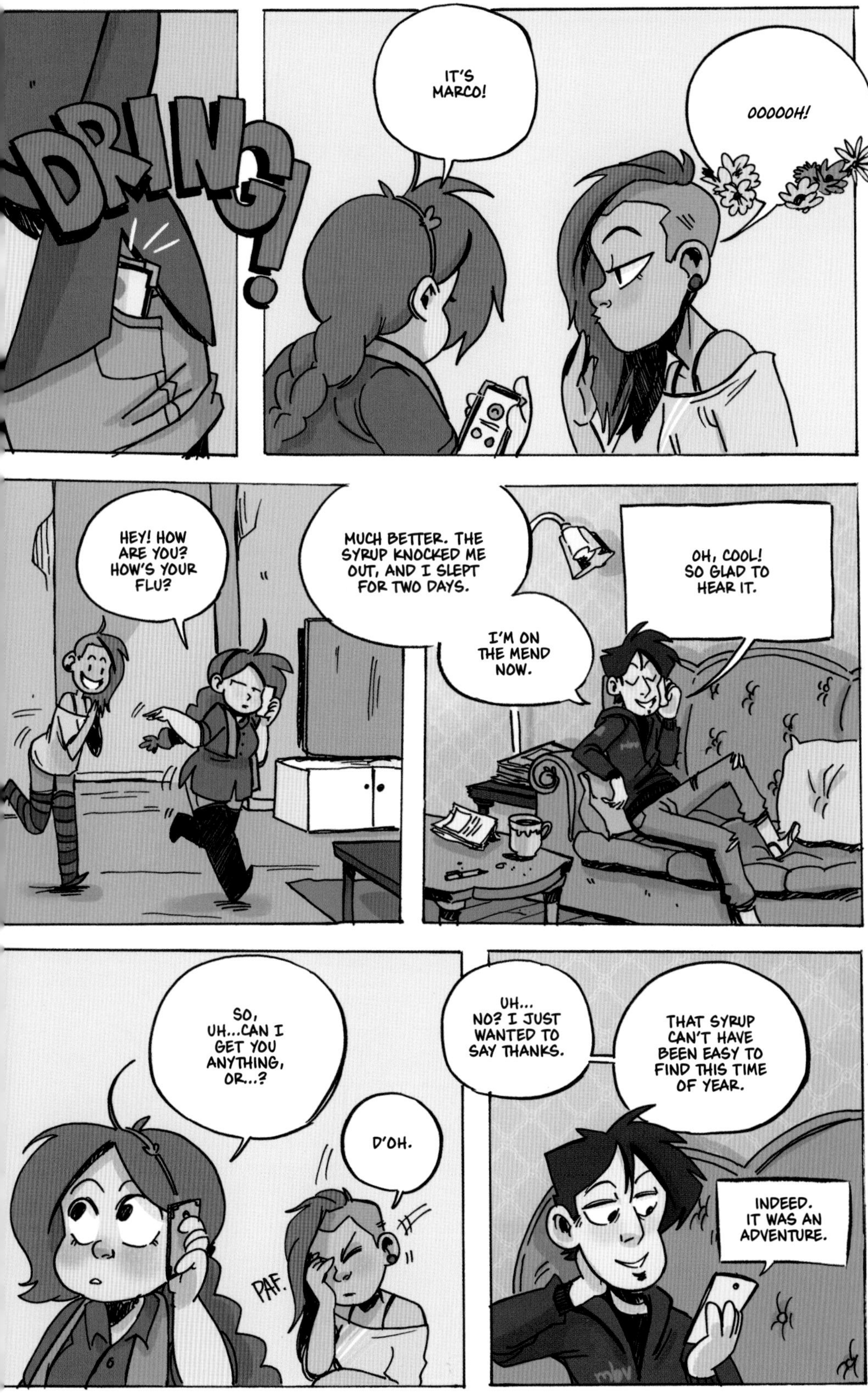
DRING!
IT'S MARCO!
OOOOOH!
HEY! HOW ARE YOU? HOW'S YOUR FLU?
MUCH BETTER. THE SYRUP KNOCKED ME OUT, AND I SLEPT FOR TWO DAYS.
I'M ON THE MEND NOW.
OH, COOL! SO GLAD TO HEAR IT.
SO, UH...CAN I GET YOU ANYTHING, OR...?
D'OH.
PAF.
UH... NO? I JUST WANTED TO SAY THANKS.
THAT SYRUP CAN'T HAVE BEEN EASY TO FIND THIS TIME OF YEAR.
INDEED. IT WAS AN ADVENTURE.

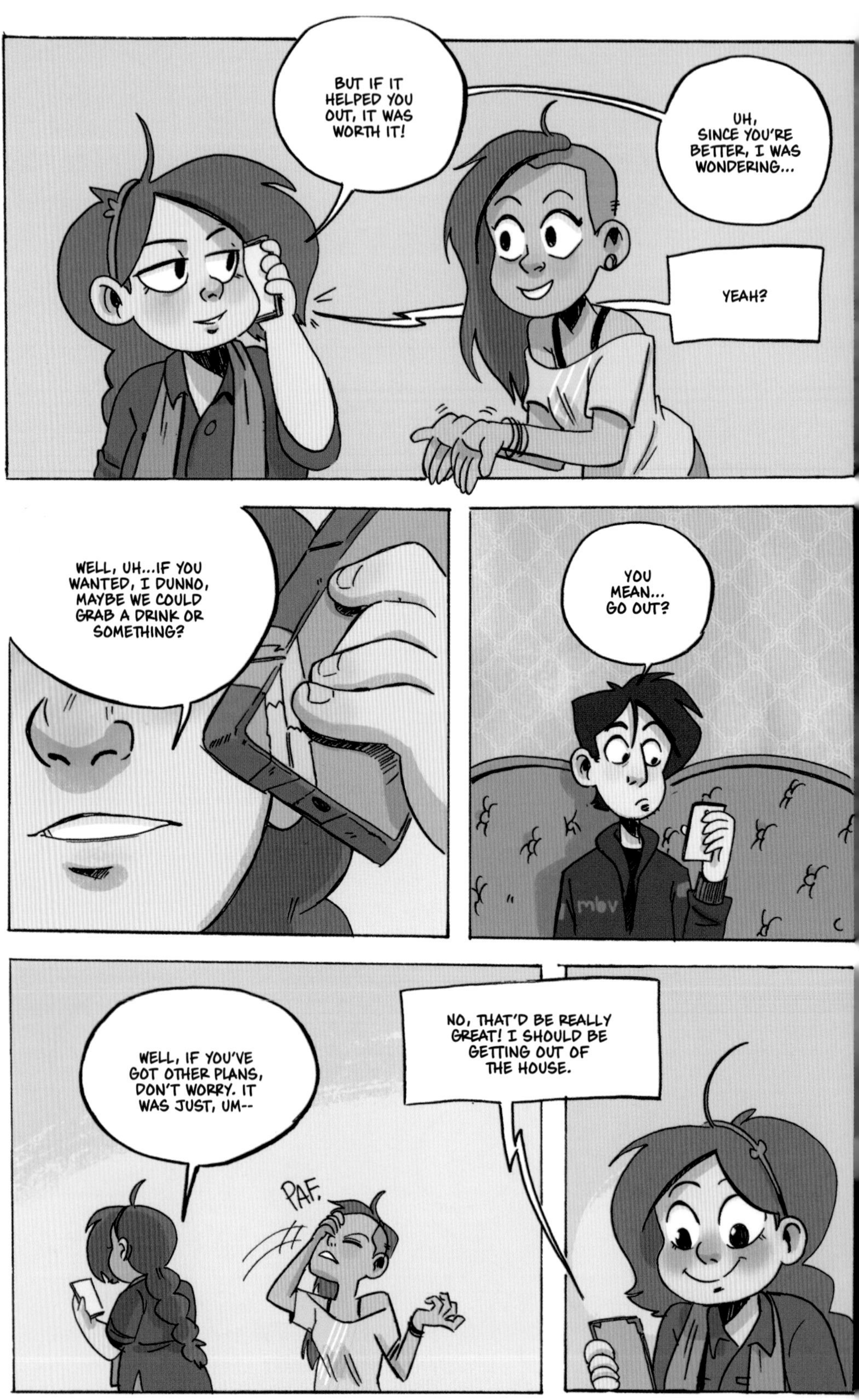
BUT IF IT HELPED YOU OUT, IT WAS WORTH IT!
UH, SINCE YOU'RE BETTER, I WAS WONDERING...
YEAH?
WELL, UH...IF YOU WANTED, I DUNNO, MAYBE WE COULD GRAB A DRINK OR SOMETHING?
YOU MEAN... GO OUT?
mbv
WELL, IF YOU'VE GOT OTHER PLANS, DON'T WORRY. IT WAS JUST, UM--
PAF.
NO, THAT'D BE REALLY GREAT! I SHOULD BE GETTING OUT OF THE HOUSE.

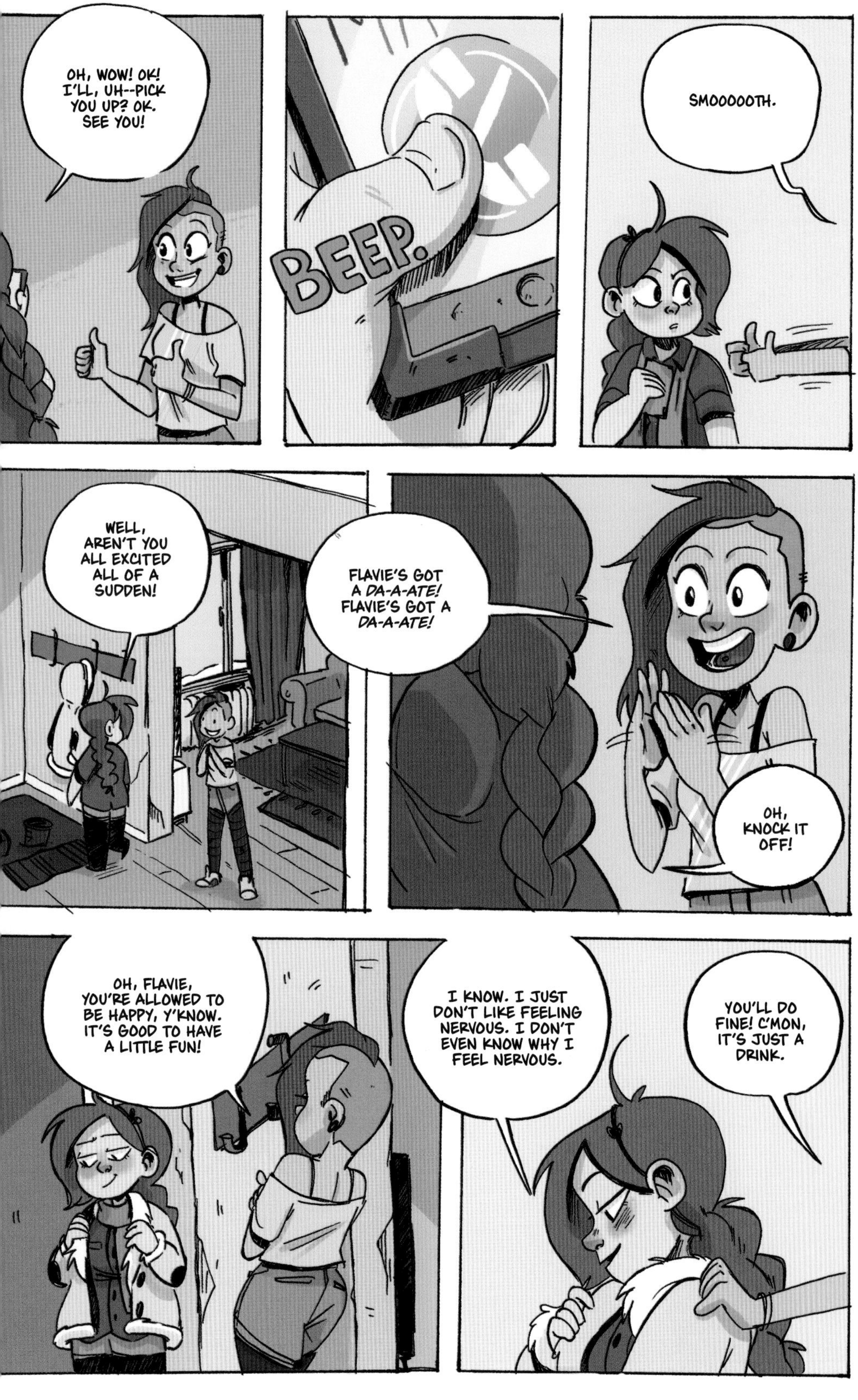
OH, WOW! OK! I'LL, UH--PICK YOU UP? OK. SEE YOU!
BEEP.
SMOOOOOTH.
WELL, AREN'T YOU ALL EXCITED ALL OF A SUDDEN!
FLAVIE'S GOT A *DA-A-ATE!* FLAVIE'S GOT A *DA-A-ATE!*
OH, KNOCK IT OFF!
OH, FLAVIE, YOU'RE ALLOWED TO BE HAPPY, Y'KNOW. IT'S GOOD TO HAVE A LITTLE FUN!
I KNOW. I JUST DON'T LIKE FEELING NERVOUS. I DON'T EVEN KNOW WHY I FEEL NERVOUS.
YOU'LL DO FINE! C'MON, IT'S JUST A DRINK.

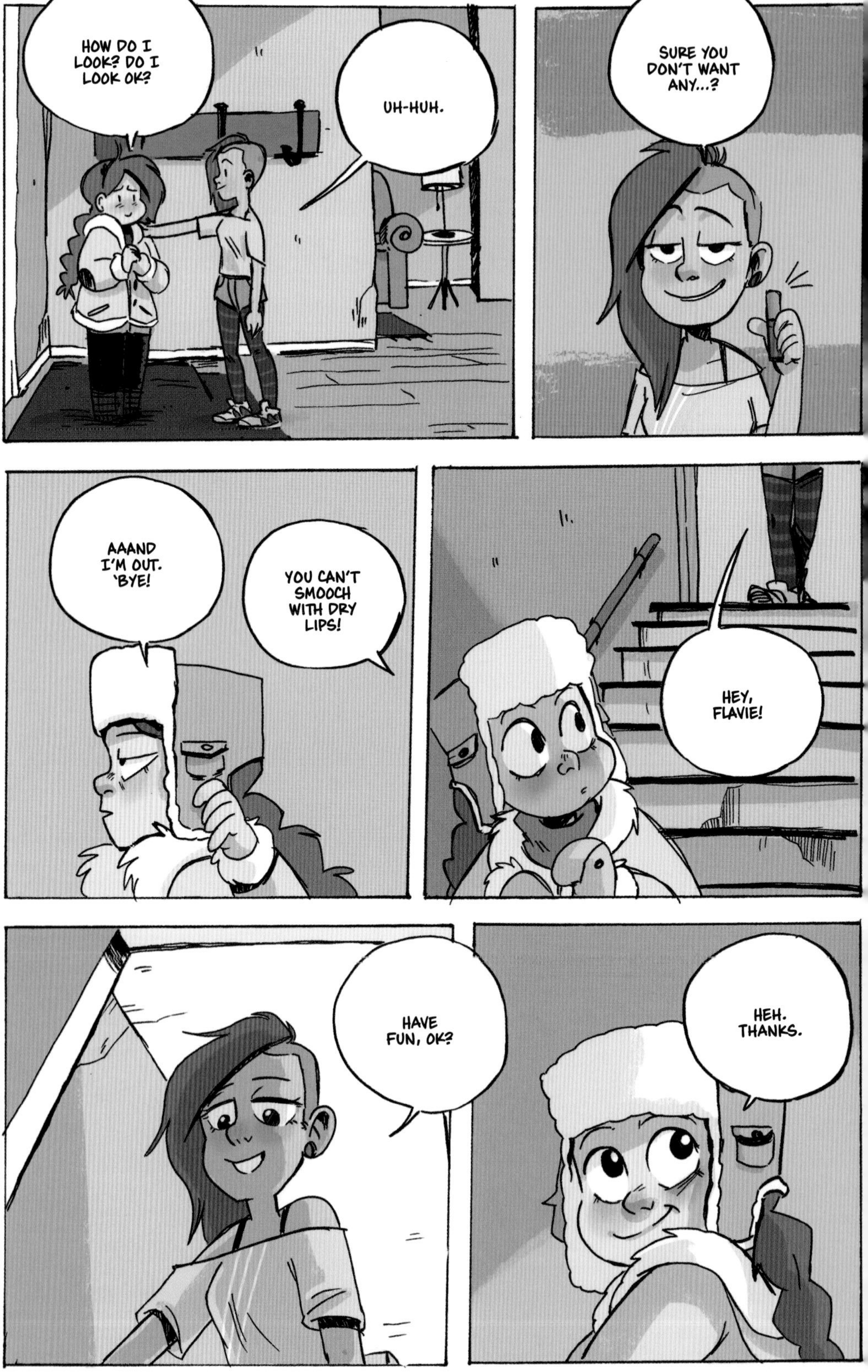
HOW DO I LOOK? DO I LOOK OK?
UH-HUH.
SURE YOU DON'T WANT ANY...?
AAAND I'M OUT. 'BYE!
YOU CAN'T SMOOCH WITH DRY LIPS!
HEY, FLAVIE!
HAVE FUN, OK?
HEH. THANKS.

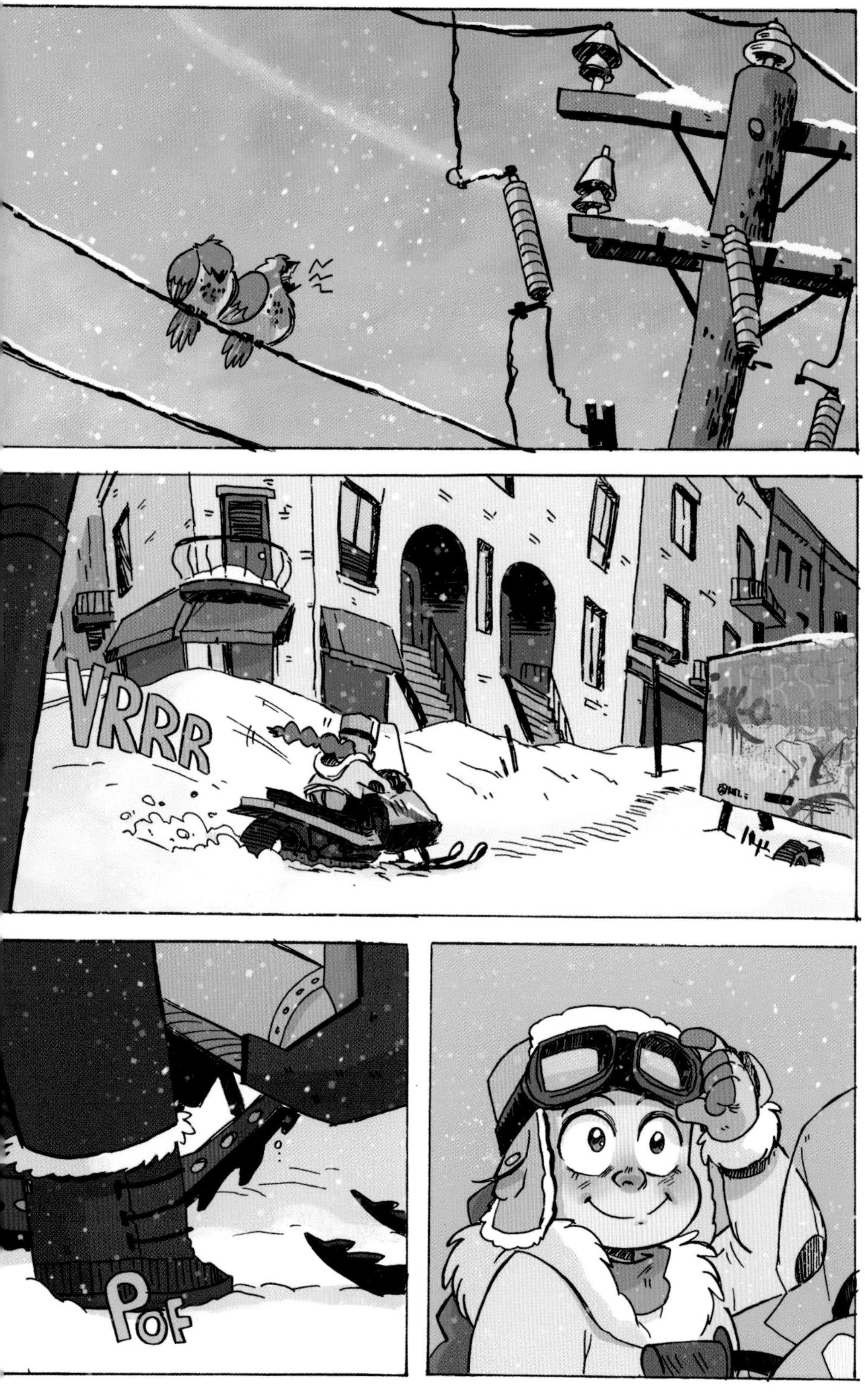
VRRR
POF

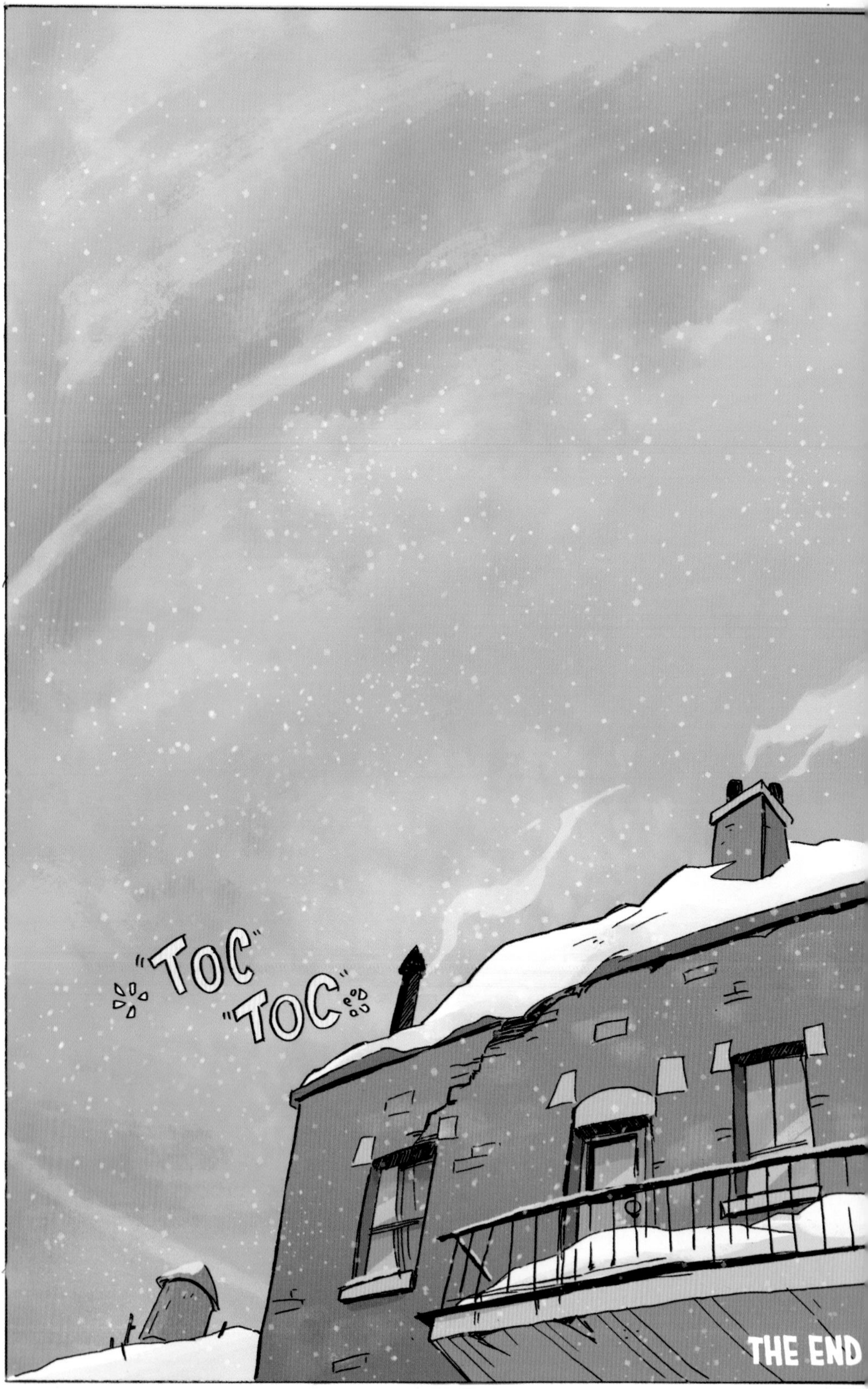
"TOC"
"TOC"
THE END

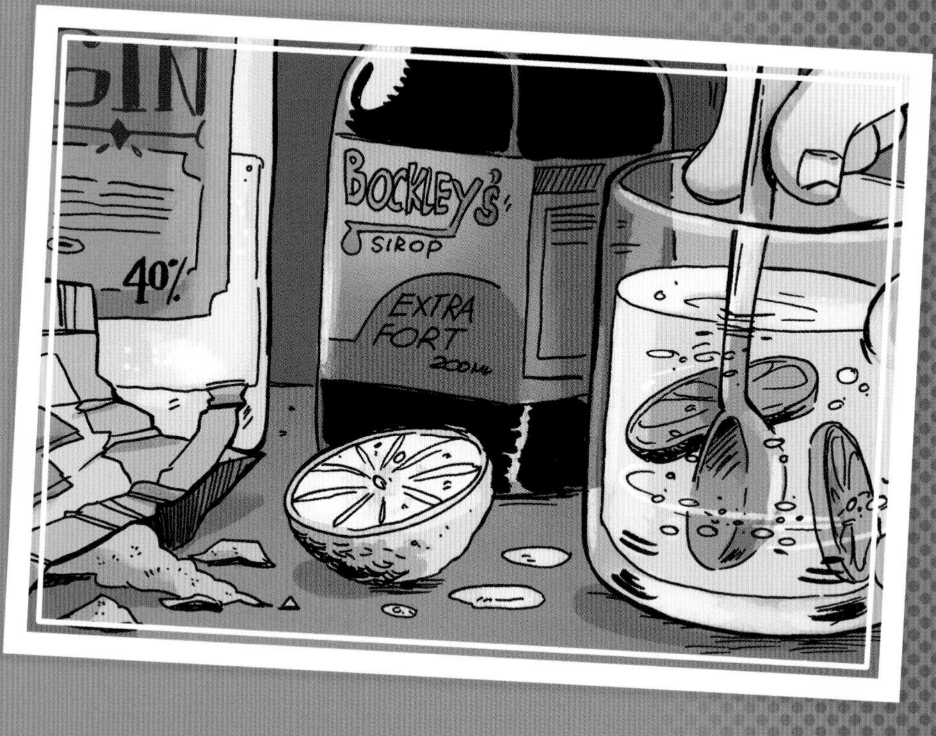

GIN
40%
BOCKLEY'S
SIROP
EXTRA FORT
200ML

DEVELOPMENT SKETCHES

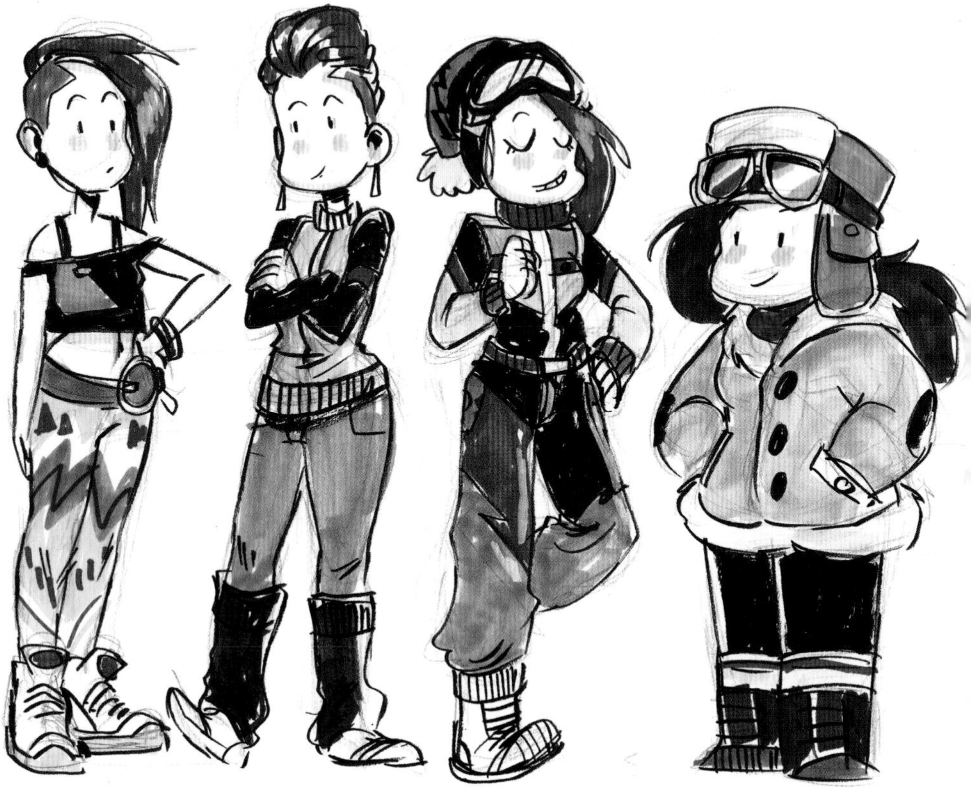

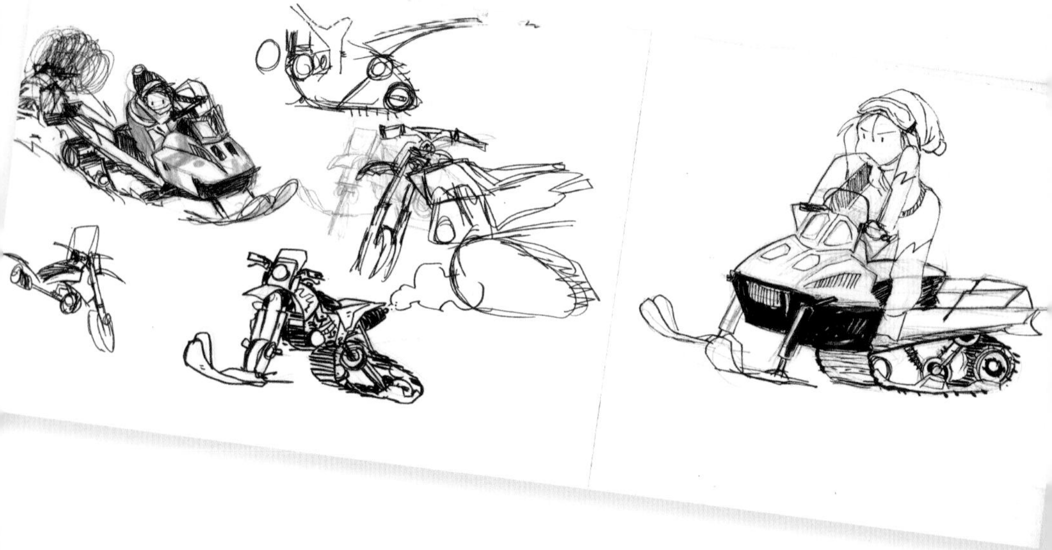

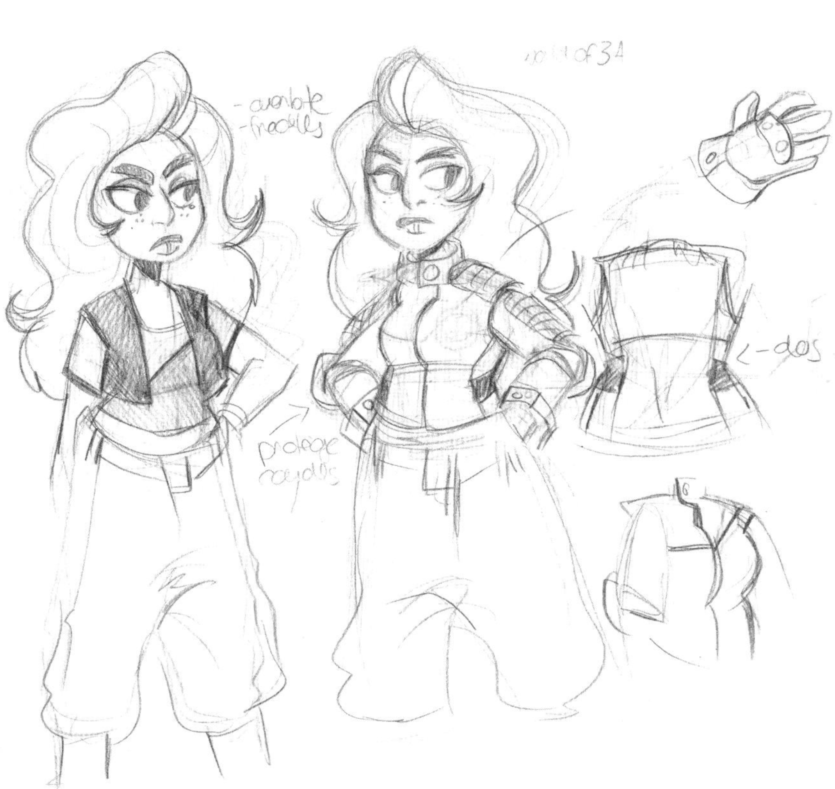
- freckles
<- dos

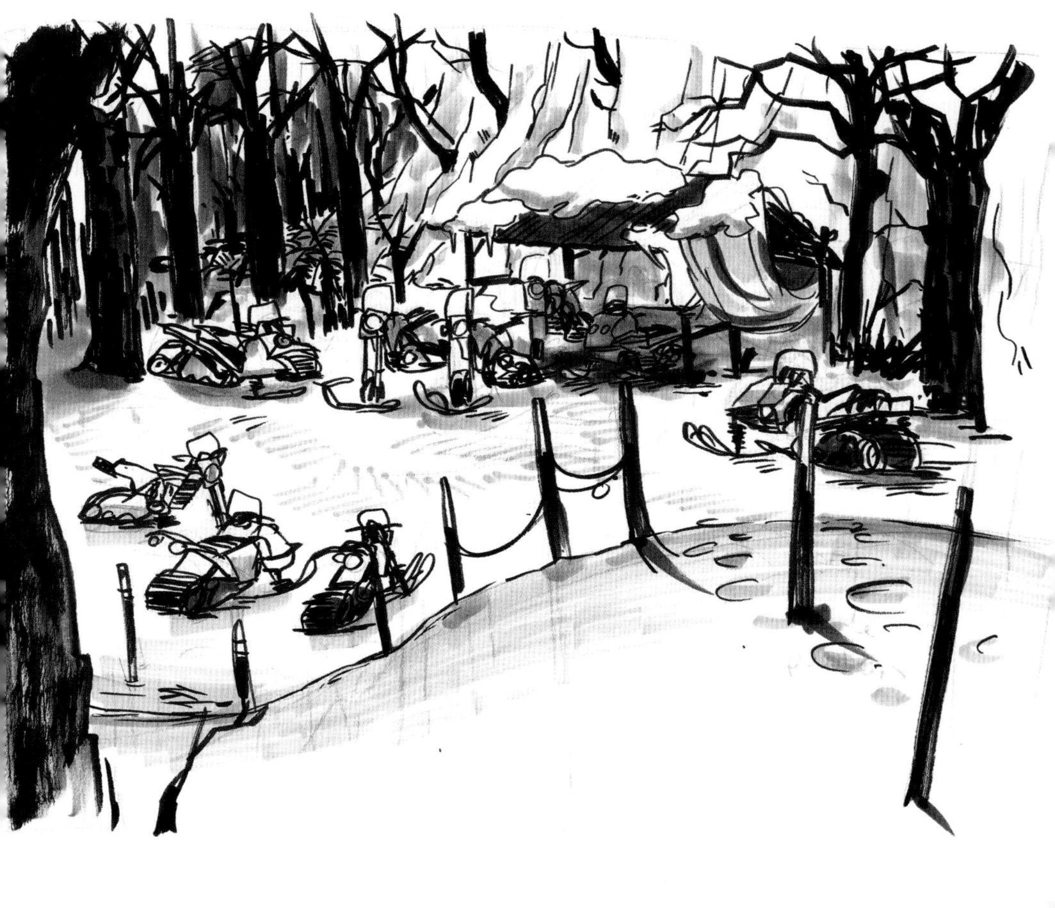

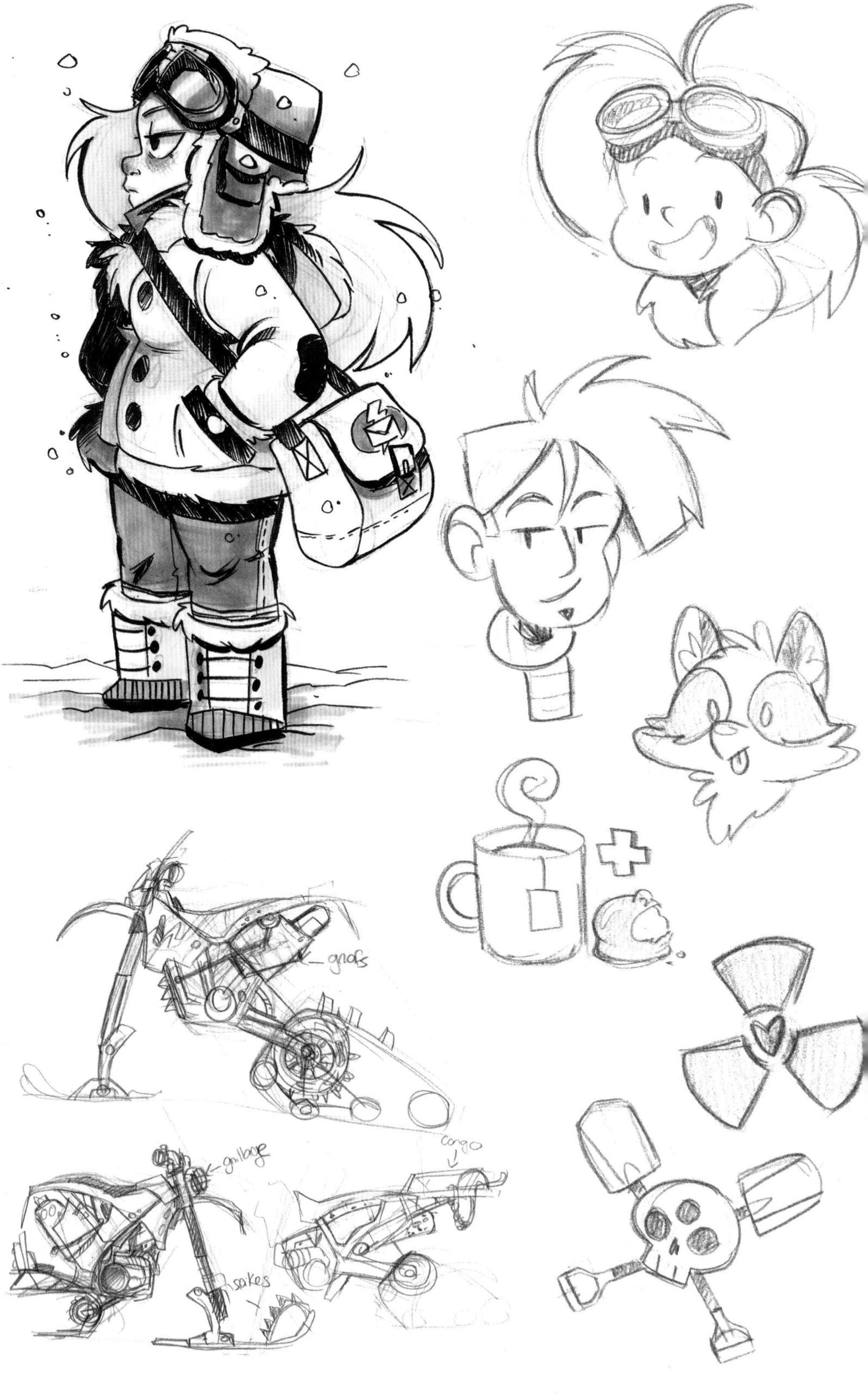

gnofs
grillage
cargo
spikes

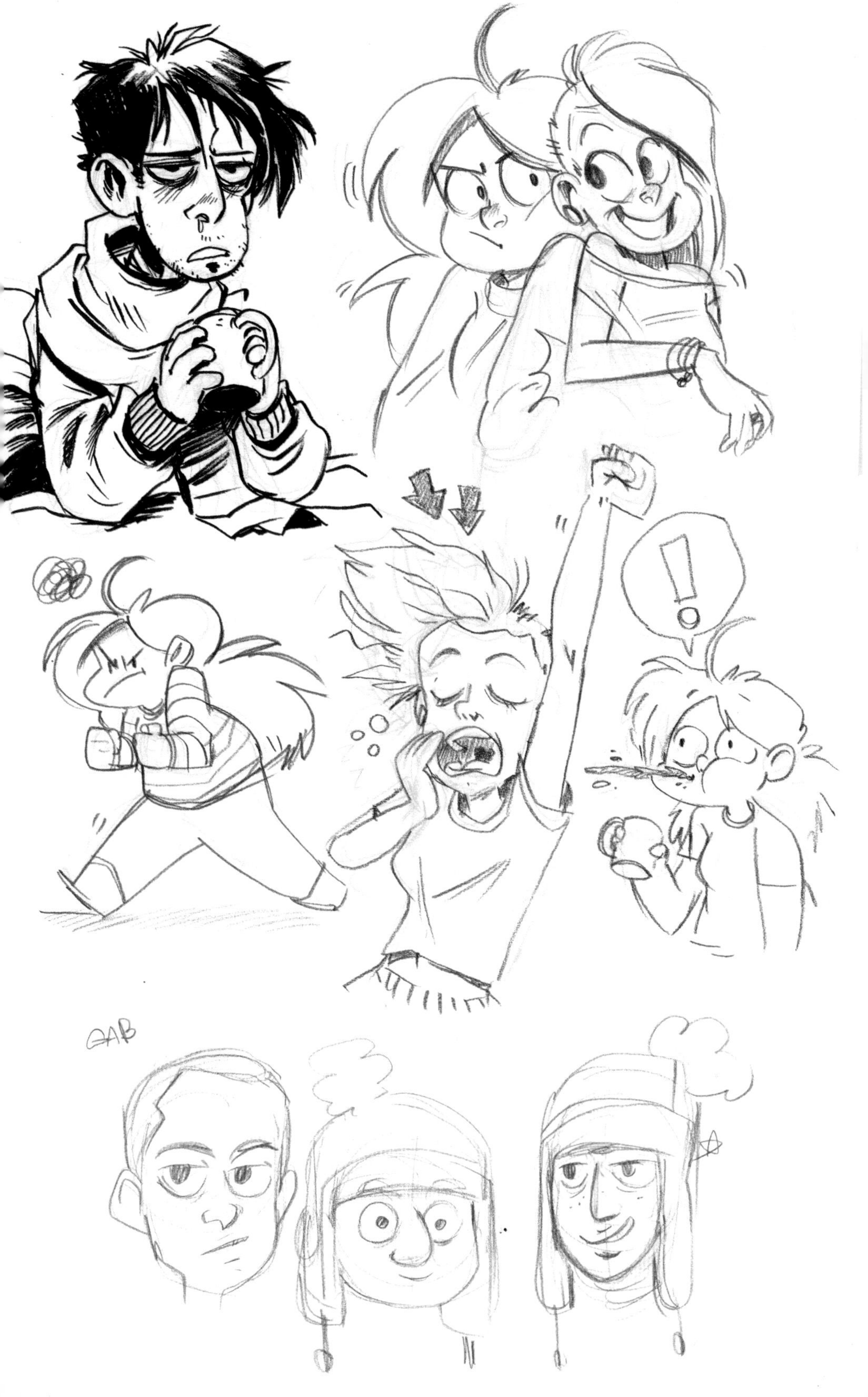
!
GAB

ABOUT THE AUTHOR

Caroline Breault (aka Cab) is a comic artist based in Montreal and the creator of the graphic novel series Hiver Nucléaire (aka "Nuclear Winter"). A full-time resident at Lounak Studios, she also works as a colorist and a freelance illustrator. In 2017, Cab received a nomination for the Joe Shuster Awards for best cartoonist. In reality, she does not like winter one bit but thinks it looks really pretty.

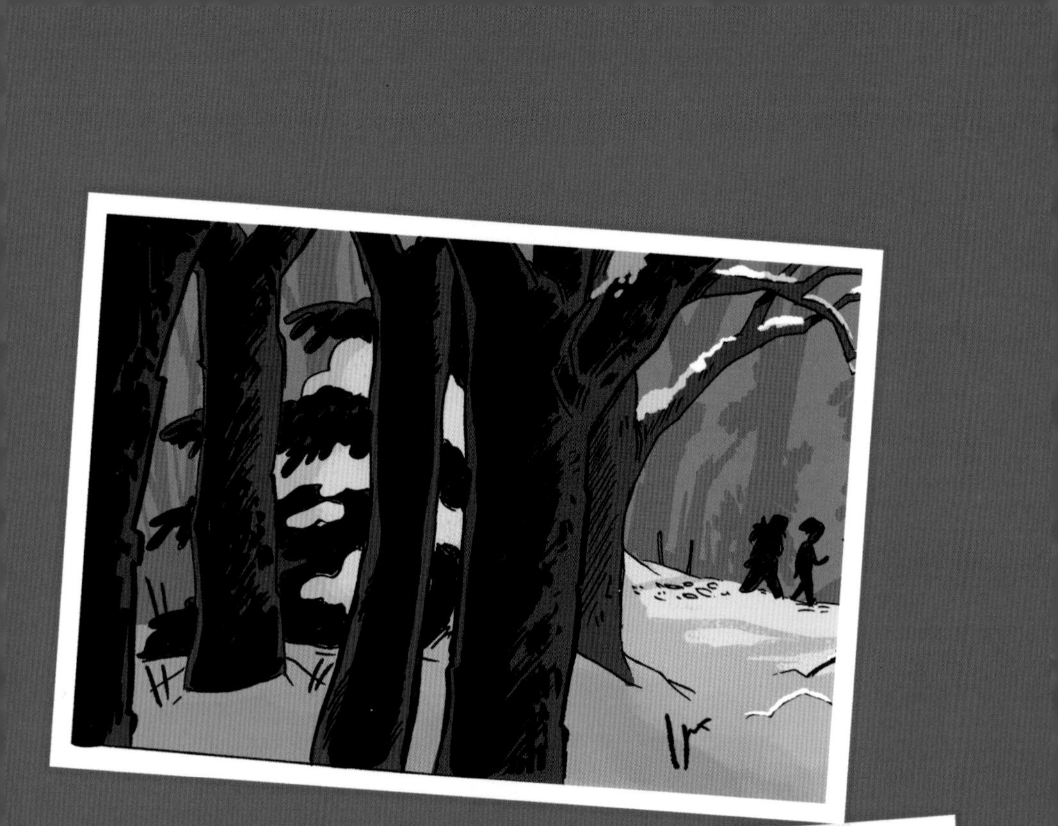

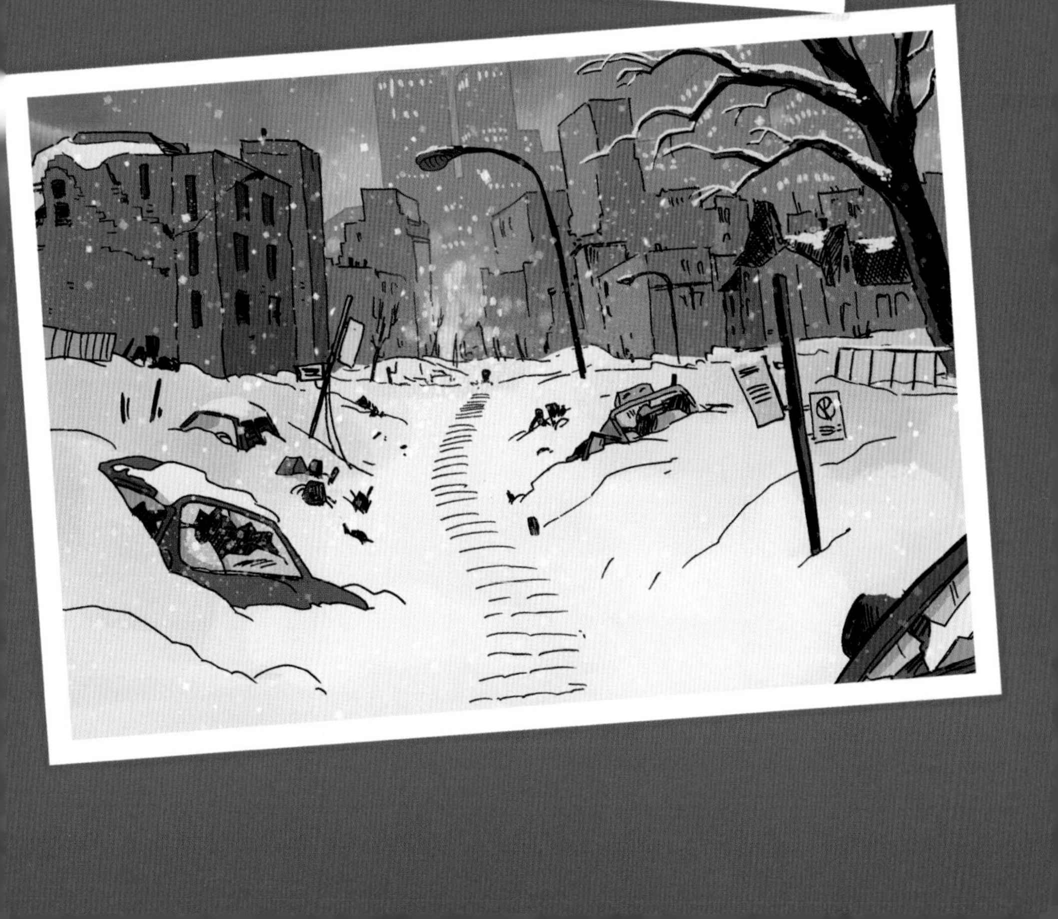